Cr

T0208281

Pros and Cons

Criminal Justice: Pros and Cons

PAUL J. WILLIAMS

iUniverse, Inc.
Bloomington

Criminal Justice: Pros and Cons

iUniverse books may be ordered through booksellers or by contacting:

iUniverse
1663 Liberty Drive
Bloomington, IN 47403
www.iuniverse.com
1-800-Authors (1-800-288-4677)

Because of the dynamic nature of the Internet, any web addresses or links contained in this book may have changed since publication and may no longer be valid. The views expressed in this work are solely those of the author and do not necessarily reflect the views of the publisher, and the publisher hereby disclaims any responsibility for them.

Any people depicted in stock imagery provided by Thinkstock are models, and such images are being used for illustrative purposes only.

Certain stock imagery © Thinkstock.

ISBN: 978-1-4502-8685-5 (pbk)
ISBN: 978-1-4620-2725-5 (cloth)
ISBN: 978-1-4502-8686-2 (ebk)

Printed in the United States of America

iUniverse rev. date: 07/11/2011

CONTENTS

DEDICATION

These Memoirs are dedicated to Réal, Vic, Marcel, Jacques, Claude, Bobby, Frank, Jackie and Jay whose troubled lives contributed directly to my personal and professional growth.

PROLOGUE

Some forty years ago I embarked on a journey that would lead me through the violent world of criminality, both within the confines of a penitentiary and in community parole supervision. While still in the university setting, I had envisaged a promising future in the comforts of a private office, with the support of professional colleagues. The ensuing reality bore little resemblance to my reverie.

My particular odyssey would be through a minefield of suppressed violence and deceit, occasionally uplifted by the hope of change, only to be thwarted later by the duplicity of power games. Despite this, my career has been a rewarding one. The relatively few successes have adequately compensated for the many setbacks in this complex field.

I started working at St. Vincent de Paul penitentiary, April 24th 1962, simply because there were no positions available elsewhere for an inexperienced psychologist. I had recently graduated from the university and had filled out a series of application forms at various employment settings to no avail. An interview at "the Pen" proved successful to the extent that I was offered a position of Classification Officer, since the three psychologist positions were currently filled. Although this was somewhat deflating to the inflated ego of a newcomer, I accepted the job and have never looked back.

As it turned out, the penitentiary erupted in a major riot less than two months later and the resident Psychologists resigned. No doubt they were aware that there would be little opportunity to ply their trade in the physical and emotional detritus left in the wake of the uprising. I lacked the experience to make this judgement but now consider my stay as the first of many serendipitous happenings that blessed my career.

There are many people who have laboured assiduously in the correctional field for thirty years or more. I consider myself fortunate, however, to have been exposed to various settings in different jurisdictions along the way. This afforded me a more comprehensive experience that widened my view of criminal justice and enhanced my development as a person.

The first victims of crime are the offenders themselves. This is not meant as an excuse for their behaviour but merely as a hint of an explanation. I believe that we, as a society, have a serious obligation to the prevention of crime and one valid approach lies in the treatment of the offender. This is a complex notion that includes knowledge of delinquent dynamics, an awareness of societal resources and insufficiencies, along with an in-depth understanding of the effects of the deprivation of liberty.

Incarceration is society's primary manner of responding to behaviour that contravenes established law. There are other means as well but if the behaviour is considered serious enough or repetitive enough, imprisonment is the outcome. Some believe it is not used often enough, others that it is meted out too easily; some hold that it is not sufficiently harsh, others proclaim that the simple deprivation of freedom is punishment enough. In fact, both the law and government correctional documents state that incarceration is to be used as a last resort. Official written proclamations, however, do not always reflect the reality in practice.

Incarceration, then, as a means of neutralizing criminal behaviour, is indispensable. It must be used prudently, however. Canada has the dubious reputation as the country with the second highest incarceration rate in the western hemisphere. This reflects a knee-jerk reaction to media hype, rather than a planned response based on informed opinion and expertise. This situation prevails even though the crime rate across Canada has been in a decline over the last three decades. Strident attention, rather than mere lip service, must be paid to the spirit of the law as well as stated correctional policy; incarceration is to be employed as a last resort.

Equally important, however, is the manner in which the incarceration process is carried out. Deprivation of liberty is a serious matter and must be treated as such. The simple removal of someone from society does not necessarily solve the problem, either for the offender or for society as a whole. That portion of the sentence to be served in a correctional institution must be designed in such a manner as to enhance the chances of the offender to reintegrate into the community. The post-release phase of the sentence, to be served under supervision in the community, is an integral part of the correctional process and must be directly related to the institutional experience. Thus, reintegration of the offender neither begins nor ends upon release from prison but must be an essential ingredient inherent in the institutional experience.

Prisons and penitentiaries are the dwellings in which offenders are housed. The average cost to maintain a person incarcerated in a federal penitentiary now surpasses sixty thousand dollars per year. The overall budget of Correctional Service Canada surpassed the annual billion-dollar mark in 1996 and has been increasing since. There are many reasons why this cost is so high and much dispute as to whether or not the entire process is justifiable. Suffice it to say that society has a right to a minimum expectation; an individual should not emerge from the incarceration experience less equipped to deal with the demands of freedom than prior to admission. Perhaps one could argue that the individual should come out of the experience better equipped or, at least, that every effort had been made to accomplish this. It is trite to allude to protection of the public if the idea of change, in the sense of personal growth, is not inherent in the correctional equation. It is equally banal to exclude the notion of providing realistic help to the offender. Society deserves some level of satisfaction from a system so costly in human as well as monetary terms.

One of the uppermost challenges facing an organization that provides a helping service is to keep the essential goal of the service in the forefront. This holds true for community-based organizations as well as government agencies. Secondary issues and concerns can make the organization or those who work for it more important than the clients they serve. Whereas the profit motive keeps a check on profit-making corporations, social service delivery systems have no such innate, systemic control. The fact that schools are to educate students and hospitals are to treat patients are examples of truisms that sometimes recede into the background in practice, as labour movements jockey to secure the optimum for those they represent or when political expediency rises to the fore.

In the correctional field, several factors may come into play and cloud the ultimate goal of the service. The most incessant impediment stems from the nature of the subject matter itself, delinquency, personified by the offender. The offender, particularly the persistent offender, is seldom motivated towards internal change. This presents a unique challenge to caregivers and renders their task an especially difficult one. Basic differences in the perception of needs and goals create a pronounced antithesis between caregiver and client, creating antipathies that must be recognized. If they are not addressed, the caregiver's role is never actualized and a truly helping service is impossible.

With today's advanced technology, prisons and penitentiaries have streamlined their service delivery. There are more correctional programs available than in the past, easier access to educational and vocational assistance and added functions to address ethnic and cultural diversity. Despite these developments, however, the overall tenor of the institutional climate has become increasingly impersonal. Wardens have retreated to a bureaucratic hideaway, making fewer hands-on decisions while delegating to a myriad of faceless committees. Institutional parole officers, better educated than in days past, perform at a comfortable distance as "crimino-technicians," diligently perusing files and busily collating computer-provided information of arguable accuracy.

The true test of the cogency of a specific law is its applicability to everyday life in society. Similarly, the validity of a correctional system, with its articulated policies and practices, lies in the degree to which these decrees from on high are translated into action in the operational field. The ultimate responsibility rests with senior officials, not only to enunciate a mission statement and a set of core values, but also to ensure that these can be and are put into practice. Otherwise, the exercise becomes mere window-dressing designed to enhance an image.

My personal experience with the federal correctional service suggests a growing discrepancy between the authorized printed word and actual practice. This, in part, is the result of an unmanageable bureaucratic explosion over the past thirty years. It is also due, however, to an insatiable desire to polish an image for popular and political consumption. While senior representatives of the government agency seem bent on preaching their correctional gospel to an international audience, a closer look at everyday practice at the field level reveals problems that need addressing.

*   *   *

I called from my office in Leclerc Penitentiary to the officer on duty at 3GH, a penitentiary wing, and asked to have an inmate sent over. This was the usual procedure. I would call either the wing where the particular inmate was housed or the place where he worked. I didn't make out passes in advance, as most others did, simply because my work schedule was haphazard. The contract called for my presence an average of two and a half days per week. I chose the days and the choice was, in part, contingent upon obligations elsewhere.

René, an inmate whom I had first met more than thirty-five years before and who was excellent at referrals, had referred Jimmy to me. He knew what I could and could not do. He was also adept at screening out those inmates who would see anyone at anytime so long as it got them out of work or some other irksome obligation. As a matter of fact, René was much less tolerant than I and would usually admonish the individual he was sending over, ". . . don't start with the bullshit and take up his time for nothing." This caution usually proved to be a time saver.

When Jimmy arrived I was somewhat taken aback by his youthful look. I knew he had just turned twenty-two but he had the physical appearance of a teenager. Standing at about five-eleven, lean, bright blue eyes and a carrot top, it was not surprising he featured a slight scowl. After all, this kid had to have some hint of threat about him, if he were to survive in the jungle.

"How's it goin' man?" I exclaimed, reaching out to shake his hand. His firm handshake belied what, on first sight, seemed to be a slim physique. In fact, he had the well-toned musculature of an athlete rather than the build of those artificially developed mesomorphs who strutted across the yard to and from the weight pit.

> "I'm having trouble sleeping and wanna know if you could prescribe something," he stated politely, as though he were at the head of the line at the neighbourhood pharmacy.

I explained to him that I was not a medical doctor and, as such, could not prescribe medication. I then hesitatingly offered him a cup of coffee. I was always glad to share the pot of coffee I prepared in the morning: Not only because a full pot was too much for any one person and was strong enough to revive the brain-dead, but a cup or two helped create a more pleasant ambience to compensate for the stark décor of my penitentiary office.

In truth, my coffee had become somewhat of a legend. Those who knew me politely declined my offer. Those who knew me better, laid it out, "This is the worst concoction ever served, it makes our worst home brew a delight." But I was never convinced. I could drink it, why not the others? So, I affably offered it to all first-comers. Some became last-comers; others firmly refused the libation.

Jimmy accepted my cup of coffee and finished the pot with me. He spoke of his difficulty sleeping, a plight which had plagued him since his incarceration. He was in his third year of a life sentence for second-degree murder. This made him eligible for full parole after the completion of ten years. Most inmates with a similar sentence, in an effort to maintain some semblance of mental and emotional stability, think and behave as though the ten-year mark was an automatic release date. They know this to be factually incorrect but, at least, a specific release date helps quieten the anxiety and depression engendered by the nebulous quality of a life sentence.

Jimmy, however, had not reached that point as yet. He was still living in the largely illusory world of the appeal. This provided some faint hope but also reinforced an emotional defence against speaking about the crime: "my lawyer has instructed me not to talk about it until my appeal is over." If these same lawyers were privy to the ongoing trauma some of their clients experience because of this blanket prohibition, they may well be more discerning in their counsel. Catharsis is a rare luxury in the emotionally repressive atmosphere of the penitentiary. In this unhealthy milieu, where feelings other than anger and hostility are frequently interpreted as a weakness, the clinician is often at pains to create a climate of trust and provide the solace necessary to solicit deeply buried feelings of grief and remorse.

Nevertheless, Jimmy was able to speak of other revealing facets of his young life. Even in that first interview, the scowl quickly transformed into an engaging smile. Over a period of two and a half hours, interest areas within the sphere of literature, music, films and sports were uncovered. It was the institutional bell, the signal to return to the cell area for the official midday count, that interrupted our conversation. Jimmy sat bolt upright at the sound,

> "thanks for your time, I really enjoyed talking, I hope you'll call me again. The coffee was really good!"

I looked up expecting that impish grin I noticed had accentuated some earlier witticisms. I was startled to see a serious look of sincerity. I knew immediately I had found a new pal. Ol'Red was okay!

For the next two and a half years I followed Jimmy along his journey, on a weekly basis. If he arrived early and the mugs had not been laid out as yet, he would cast a furtive glance toward the percolator and with an audible sigh of relief attend to "setting the table." These sessions, officially referred to as individual therapy, took up the entire Monday morning. He would recount the weekend's activities, mainly sports, both as a spectator and as a participant. A voracious reader and an avid music buff, he would quote from various sources and punctuate the dialogue with insightful comments and clever repartee. His complaints of insomnia quickly disappeared as he developed the technique of reading well into the night before finally dozing off. This seemed to be to his satisfaction, although less so to those who expected him to be at work in the morning. "I'm not a morning person," was his brief explanation to the staff.

A solution was found when they appointed Jimmy as cleaner on the wing. This entailed approximately thirty to forty-five minutes of mopping a day. This "work assignment" was duly incorporated into his "correctional plan," undoubtedly an integral part of the overall plan to prepare him for the world of work upon release into a competitive society.

Jimmy's prowess at sports was considerable. He was above average in all the institutional contests but excelled particularly in football. He had played organized football as a teenager and was proficient enough to have earned a scholarship, a reward cancelled by his incarceration. He was highly competitive, a necessity to gain respect in the Pen but a double-edged sword, since fierce competitiveness could be interpreted by the less talented as a means of showing them up. He played with the reckless abandon of youth, impervious to any danger, on or off the field.

The fact that Jimmy had eventually completed high school was a minor miracle. He was certainly of above average intelligence and possessed an inquiring mind. His personal life from the early developmental years on, however, can best be described as a horror show. His early school years and adolescence give true meaning to the expression "street kid."

Jimmy never met his natural father nor ever knew who he was. He was in the hands of a drug-addicted mother and a string of abusive and addicted male figures. He began roaming the streets of Ottawa at age eight, sleeping in parked cars and apartment hallways. The many attempts to have him placed by Children's Aid, resulted in the characteristic absconding from the placements "in search of mom." He usually ended up back in the streets and attributed his being fleet of foot to these early experiences.

> "I became really good at runnin' when I was spotted. I could leap over backyard fences like Jordan goin' for a slam-dunk," he recounted with eyes shining as though he were living the moment.

Every now and then his mother would stabilize somewhat as she began once again with a new partner. He could remember only one, Art, who "treated me good." Further probing revealed that his acceptable treatment was defined by the fact that, "Art didn't beat my mother. He wasn't a heavy user either; he just hung around the house. He was with us for almost two years." This latter statement was uttered with a sense of approbation; Art was the most stable male figure Jimmy had met.

The growing sense of abandonment, reinforced by the regular disappearances of his mother, finally took its toll. He was about fourteen when he accepted placement with a family on a farm just west of Ottawa. His acceptance was as much due to the fact that he had written his mother off, as to the genuine interest and kindness of this new family. They had three or four other youths there "but you felt right from the start this family was in your corner. We used to rap about it among ourselves."

Jimmy's own life stabilized somewhat in that he was able to stay in school. His previous nomadic existence had wreaked havoc with his school performance but his strong intelligence and emerging sense of wanting to accomplish something, however vague, now held him in the one school and gave him the opportunity to catch up. The early emotional scars, nevertheless, left their imprint and affected his social development.

Jimmy excelled in sports in school, particularly football. Although this made him popular with the school peer group, the absence of a sense of basic trust pushed him toward the fringe element. It was within this group of insecure adolescents that a denial of feelings was interpreted as strength. Here he was able to relate to others who would not open any emotional doors. The hurt centred on Mom was now repressed, only to emerge occasionally and momentarily, over coffee, in the sparse confines of a penitentiary office much later.

I have made it a practice not to limit my work with the inmates to an office setting. Obviously, there are times and subject-matter which dictate the more official ambience of a traditional desk and chair encounter; equally obvious, at least to me, is that there are times and occasions when the contact is less formal and, because of this informality, a strengthening of the relationship may come about. Given the nature of the correctional setting, the inmate serving a sentence and the personnel administering the sentence, the relationships are usually unidirectional, from supplicant to decider. Over an extended period this creates a climate that can be ultimately counter-productive. I try to counterbalance this with a casual approach. There is some validity to "street work" in the gym, the yard or on the wing.

Jimmy was a member of the Lifer's Club and helped organize the annual day for a group of physically and mentally challenged people. The guests were bussed in on a Saturday morning, played various games with the inmates and shared lunch as well as liquid refreshments throughout the day. The activities went on from nine-thirty to three-thirty in the gym. Some members of the staff would come in and I made it a point to bring my son and daughter with me. I wanted them to have first hand experience of what a penitentiary is like, meet some of the men and perhaps test the veracity of some of the "war stories" I recounted at home.

Both my son and daughter were touched by the graciousness accorded them by all the inmates they encountered and remembered for sometime afterward Jimmy, himself. I had been working with him for about a year at this time and the transference that had developed ticketed me as a benevolent father figure. Jimmy was initially reserved with my son and daughter and seemed to be tripping over himself to try and do the right thing. He seemed to breathe more easily when they accepted his offer of a Coke as it gave him a moment's respite from the social pressure when he left to get the soft drinks. We relaxed over our soda around ten in the morning. At least it beat my coffee!

It was while pondering over this encounter sometime later that I put Jimmy's youth and life situation in perspective. He was the same age as my son, twenty-three. He was serving a life sentence for the murder of a friend's abusive stepfather. Involved in a correctional system that had become so impersonal he was considered a "lifer" who had a "case management officer", more than a young adult person. My son had had his problems during his adolescent years; some serious enough to warrant close attention. At least he had had parents to whom he could and did turn. The best Jimmy had was a substitute, perhaps a designated hitter. Evidently, this best wasn't good enough!

The Monday morning sessions continued regularly. The thrust of the counselling was towards encouraging and reinforcing certain positive steps Jimmy was able to take. Although adept at sports, he was less comfortable in the more mundane social relationships, greeting many but courting few. It was obvious the competitive ambience of athletic encounter suited him; in a sense, his early experience of self-reliance for survival served him well in this arena. He was less well equipped for everyday social encounters.

In the circumspect world of the penitentiary, social graces take on new meaning. On the one hand, the inmate often feels obliged to behave in an expected manner so as to gain the necessary recognition as one who is "changing" and "benefiting" from the contrived programming of the institutional life. At the same time, survival within the real cultural milieu, defined by the power structure within the inmate population, requires a certain posturing that basically defies conformity to norms established by the authorities. This paradoxical situation demands a balancing act, difficult for neophytes but, unfortunately, commonplace for those on whom the process of incarceration has taken its toll.

Jimmy had difficulty coping with both horns of the dilemma. The residue of his developmental experience shut the door to trust and confidence in those who exercised authority, effectively curbing any meaningful participation in prescribed programs. Likewise, the not-so-subtle demands of the institutional sub-culture seemed to him another imposition by others. Others had defined his life up to now; where and with whom he must live and in what style; persons and circumstances outside his control had dictated all. The result had been severe emotional pain, assuaged only by absconding. His present situation allowed only for a certain degree of emotional withdrawal, disguised by a carapace of curt and sometimes caustic verbal response. This would keep "them" at a distance.

As time passed, Jimmy showed minor signs of increasing autonomy. He had approached the school supervisor about possible correspondence courses at the university level. He had begun to write a short story, bringing it to my attention for approval and encouragement. Finally, he obtained a job transfer to the institutional canteen, a move initiated and facilitated by one of his closer friends, another sports addict. This latter step was somewhat of a challenge as the work assignment entailed some responsibility. For some years now the inmates operated the canteen. The ordering and selling of canteen articles called for a transparent balance. This placed those who worked there in the sometimes delicate position of preventing, or at least controlling, the abuses which fund the various illicit trades common in penitentiaries. It is a job many inmates will avoid.

One Thursday afternoon I was "making my rounds" through various parts of the institution. I was looking forward to a long weekend and thought I'd touch base with as many men as possible before leaving. About three-twenty, I was coming through the gym from the main yard. Jimmy was shooting hoops with some of the Brothers. He was the only white guy who played regularly with the Blacks. The mutual respect was evident.

"What's happenin' Doc?" he said light-heartedly.

"Gettin' ready to split. Long weekend for me. Where are you off to?" I needled.

"Same ol' shit here. But, will you be back Monday?"

"Yeah, I'm here. I'll call you up for nine-thirty."

"Don't forget the mud. I need my fix if I'm gonna stay awake all week," he joked, casting a quick glance at his audience. I performed the ritual handshake with each man and left.

Monday morning remains ingrained in my mind though it is now several years past. As I sauntered past "Control 30," a security control post on the way to my office, an inmate sidled up to me.

"How's it goin' this mornin' . . . too bad about that kid who got it!"

I turned to him abruptly but before I could utter a word, "the redheaded, English-speaking kid."

Although I knew instantly, I could feel it in the pit of my stomach, "What happened?"

"He got shived near the Socio, staggered to the gym and was dying in a pool of blood before them fuckin' screws finally got 'im to the hospital. He died there," he blurted out in one breath.

He then slipped away as furtively as he had approached me a moment before. I was shell-shocked for the moment. There are no long discussions over death in the Pen. Although I was never able to confirm this, I believe this inmate was sent to prepare me by others. A number of the men knew that Jimmy was seeing me on a regular basis. They knew I cared. Nobody on staff ever mentioned a word to me.

Some weeks later there was the mandatory Administrative Inquiry. A body of three people, one from outside the system, conducted interviews and studied written policies, procedures and technical implements such as cameras, static security posts, etc., for possible lapses. It was established that Jimmy had been playing basketball when approached by an inmate who told him someone wanted to see him at the Socio. He was next seen staggering back to the gym where he collapsed. The several knife wounds proved fatal and he succumbed to his injuries approximately an hour later in the hospital. No assailant or accomplices were ever positively identified.

This was certainly not the first inmate with whom I had worked regularly to be killed. In a sense, though, he was the closest. He was the last man I spoke to before leaving for the long weekend; our agreement had been to meet Monday morning; I always prepared mentally for my counselling sessions. More important, however, was the fact that Jimmy really had no one in the world. There were visitors he sometimes alluded to, but they were always coming "any day now." Although he insisted vehemently that his mother was in the past, I always suspected that if, by some miracle, she had been able to visit, he would have spirited himself to the visiting room "like Jordan goin' for a slam-dunk."

This was never to be. Although I could not have hoped to fill the void Jimmy experienced, I do hope that I provided some meaningful measure of human contact. It all ended October 31st, 1998. In a whited sepulchre, a veritable cauldron of seething hate, anger and pretence, a twenty-four year old man lost his life.

ACKNOWLEDGEMENT

I would like to acknowledge the perseverance of Ms. Susan Pelletier in typing and re-typing the original manuscript.

As well, the friendship of Gaston St-Jean, reflected in his untiring patience while making valuable suggestions, is greatly appreciated.

INTRODUCTION

"Pros and Cons" is an expression that has different meanings to different people, depending on the given context and contingent upon the viewpoint of the speaker and the listener. A common usage of the term refers to the two sides of a particular issue. The two words, taken separately, are sometimes used as diminutives for professionals and convicts; a further colloquial use of the word "cons" implies the deceitful manipulation of another.

In the treatise to follow, the interpretation of "pros and cons" is left up to the reader. Is society well served by our use of incarceration as the principal means of dealing with the offender? Certainly what follows is about both professionals and convicts and a good amount of conning is recounted. What the reader must determine is whether the real professionals are those who profess to address the problem or those who have been convicted. Similarly, who is doing the conning?

Criminal Justice as a whole and the correctional system in particular, with its inherent mechanism of conditional release, becomes a subject of wide public interest when a major event occurs. There is usually a media feed frenzy when a gruesome murder, a prison riot, a hostage taking or some similar spectacular incident takes place. Although it is the media's responsibility to report these events, undue emphasis on the dramatic can result in unwarranted conclusions. Unfortunately, the general public's knowledge of corrections, its players and its problems is almost entirely limited to media accounts of such episodes. A perilous corollary is that policy makers, in deference to this contrived public opinion, are wont to counsel change founded on biased and incomplete information.

Criminal Justice, which incorporates the correctional system, must be a concern for all at all times. The openness of our court system is to ensure that justice takes place and that there is an appearance of justice as well. This fundamental transparency is an important benchmark of a healthy system but must not be limited to the judiciary. Although a certain veneer of candidness has emerged in corrections and parole over the past several years, the portrait is a mere adumbration of the reality. Political consolidation and correctness, bolstered by the bloated bureaucracy of a government agency bent on creating and preserving an image, have all but muted the voice of informed criticism from without and implanted an internal structure of intellectual and functional inbreeding.

Corrections is a people business whose ultimate efficacy is reliant upon the interpersonal relationships among its various players. Most administrators acknowledge that correctional personnel should somehow share a common goal. Although the term "team approach" is presented in official communiqués, closer scrutiny leads to question whether the "game" is the same one for all concerned. In any case the offender population, that people element without which there would be no game whatsoever, must be perceived and accepted as an integral part of the maze of interpersonal relationships. This latter group, comprised of individuals detained against their will, is the raison d'être of any correctional system. They must be dealt with honestly and openly if one is to expect of corrections something more than temporary, preventive warehousing. Concepts such as compassion and respect, anathema even to some practitioners but innate in true justice, must be actualized if only to keep at bay the emergence of an ersatz justice system, ultimately characterized by the din of jackboots marching in cadence.

ST.VINCENT DE PAUL PENITENTIARY

~ the Pen

Cell Block one was a stone fortress within the walls of St. Vincent de Paul penitentiary. Its interior, Segregation, was a combination of cement and steel, peopled by uniformed guards and differently uniformed inmates: the watchers and the watched. One of the guards was armed and observed from an elevated steel cage.

The steel steps made a clanging noise as I climbed to the second tier, adding to the pervasive metallic din. I had previously sent a written request to each man in segregation asking for his participation in a research project for my thesis. Most of the inmates housed here were awaiting a court appearance on charges emanating from the recent riot that had devastated the penitentiary. This was truly a captive audience, detained in the cell twenty-three hours a day. They were eager for any sort of diversion and, consequently, all but one of them had replied to my request. I was on my way to see the one who hadn't.

Jean-Guy was in Segregation but not because of the riot. He had spent the greater part of the past five years in one form of isolation or another. Since his admission to the penitentiary at seventeen years of age, he had been considered a "trouble-maker," "muscle man," "un bras," some of the many terms used in the colourful jargon of the Pen.

He was serving a twelve-year sentence for manslaughter and aggravated assault, the culmination of several years of gang fights. During the first five years of his sentence, he had become somewhat of a legend. He had initially been refused transfer to the Federal Training Centre, flagship of the Canadian Penitentiary Service at the time. This institution had been designed for first penitentiary offenders, under the age of twenty-five and specialized in trade training. The rationale was, if one were able to separate the first penitentiary offender from the older inmates and expose him to specific trade training, a re-made individual would somehow emerge. Although a certain classification of offenders and trade training are positive steps, these elements alone are a simplistic approach to a complex problem.

In fact, Jean-Guy met with the criterion of first penitentiary offender under the age of twenty-five. His street reputation, however, reinforced by his early adjustment difficulties quickly ticketed him as a young tough, too disruptive for the relatively new and progressive institution. The Federal Training Centre was one of the first in a long line of progressive institutions to come. None of these new institutions would ever effectively uncover and contend with the multi-faceted problems that brought men into conflict with the law. What would emerge instead, was a more refined selection system that would attempt to tailor the offender to the institution. The bottom line: quiet and smooth-running institutions, a policy that was to be enforced and reinforced through the collusion between a growing administrative bureaucracy and an increasingly powerful labour movement over the ensuing years.

Instead of transfer to the new institution, Jean-Guy was assigned to the Y Block of St. Vincent de Paul. Here, the inmates were under twenty-one years of age, required to wear the letter Y along with their Pen number affixed to their cap, jacket and pants. This was intended to separate the younger offenders from the older ones, "*les serins*" from "the wolves." Although sleeping and eating accommodations, as well as certain Y Shops, remained apart from the general inmate population, recreational activities, for the most part, allowed for intermingling.

It was only a matter of time before Jean-Guy took control of the Y side, along with some older, more experienced inmates; taking control included anything from collecting canteen articles as protection, to demanding outright sexual favours. It was not long before the institutional authorities took action. He was removed from the Y Block and placed in isolation for punishment and control.

In those years, the institutional Warden reigned supreme, with power shared only with his immediate delegates, the Deputy Warden and the Chief Keeper. As there was no regional authority and communication with the central authority in Ottawa haphazard at best, there was no independent court of redress should any abuse arise. Isolation, suspension of visiting privileges, loss of "good time," corporal punishment, sudden and unannounced transfer to another region of the country, or any combination of the above were the principal disciplinary measures. Discipline was the euphemism for punishment and control, the means to maintain a quiet institution. This ultimate purpose has not changed in forty years; only the methods have been modified. Fundamental issues as delinquent mechanisms, reactions, behavioural patterns, as well as the effects of the deprivation of liberty, are no better dealt with in contemporary correctional institutions than in those days. If anything, today's prisons and penitentiaries better reinforce delinquent mechanisms. The physically brutal system of the past has been replaced over the years by an increasingly impersonal, bureaucratic mentality that ensures constant manipulation by both sides. The Chief Keeper of the 'fifties and early 'sixties knew every guard and almost every inmate by his first name. Today the ever changing management teams have little time to get to know each other, let alone the inmates, as they peruse the mounds of directives, memos, regulations, etc., which cross their desks daily. Today's experts in corrections are certainly expert in the compiling and reading of files; limited time is spent establishing direct contact with the offender.

Although the immediate goal of neutralizing Jean-Guy through isolation was accomplished, the long-term effect was more dramatic. In an attempt to return to the general inmate population, he eventually took two guards hostage while in isolation. After verbal agreements had been reached, but later abrogated by the authorities, his efforts ultimately resulted in an additional two-year sentence and transfer to Kingston Penitentiary (KP).

In the circumscribed penitentiary world, an inmate's reputation often travels faster than he does, despite elaborate security measures. That amorphous grape vine frequently outdistances even today's technological expertise. Jean-Guy had become legendary by the time he was welcomed at KP, particularly by the minority, French-Canadian inmate group. His previous exploits took on a dimension that only time and distance can enhance. Since the only fundamental difference between Kingston and St. Vincent de Paul was a linguistic one, identical problems arose. Although the Kingston authorities wrote their prescription more quickly, the treatment was the same: displacement of the problem. Jean-Guy was returned to St. Vincent de Paul within a year and immediately reassigned to the newly opened Segregation in Cell Block one.

Our democratic society has chosen the deprivation of liberty as a means of dealing with those individuals who constantly transgress existing laws and are caught. This is the fundamental *raison d'etre* of prisons and penitentiaries. Within the institutions, however, there are several means of dealing with unacceptable behaviour. One of the most common is to segregate the individual from his peers. This is the extreme deprivation of liberty; a prison within a prison. Society pays a monetary and human price for its use of the deprivation of liberty; a higher price tag comes with use of the extreme deprivation of liberty.

Incarceration is sometimes necessary. Individuals, who repeatedly come into conflict with the law and those who present a danger to others because of aggressive behaviour, must be neutralized. However, society has a duty to attempt to discover the causes of this behaviour, if only to prevent it recurring. If incarceration is to be valid, serious attempts must be made to help the individual return to the community, prepared to cope with the demands of freedom. In fact, many offenders return unprepared for responsible living; the manner in which the process of incarceration unfolds comes into question.

The effects of the extreme deprivation of liberty are even more consequential. The daily routine in Segregation was twenty-three hours of cell time with one hour in a special exercise yard, weather permitting. Visits were allowed on a monthly basis, always within the hearing of a guard. Canteen privileges were significantly reduced and the threat of corporal punishment, in the form of a strap applied to bare buttocks, was ever present.

The most debilitating of all sentences, whether meted out by a court of law or by institutional authorities is one of an indeterminate nature; one in which the termination date remains nebulous. Although safeguards have been instituted to ensure a sense of acting fairly when isolating an inmate from his peer group, the result is still an indefinite sentence. After having followed many men in Segregation over several years, I have often observed a significant build-up of diffuse hostility over time. These feelings are eventually expressed in one of three ways: outwardly, along a continuum from verbal aggression, through physical attack and sometimes culminating in homicide; inwardly, through auto-mutilation and suicide; or through psychological withdrawal, spanning anywhere from schizoid behaviour, through clinical depression, to complete psychotic withdrawal.

Some months after his return from KP and his admission into Segregation, Jean-Guy viciously attacked a guard with a "home-made shiv." As the inmates alternated in serving the meal trays in each wing, he took the opportunity, during this brief period of freedom from the cell, to stab the guard repeatedly, blinding him in one eye and rendering him partially paralysed. He was charged with attempted murder and held in a cell on a solitary wing of Segregation while awaiting sentence on this last charge. It was during this period that I was to meet him for the first time. He had been sent the same written request as the other inmates in Segregation. Each of the others had put a checkmark in the <u>Yes</u> box on the request form and had returned it to my office. Jean-Guy had not replied.

I had started working at the penitentiary less than a year before this incident. It was my first job as a psychologist, although I did not have the university degree; I had completed the required courses but had not written the thesis had as yet. This posed no problem working for the Canadian Penitentiary Service since several psychologists in their employ at that time did not have the official university degree.

I had come to the penitentiary quite by chance. Several applications at various hospitals had proved fruitless, so I tried the Pen. I have never looked back and have never regretted the decision to work in corrections. The fact is, I have stayed with it over the past five decades. Despite the violence, treachery, and helplessness that permeate the institutional milieu, if one remains sensitive to human frailty and maintains a desire to search for solutions, one can survive and reap some reward. Although the problems frequently appear insurmountable, there is no more interesting field, pregnant with potential for meaningful change.

The real tragedy in corrections is that, in my experience, little change of any consequence has taken place over the last five decades. A penitentiary has evolved into a "Correctional Facility;" guards have assumed the title of "Correctional Officer" or "Living-unit Officer;" inmates are frequently referred to as "residents;" stone walls have been replaced with double-link fences. By the same token, the most common inmate label for a guard, correctional officer or living-unit officer remains "a screw" and the frequently heard institutional term for an inmate or a resident is still "*un bagnard*." Perhaps these lasting epithets are a more accurate barometer of change, or lack of, within the institutional milieu.

The sites of correctional facilities, frequently chosen for purely political reasons, are now often some distance outside the large metropolitan area, from where the majority of inmates come and where their families still reside. Correctional officers are now expected to fulfil a nebulous role of counsellor and suppressor, a paradoxical portrayal lacking credibility. As a result, the gap between the watchers and the watched is enlarged. Inmates have now gained many rights, without any of the inherent responsibilities, thus effectively precluding the acquisition of that basic human right: the right to be able to live in freedom. The wire fences that have replaced the stone perimeter of the correctional facility blend in well with the overall institutional milieu, affording no more than an opaque view of the outside world.

*   *   *

As I reached the second tier, I was immediately before the barred door that separated the wing from the central part of the cellblock. Behind this door stood Jean-Guy, clothed in a towel as he stepped out of the shower. I introduced myself and mentioned that I had not received a reply from the request I had sent him.

"Yeah, I got it, what does dat mean? What do I have to do?", he queried in accented English.

After a brief explanation of a need to have some figures drawn, as part of a research project for my thesis, I awaited his reply. It was brief.

"*Behn oui*, I can do dat!"

Such was the inauspicious beginning to a relationship that would span ten years. During this period, I was to grow as a professional in the field of corrections. Jean-Guy was a key figure in unlocking doors to the violent world in which he lived and through him I gained my first insights into the importance of the institutional milieu. He made progress as a more autonomous person, until his tragic end. Nevertheless, I believe the clinical information gleaned from the longitudinal study of Jean-Guy, if put into practice, would afford a more meaningful approach to the serious problems of crime and delinquency.

He was the second of six siblings in a family raised in the "red light" district of Montreal during the 'forties and 'fifties. His fondest memories were of his mother, grandmother and older sister; his bitterest feelings reserved for his father. The extended family, comprised of grandparents along with several aunts and uncles, was close-knit and directly influenced his formative and early school years. It afforded tenderness and concern that fostered emotional security. However, there were six maternal uncles, all of who worked "sur la Main" as bouncers, collectors, etc., and who favoured aggressive acting-out as the preferred means to problem solving. This created a marked ambivalence in Jean-Guy's evolving perception of role models and life situations. It was to characterize his interpersonal relationships throughout life. His fierce loyalty to those he considered friends, was equalled only by a deep-rooted animosity toward those he perceived as adversaries. This good/bad splitting of object relationships was further complicated by an overly charged, poorly controlled affectivity.

Jean-Guy's adjustment to school life was tenuous at best. His frequent fights were an attempt to establish himself as a peer group leader and brought about problems with the school authorities. These aggressive exploits directly influenced his developing self-image, which itself was becoming a growing source of inner-conflict. The macho image, fostered and rewarded by the male members of the family, led to increased controls put upon him by his father who was responding to numerous complaints from the school. Years later, while in the penitentiary, he still was confused by the demands that had been made upon him:

> "My old man bought me weights before I was eight, 'den when I get 'ome from school, he beat 'de shit outta me for fighting, even 'dough I won da fight!"

Jean-Guy was never able to speak with ease about his mother. He once related an incident that was obviously still a major source of emotional pain. As he recounted the story, tears welled up in his eyes.

His mother had a serious tubercular condition and was hospitalized frequently. Her last hospitalization was when he was twelve years old. At the time, he was vaguely aware that she was dying. He would sit on the curb outside the hospital after supper, look up and wave to her through the window some stories up. Hospital regulations did not allow visitors his age.

One evening, upon returning home from one of his hospital visits, he found his father in bed with his sister's sixteen-year-old girlfriend:

> "can you see 'dat, my fodder's fucking 'dis broad and my mudder's dying in 'de 'ospital," he blurted out angrily.

He turned his head away from me, momentarily remaining silent and trembling slightly, then promptly demanded to return to his cell. During the many years I worked with Jean-Guy after that, the subject remained a delicate one. When I alluded to his mother in any way, he would simply grin defensively and say,

> "I know what you're doing! You want me to talk about my mudder . . . you t'ink you can make me cry . . . ha! ha!" He then pleasantly but firmly changed the subject.

I often wonder what would have happened if this matter had been explored at the time it occurred. He was twelve years of age, five years before he would enter St. Vincent de Paul with a lengthy sentence. Is it possible some of his street violence could have been avoided? I also wonder whether an attempt to explore this sensitive area at the outset of his sentence would have reduced his later institutional violence. As to the first question I can only say that anything's possible. The response to the second, however, is an unequivocal yes. The reason is simply because of the positive experience we had dealing with Jean-Guy in a different manner over the ensuing years. Not everything went smoothly at all times, but some observable, positive changes did come about.

* * *

Two interdependent elements of importance to a correctional institution are a clear *raison d'etre* coupled with well-defined roles for the personnel. Regardless of the specific job one may have in the penitentiary, the individual worker is never working in a vacuum. The institution is a truly closed milieu and the impending deprivation of liberty has an effect on all, even those exposed to it for eight-hour periods.

Unfortunately, not all realize this. Higher placed administrators and professionals frequently see themselves as, somehow, above it all. Nonetheless, all are touched by the deprivation of liberty: the administrator who gives more importance to directives and procedures than to the individuals who people the institution; the psychiatrist who is duly concerned with the correct diagnostic label but overlooks the nefarious effects of the immediate milieu; the psychologist who fails to realize that the interpretation of responses to projective stimuli often reveals more of the one making the interpretations than of the one giving the responses; the case management officer who manages cases instead of dealing with people.

Over the years I have worked with many talented and concerned guards and instructors. These were the individuals who traditionally held the frontline jobs, those who had to fend for themselves on a daily basis. Early in my career I was appalled at the lack of formal training these people had, yet surprised at the competency some had in dealing with difficult inmates. Later on, when training programs had been established at the Staff College, I began to realize that front-line, supervised experience resulted in better learning than a theoretical, didactic approach.

An example comes to mind that should elucidate my point. Immediately after the riot of June 1962, inmates were under twenty-four-hour lock-up for an extended period of time. This procedure was put into effect so as to resume control and gradually process inmates for transfer to lesser security institutions. The transfers were necessary because of extensive cell damage. Nevertheless, the institution still housed over a thousand inmates and had a large staff complement. People had to be fed. The personnel had to carry out many of the chores usually done by inmates. I volunteered to help out in the Dishwashing section. This was heavy work that entailed the manipulation of large, metal food containers. The officer-in-charge was a physically impressive man who had that rare talent for getting those under him to work while, at the same time, maintaining good inter-personal relations. I got to know him quite well under these circumstances and later learned that his skills were equally proficient with the inmate population. He seldom refused an inmate assigned to him and consequently ended up with an undue number of more difficult inmates. I asked him to take a few on occasion. He knew how to handle men, particularly difficult men.

Some years later he was promoted to Living Unit Supervisor at Cowansville Penitentiary. The Living Unit system was first implemented in certain medium security institutions across the country in 1970. The underlying rationale was that the Living Unit (LU) Officer worked more directly with the inmate on the Unit where he lived, assuming the dual responsibility for discipline within the Unit while, at the same time, participating in the counselling of inmates. The immediate boss of the LU officers was the LU Supervisor.

One day I happened to meet my friend from Cowansville at the Regional Staff College. After the usual pleasantries, I asked him about his job on the Living Units. What I remember of the conversation was his stated involvement in the counselling of inmates, which included the interpretation of dreams. I couldn't believe my ears then and still have a queasy feeling when I think of it today. What a waste. A competent man with a rare expertise at handling the more difficult inmates under adverse conditions was somehow being converted to the hocus-pocus world of pseudo-science. I don't believe there is any one person responsible for this aberration but, rather, a system that had lost sight of basic priorities.

This is a people business. The problems emanate from the behaviour of people; the solutions come about through the healthy interaction among people. Correctional institutions, if they are to have any meaning, must be organized in such a way as to identify and deal with the real needs and problems of the incarcerated population. At the same time, the true potential of the personnel must be actualized. There is nothing to be gained by making pseudo-psychologists out of correctional officers or, for that matter, by attempting to make competent administrators out of those with a purely clinical training. Roles must be clearly defined within the parameters of the *raison* d'etre of the institution and the potential of each incumbent realized. Since the front-line workers have daily contact with the inmate population, their role definition takes on a particular significance. Their individual potential must be explored to the maximum, so as to develop and maintain a viable and encompassing decision-making process.

The correctional system, with its burgeoning bureaucracy and depersonalizing institutions, has become an increasingly debilitating system for all concerned. It is frequently easier to understand those inmates for whom incarceration simply reinforces delinquent mechanisms, than the few who seem to emerge relatively unscathed. Similarly, too many young workers with a certain potential become, over time, experienced bureaucratic clones of those above them.

The senior institutional administrators of the 'sixties had come up through the ranks. Although their academic level was lower than that of their counterparts today, they usually had had their baptism of fire on the front lines. Many of today's institutional administrators are university graduates in the social sciences. Despite what one might expect from this academic background, too many become entangled in unquestioned policies and procedures from on high, mouthing the platitudes of "corporate objectives" and "core values," while seemingly unable to put into practice the simpler basics centred on human contact.

*   *   *

My own work with the inmates at St. Vincent de Paul penitentiary, and particularly with Jean-Guy, was greatly facilitated by certain key figures. Michel LeCorre was the man who became Warden of an over-populated, seething penitentiary, two weeks before it erupted in the most devastating riot up to that time. He was an intelligent man with excellent organizational ability. He exuded a sense of security, which allowed him to use those around him in a manner beneficial to all. He was a strict disciplinarian with staff and inmates and naturally incurred the wrath of some on each side.

When LeCorre became Warden I had all of three months experience in the penitentiary. Since I lived in the centre of Montreal but had no car I depended on a daily lift from a co-worker. One week I missed my lift twice and arrived at work more than an hour late on two consecutive mornings. In those days, everyone punched the time clock. I received a call in my office from the Warden's secretary, advising me that he wanted to see me. We had not been formally introduced as yet, so I was looking forward to the meeting. I had been spending a lot of time with the rioters in Segregation and was certain LeCorre wanted some in-depth insights into the personalities and behaviour patterns of segregated men.

My French was quite limited at that time and LeCorre's Breton accent produced a sound foreign to my ear. Comprehension was considerably reduced and this led to some misunderstanding at the outset. When he said something in rapid-fire French and pointed to his watch I thought he was asking the time. When I looked at my watch and gave him the time he glared at me with a look that clearly said: "*mon dieu*, not another shrink!" We were finally able to understand one another, or I should say, I was able to understand him. He did the talking. I did the listening. A psychologist a psychologist may know certain techniques for working with difficult inmates but a psychologist, like anyone else, may not be late for work!

The other side to this autocratic approach was that it let one know where one stood. Although I had left his office sheepishly, I soon realized that his ability for direct confrontation was an asset, which was later to serve me well. In the same way that LeCorre had no difficulty telling the psychologist he had the same responsibility toward institutional regulations as others, he was secure enough to recognize and accept the capabilities and advantages of those who worked on a more direct basis with the individual inmate. His own duties and preoccupations as Warden kept him remote from the internal daily life of the institution. His experience with front-line work, however, allowed him to listen to and appreciate the counsel of others. He was the chief administrator of the penitentiary and, although he had a good grasp of delinquency, he never fancied himself a clinician and was able to accept those who were and profit from their expertise.

It was principally through Michel LeCorre that we were eventually able to extricate Jean-Guy from a living situation that contributed directly to his dangerousness. He recognized the necessity for Segregation as a means of temporarily defusing a specific, explosive situation with certain individuals. He was also quick to realize that simply separating individuals from problematic circumstances did not solve the problem. The inherent dangers in warehousing a group of aggressive individuals together for an indeterminate period became increasingly clear to those of us who worked regularly with segregated men. The process of segregation caused a specific malaise that gradually generalized, enveloping the total personality and increasing the chances of reoccurrence with more explosive results. These were important issues and steps had to be taken to implement healthy, corrective measures. In the case of Jean-Guy, it took a good amount of courage on LeCorre's part to help, since there was strong resistance to any change that could be interpreted as permissive. The resistance came from sources as close as most of his assistants.

* * *

The senior correctional officers in the penitentiary during the 'sixties were called Keepers. There were six to eight of them and each was responsible for a specific sector within the walls. Their principal task was to assure security. Cell Block One was the highest security area of maximum security, St. Vincent de Paul. There was one man directly in charge of the segregated inmates and their guards who were sometimes referred to as the "goon squad." The Keeper: Gerry Landry, the toughest of them all.

I would like to state, at the outset, that my overall experience with the guards in Cell Block One was a positive one. I learned a lot from them and, hopefully, they learned something from me. They were a rough group of men who reacted swiftly and vigorously to verbal and/or physical abuse. I suspect that a few of them occasionally instigated trouble and I certainly don't condone this behaviour. I believe, however, it would have been reactive behaviour rather than pure malice; a delayed reaction to the pervasive pressure of a totally suppressive regime. Although I received several complaints from segregated inmates over the years, the fact is I rarely observed troublemaking instigated by the guards. Our relationship, tenuous at first, mollified over a period of time. In the beginning I was greeted with stony silence and seen as an intruder. I was granted a begrudged, basic cooperation, enough to allow me to conduct interviews. This coldness dissipated gradually and I began to be perceived as help rather than hindrance. Eventually, a number of the guards overtly cooperated by referring inmates to me.

One day I received a call in my office from Cell Block One. The guard told me an inmate was asking to see me in my office. He was escorted according to the procedure of the time, handcuffed to one guard and followed by a second guard who kept the key. At my request, the handcuffs were removed as the inmate entered my office and the guards remained behind the closed door in the hallway.

Harry was a young tough in his mid-twenties, serving a third penitentiary sentence. He was in Segregation for the riot, awaiting formal charges and subsequent court appearances. I had interviewed him once or twice before the riot so, in a sense, we knew each other. Although his manner of speech indicated a certain cultural deprivation, he obviously possessed strong "street smarts", an asset for survival in his violent world.

"Mr. Williams, we have a fuckin' bug on the wing whose gonna get shived tonight if you don't do something. We had a meeting, me and the other guys on the wing, and we all agreed I should come and see you. We don't want no trouble, we got enough as it is, but 'dis guy's gonna drive us nuts! He rants and raves in his cell day and night, sayin' he's gonna kill 'dis guy and 'dat guy. The best is, the guys he's namin' aint even in 'de joint. You gotta do somethin', or we will. 'Dis guy could be dangerous for any of us, it's not his fault . . . but we're not takin' no chances."

The mini-speech was delivered in one breath; it was obviously a serious matter. This was a peculiar situation. Inmates normally don't report incidents before they happen. Certainly many of the men in Cell Block One had few qualms about rectifying a threatening situation in their traditional manner. On the other hand, they were in a highly restricted area where it was more difficult to handle the matter surreptitiously. If I were to be of any help, I simply had to remove the "bug" from Segregation and, at the same time, maintain Harry's anonymity. Although he had the okay of his wing mates, this way of dealing with a problem is not generally accepted; speaking to someone "up front" about internal matters is just not done.

I find it difficult to imagine an incident like this being easily handled today, but this was 1963. This predated "risk factor scales," "notorious cases," and "administrative inquiries." In this simpler time, I was able to explain the situation to the Warden, without identifying Harry. The "bug" was removed from Segregation and placed in Psychiatry. The institutional Psychiatrist later diagnosed him as having suffered a reactive psychosis with accompanying hallucinations and a developing delusional system. Although the inmate terminology "bug" did not allow for a differential diagnosis, the entire incident proved to be positive. It was the first of many that would help me realize that the best institutional diagnosticians were often the inmates themselves. If only we could learn to create a positive milieu that would encourage and reward healthy social behaviour and attitudes.

I visited the inmates in Segregation on a daily basis for a long period. A guard would unlock the door to the wing where some twenty men were locked behind the barred doors of individual cells. I was then left in the relative privacy of a corridor stretched out in front of cells one to twenty. Interviewing under such circumstances was time saving but limited to matters common to all or many of the men. It also had a certain cathartic value for individuals subjected to a physically and emotionally deprived routine. Topics of a more confidential nature were discussed in the privacy of my office.

*   *   *

A common allegation against the validity of private interviews with institutionalized delinquents is that, in such a setting, the inmate is playing a role, putting up a good front to get something. There is a certain amount of truth to this. In fact, the imposed lifestyle in a correctional institution reinforces this type of manipulative posturing. If an inmate wants to get a job change, a telephone call, an extra visit, a parole, he must learn the tune being played, then dance to it. In a large impersonal institution this superficiality frequently passes as meaningful change and is rewarded. Unfortunately, a process such as this favours the better organized, not necessarily less delinquent, individual and discriminates against those who are personally disorganized.

However, a competent interviewer is sensitive to delinquent mechanisms and takes them into consideration when evaluating the content of the interview. Once a certain trust had developed between inmate and interviewer, the inmate is increasingly able to drop his defences and reveal his true self. Obviously, this scenario is enhanced in more private surroundings where the inmate is not directly subject to peer group demands. It was in the privacy of my office that tough men cried, leaders revealed their real fears and "hard rocks" spoke haltingly of their impoverished upbringing.

The phenomenon of delinquency is distinct from mental illness and major emotional maladjustment. There are mentally ill offenders; however, they are in the minority. Likewise, there are certain offenders who manifest neurotic symptomatology. Nevertheless, if the neurosis is successfully treated we are usually left with a neurosis-free offender. What one finds all too frequently in penitentiaries are men suffering from reactive psychosis. This may be due to a gradual build-up, over a long period of time, of self-defeating situations that culminate in a break with reality; it may also be a reaction to the severity of the sentence itself or simply to the daily stresses of institutional life. Fortunately, reactive psychosis is readily treatable if correctly diagnosed. The most difficult to treat are those individuals who have the basic delinquent personality make-up with an overlay of mental illness symptomatology.

I first met Al toward the end of my first year in the Pen; to this day, I don't know why he didn't surface earlier. He worked in the dishwashing and was considered a hard worker. Although hard workers were appreciated by the administration and compensated accordingly, their inmate co-workers did not generally accept them. An inmate who worked hard was perceived as showing-up the others. This was seldom tolerated and controlled by threat or overt force. In Al's case, however, the need to work hard as a means of doing his time was recognized by others. Their acceptance, a marked departure from the norm, was due in great part to Al's irritability, which generally dissuaded others from slowing him down.

Al was a well-built black man from a Nova Scotia ghetto, then known as Africville; an ex-boxer with a reputation for success in the ring, both on the outside and in the institution. He was one of some twelve to fifteen siblings; the exact number was of no relevance to him. He was doing a twenty-year sentence for manslaughter; convicted for the knife slaying of a white man, in what he perceived as a racially provoked fight on the part of the victim.

When inmates first came to my office, they were usually there for pragmatic reasons. It may be for the luxury of a tailor-made cigarette, a 'phone call or a plea for support in a bid to transfer to medium security. In any case, the pragmatism was usually obvious. Al was different. He came to talk, not to be heard, just to talk. He rambled on, never asking any questions. If I were able to get in a quick question in one of his brief pauses to light a cigarette, he basically ignored it and simply rambled on, not always coherently. There was never any hostility directed toward me but rather a strange, non-verbal appreciation of the fact that I just sat there and listened. I had the feeling that most inmates gave him a wide berth to begin with and if ever cornered by him at work, for example, would split at the first opportunity.

Listening, or rather hearing, was no problem. Al recounted exploits at a rapid pace and always at high volume. His voice grew louder as he got emotionally caught up in his own story and phrases were regularly interspersed with loud bursts of laughter. What was particularly disconcerting was that it was impossible to relate the laughter to the verbal content. At times I felt that not only I, but Al too, was simply an observer. For example, he would relate his experience in court when sentenced for the present offence and within a relatively brief period of time, he had turned toward the wall and was addressing the judge, jury and prosecutor, alternately in the past and future. As he reached an emotional crescendo, the aggressive verbiage he directed toward the court figures was accompanied by loud peals of laughter. When he had determined the interview over, he simply put away his cigarettes, shook my hand fervently and said, "thanks man . . . great seein' ya . . . ah gotta git back now."

On more than one occasion, the noise emanating from my office brought a worried Chief Keeper to my door. He would peer through the glass momentarily and then return to his office nodding in disbelief. He once asked me if I felt safe with Al in my office. I assured him that everything was okay and then muttered under my breath that I only wished I knew what the hell was going on.

Despite the many uncertainties, I feel that the climate of those times was healthier than today's and should have developed more positively. In today's institutions, incidents such as described above would be suppressed by a reactionary and amateurish Preventive Security, which would ultimately prevent learning more than anything else.

Some months later, I was instrumental in helping both Al and the institution in a potentially explosive incident. He had applied for transfer to Kingston Penitentiary and was on the waiting list. A hostage-taking incident the previous week had increased the tension in the institution and pushed many to over-react. A combination of anxiety built up by the uncertainty of the transfer, combined with heightened feelings within the general inmate population, finally proved too much for this fragile individual. He made the offhand remark, "I guess you have to take a fucking screw hostage to get outta here". When this was overheard, steps were taken to place him in Segregation. These steps were partially successful. They were able to get him to Cell Block One but he refused to go into a cell. He asked to see me, and I credit Keeper Landry with the good judgement of calling me in an attempt to avoid violence.

When I arrived at the Cell Block, Al had been placed in a wing of some twenty empty cells. I asked the Keeper to allow me to enter the wing alone, to lock it behind me and withdraw out of sight. Keeper Landry knew me fairly well by this time and complied with my request. I was simply afraid that if Al became emotionally agitated, the uniform might trigger off some acting-out. I was thinking of my own security.

Al was calm enough, more so than I was, and readily accepted a cigarette. It didn't take long to realize that he accepted his situation; he was in Segregation and he was here to stay until the transfer. I assured him that I would do my best to accelerate matters. This assurance had a noticeable effect on him and the only other point seemed to be that he feared being on a wing by himself. Although he avoided the word fear, his demeanour was telling.

Since I knew all the men in Segregation, I suddenly realized that one wing had three or four guys who had been transferred from Dorchester Penitentiary, from where Al had originated. The next steps were clear: get the okay from the guys on the wing and get the okay from Keeper Landry. The demands were reasonable, the problem was solved, and the violence had been avoided.

Al was eventually transferred to Kingston Penitentiary some short time later. I never heard from or about him since. Although I could never arrive at an accurate diagnostic label for Al, I did ask him once if he would like to speak with the Psychiatrist. I even offered to go with him.

"You axin' me go see that guy? No way man, that mothafucka's crazier'n me!"

*   *   *

The vanguard of prison reform has often been embodied in various religious groups. Similarly, individuals who have sought to defend inmate rights, represented them in courts and before administrative tribunals, acted as principal mediators between the offender and his family, have frequently been representatives of a particular organized religion. The tradition is an ancient one and continues today.

Despite this, the role of the penitentiary Chaplain has often proven to be an ambiguous one. This probably says more about how correctional institutions have evolved than the chaplaincy itself. The role has seemingly developed gradually over the years from the isolated individual who provided solace in times of distress to the more professional team player who dispenses more progressive theological concepts, sometimes laced with up-to-date social work terminology. The latter is seemingly preoccupied with inmate rights within established institutional living, the former with the inmate as a person. My own experience indicated that, although some organized religious groups were more active than others, the long-term concern belonged to individuals regardless of their particular school of beliefs.

Bill McCarthy was an Anglican priest and veteran of the Korean War. He was also a product of the north end of Montreal, a recruiting ground for future penitentiary inmates, a district known at the time as "Mile End". He had the respect of a multitude of the city's indigent alcoholics, as well as many of the "west-end gang." "The Rev," as he was respectfully referred to by many of his "clients", tirelessly supervised the Old Brewery Mission for more than thirty years. Over this period of time, he had successfully integrated many graduates of our prisons and penitentiaries into the work at the Mission, allowing them to regain some much needed self-worth, as they provided realistic, street-wise help for the helpless and homeless. If organized religion of any label has a job description for its ministers, it must certainly include McCarthy's activities. Had he had the chance to read this, undoubtedly this self-effacing man would have been livid.

I first met Bill McCarthy shortly after the riot in 1962. He was substitute Chaplain at the Pen, replacing the ailing legendary, Rev. Sam Pollard. On the surface, no two men could be more different. Rev. Pollard was an erudite man whose English accent and command of the language, gave one the impression of speaking to an Oxford Don; McCarthy's command of the language was equally proficient, only the language was different. The impression one gleaned from his verbal expression was that he was more likely a graduate of the Canadian Navy, with a post-doctoral at the Pen. The striking similarity between the two men was their recognition of the fundamental value of the human condition. Pollard had steadfastly stood by Wilbur Coffin through to his execution and proclaimed his belief in the man's innocence up to his own death some years ago.

McCarthy had heard rumours of inmates having been beaten by guards immediately after the riot. He fearlessly used his station as Chaplain to gain entrance to the institutional hospital. He was horrified to see the deformed face of an inmate he knew, lying in one of the hospital beds. He had interviewed this man, just days before the riot and knew that his physical condition had been that of a prizefighter in training. He was now a mass of lacerations, bruises and swelling. The inmate's story, mumbled through disfigured lips and swollen tongue, was that, while in the "hole", he had been beaten by a number of guards, under the watchful eye of certain institutional authorities. His present physical condition was life threatening and the medical authorities reluctantly admitted that whatever happened had occurred since the riot.

Almost two years later, the institutional authorities felt they had an airtight case against this man as a principal leader in the riot. The prosecution was aiming for the maximum sentence for instigating a riot. The inmate defendant stunned the Court by pleading "guilty with explanation." Over the objections of the prosecution, the presiding judge allowed the testimony of three witnesses, one of whom was McCarthy. This took no small amount of courage as he had received some veiled threats because of his "siding with the cons" and had become increasingly ostracized by certain colleagues. This exclusion was the direct result of his refusal to back down from telling the truth. After two days of testimony, Judge Claude Wagner rendered his decision: one day concurrent with the present sentence. At the same time, he castigated the penitentiary authorities for having acted as judge and jury and for having meted out a sentence of brutal retaliation.

As I mentioned previously, the effects of the deprivation of liberty affect all who live and work within the institutional milieu. This becomes particularly acute in times of crisis. The riot of 1962 was under control within hours. The introduction of the Army and later the RCMP maintained the control. However, the heightened tension and anxiety lasted months and, for some, years.

As an accused rioter, the man for whom McCarthy testified was held in Segregation. After the first day of testimony on his own behalf, he was returned to the penitentiary for the night. On the morning of the second day, he was searched before leaving Segregation, following routine procedure. What was not official procedure, however, was the fact that the notes he had prepared the previous evening were confiscated and he was menacingly advised to discontinue his testimony since, "remember you're coming back here."

This scenario had no effect on the activities in court during the day but certainly increased the man's anxiety when he was due to return to the penitentiary. It was late in the afternoon when he arrived. I happened to be in the hallway of the administration building where my office was located when I heard a voice cry out:

"Mr. Williams, Mr. Williams, can I see you in your office right away it's very important!"

The guards removed the handcuffs and waited outside my office. He was obviously close to a panic state and quickly recounted the events in Segregation before leaving for court in the morning. He had just been sentenced to one day concurrent to his current sentence and was now expected to return to Segregation:

"Mr. Williams, I can't go back in there, I'll never come out. They threatened me this morning and they're serious. You gotta help me, I just can't go back there, they're really hot!"

Although I had only been working in the Pen about two years, I had learned that certain key decisions, perceived as favouring the inmate, are more easily made by the decision-maker when the inmate pleads his own case. There are undoubtedly many and complex reasons. It was late in the afternoon now, actually past lock-up time. I had no time to analyze motives but proceeded on instinct. The Deputy Warden's office was about three down the hallway from mine. I knew Mr. Brennan as a fiery Irishman who cowed many a so-called tough guy, as he sternly lectured them when they passed before him in disciplinary court. I also knew him as a man with an innate sense of justice and fair play. There were no written rules about this at the time. Brennan didn't need a book of rules. He used his head and his heart.

"Would you be prepared to speak to Mr. Brennan?

I believe this man was prepared to deal with the devil himself. The only advice I gave him was to stay cool and relate all the facts as he had related them to me. Later I was summoned to the Deputy Warden's office and asked if I would accompany the inmate to the institutional hospital. The man looked physically relieved. I'm sure Brennan believed that my presence would ease the inmate's passage through the main cellblock area, where many of the uniformed personnel were gathered to complete the lock-up. The silent, cold stares directed toward him exuded hostility and confirmed that the court decision was now public knowledge.

It was not until I took the return trip back to my office that I realized the hostile stares were not reserved only for the inmate. They encompassed all perceived to be "on his side." About a dozen silent, uniformed guards momentarily blocked my passage. It aroused in me an emotional reaction that can be rekindled more than forty years later. I believe it was this experience that solidified my belief in the nefarious effects of the deprivation of liberty and how they affect both the watchers and the watched.

ON PAROLE

~ *outside looking in*

In the mid-sixties two significant, almost simultaneous developments, in the field of corrections affected my career. One was to take place in the Quebec Region of the Canadian Penitentiary Service, despite strong opposition from professionals in the private sector: the construction of the Special Detention Unit (SDU), about a quarter of a mile behind St. Vincent de Paul penitentiary. The other was the implementation of a treatment centre for persistent offenders, under the impetus of a group of professionals from the McGill University Forensic Clinic, in Dannemora, New York some fifty miles from Montreal. Although my contact with the SDU was only peripheral in the first five years of its existence, I participated directly in an attempt to convert the institution into "a prison that makes some sense" some years later. My involvement in the treatment centre in New York, however, was immediate to its planning, inception and maintenance over a five-year period. As it turns out this was the most significant experience of my career, as much a vehicle of learning as an opportunity to deal with the multi-faceted symptomatology of persistent delinquency.

One morning in March 1964, as I drove up Montée St-François, alongside the ominous fortress-like wall of St-Vincent de Paul penitentiary, I gazed up at the manned guard tower and realized that the inmates would be trudging across the yard from the squalor of their cells to the ennui of their work area. I was not particularly preoccupied with the scheduled upcoming meeting with the staff psychiatrist; little did I realize that it would be a turning point in my career. We had met on previous occasions, usually to discuss the handling and treatment of specific inmates. He knew of my ongoing contact with the men in Segregation and had expressed an avid interest in what we termed "the extreme deprivation of liberty." As it turned out, we prepared a paper jointly on this subject some time later.

Bruno Cormier was a paradoxical figure who engendered feelings of ambivalence in those he encountered. Inmates were angered by his confrontational style, yet sought out his help in their personal misery; his outspoken condemnation of correctional institution practices of the day was a curse to the authorities who, at the same time, consulted with him as to institutional change; those who pontificated from the comfortable seat of pure theory became the brunt of his criticism but he was regularly invited to present at national and international conferences by these same people. Although slight in physical stature, he was an intellectual giant with an iron will.

As I passed through the barred gate that separated the administration building from the penitentiary yard, I saw Dr.Cormier awaiting me some distance ahead. The meeting was to be brief and, literally, "in the open."

"How would you like to come and work at the Forensic Clinic?" he asked.

For the moment I was stunned. Here we were standing in the penitentiary yard, the last inmate stragglers sauntering sullenly toward their imposed assignments, armed guards surveying the scene from their towers and I was receiving a pardon or at least a parole. I had now been working at the Pen over two years and exposure to the drab surroundings on a full-time basis brought on overwhelming feelings of helplessness that weighed heavily on me. I still enjoyed working with the men but I was becoming increasingly aware of the extreme limitations of the setting.

Bruno Cormier was a pioneer. He created the McGill Forensic Clinic, a centre that meant different things to different people. It was inter-disciplinary and afforded me the opportunity to work in collaboration with professionals who came from diverse backgrounds with considerable experience. It was not long before I realized what had really been most difficult for me while working in the penitentiary. Although there were some well-intentioned, competent people there, I worked basically alone. There was little opportunity for exchange on a clinical level. I had shared some difficult cases with Cormier but this interaction, while refreshing, was sporadic.

Thus, I resigned from the penitentiary and took up the position of Psychologist and Research Assistant at the Forensic Clinic. The multi-disciplinary team prepared written expertise for the courts, carried out clinical research in criminology and provided an outpatient service for those released from provincial and federal correctional institutions. It was only a matter of time before I found myself back at the Pen, now as a McGill research worker with a new status that enhanced my effect both with inmates and correctional officials.

The Forensic Clinic always bore its founder's imprint; it was always "Bruno's Clinic." After his retirement many years later, it staggered on for some time, mainly because he never really retired. Even throughout his debilitating terminal illness, he kept a hand on matters at the Clinic. It did not survive long after death despite the efforts of a successor.

It was not always easy to work for Dr.Cormier who was an exacting man. His insight into the psychodynamics of delinquency, however, was unparalleled and his firsthand knowledge of correctional institutions and their debilitating effect on the individual offender gave a realistic tone to case conferences. This consideration of institutional effects on behaviour is too often absent in clinical deliberations. In summary, Cormier was one of those rare social science academics who combined solid theoretical background with an on-going clinical practice.

A context such as this was particularly rewarding for me. It allowed me the freedom to maintain regular contact with and study of the incarcerated delinquent, as I spent approximately half of my time in one or another of the penitentiaries. It was at this period I began group work with inmates: with the younger offenders at the Federal Training Centre and with the hard core at St. Vincent de Paul penitentiary. The balance of my workweek was at the Clinic itself. Interviews with offenders released from institutions as part of the post-release service, as well as evaluation of offenders sent by the court, were the basis of my work there. The regular clinical case conference, under the supervision of Dr.Cormier, was the linchpin of the entire operation. The presentations were made on a rotating basis, allowing for a sharing of expertise from individuals with varied professional backgrounds and experience. The conferences served as a learning experience at a practical level, as well as the basis for the preparation of professional papers.

I shared a therapeutic group at the Federal Training Centre with a Psychiatrist colleague from the Clinic. He had previous experience with youthful offenders, in both Great Britain and Canada. The group was composed of six offenders ranging in age from fifteen to eighteen years. Two of the six were not eligible for parole, as they had not been sentenced under the Criminal Code. They had been sentenced to the penitentiary directly from Juvenile Court as "incorrigible". My initial reaction was one of disbelief; officially incorrigible at any age is questionable, but at fifteen?

Tommy, one of the incorrigibles, had been sent to the penitentiary to learn a trade; no doubt by an exasperated system personified by a judge. The system could no longer tolerate his frequent absconding from Shawbridge Boys Farm, the principal juvenile facility for English-speaking young offenders. He had initially been placed there for his own protection. His mother was a nightclub dancer who supplemented her income with occasional prostitution. She had hooked up with various male partners over the years, the last of whom had led her off to the United States in search of better opportunities. Tommy's chief motivation to escape was to recover his mom. He recounted his story to the group with the ease and detachment of an experienced raconteur. He no longer possessed the luxury of tears; after all, he was now fifteen and learning a trade.

Inherent in true delinquency, is an incapacity to perceive the source of one's problems as emanating from within. The focal point of life difficulties is projected upon externals such as family, school, peer group, police, etc. Unfortunately, the daily institutional routine gradually strips away personal responsibility and unwittingly reinforces an evolving self-centredness. The entire process ultimately precludes the development of empathy.

Weekly, for over eighteen months, we worked with Tommy and the other members of the group. However, I was increasingly certain that our approach was simply not enough. Regardless of how astute group therapists may be, the iniquitous effects of incarceration finally neutralize any beneficial accrued effects. There had to be something different. Incarceration was certainly necessary for certain individuals but did it have to be so debilitating? Was there a way in which institutional influences could have a positive effect on those living and working within? At least, could the institutional milieu favour the reinforcement of positive social responses? These questions were discussed at length with my colleague during the long car ride back to the Clinic after each group session. What was needed was not simply a more favourable environment in which therapeutic techniques could be put into practice. We felt that a fundamental alteration of the milieu was necessary so as to profit by the total institution experience, over a twenty-four hour period. This nebulous idea seemed depressingly implausible.

Shortly after the inception of the group in the Federal Training Centre, I decided upon trying one in St. Vincent de Paul. The idea came to me as I realized that one of the young men at the Federal Training Centre had been referred to us because he was constantly in conflict with the institutional personnel and spent much of his time in the "hole." Although the group had been functioning for only a short time, there already were signs of change in his attitude and behaviour. The group itself was freewheeling and verbal expression was not curbed; the one proviso was that an analysis of the underlying emotional content must be allowed. There were several levels of expression, analysis and interpretation over a period of time and much was of considerable value. It was obvious from the outset, however, that the cathartic value of free expression was somehow translated into improved attitudes and behaviours outside the group. All these young offenders were adjusting better to institutional life, according to institutional personnel. Empirically, one may question the causal relationship; we accepted it on faith.

Although I was in St. Vincent de Paul only three half-days per week now, I did keep contact with the men in Segregation. Some were now back in the general population. The idea of trying a group was brought up with Harry and Jean-Guy, both of whom were in the general population. In fact, Harry had completed his previous sentence, including the time he received for the riot, and was now beginning his fourth penitentiary term. He had completed all of forty days in freedom before being arrested, with his younger brother, for armed robbery. Jean-Guy was simply continuing his first sentence, an aggregate of twenty-four years, including an additional ten years for aggravated assault on the guard in Segregation. Both men were excited about starting a group. When I explained that I would like to have a group comprised of men who had difficulty adjusting to the penitentiary routine, they looked at each other and grinned:

> "If it's ball breakers you want Mr. Williams, we can fill up your office in a hot second!"

Despite the public's perception of penitentiaries and their inmates, in fact, most inmates complete their sentence with relative ease. I am not saying they like it. What I am saying is that a small percentage of the inmate population is constantly in trouble. Some are personally disorganized and are used by the more clever, better organized inmates to run the various internal rackets, until they are caught and punished; others are emotionally disturbed with little control over their impulsive acting-out; a few have to put up the "hard rock" front as a self-protective device in a threatening environment and, fewer yet, will simply accept no rules or regulations from anyone, including the peer group.

*   *   *

The 'sixties was a decade of considerable importance in many respects. An American President is assassinated; the war in Vietnam continues to escalate despite growing protests on the home front; flower power is in bloom and drug usage becomes more openly widespread. Many variations of group treatment, some actually emanating from schools of social science, come to the fore. The spectrum is covered: from the monotonous drone of transcendental meditation, to the piercing primal scream; from the assuaging assurance of "I'm OK/You're OK", to the severe confrontation of the encounter group; from the soothing sensation of group relaxation techniques, to the active stimulation of feelings through groping and touching. My own attempts at group therapy within the penitentiary were driven by an undeniable pragmatism, rather than in response to popular treatment initiatives: there was one of me but many inmates.

I had no misgivings about starting a group with incarcerated delinquents, as I felt comfortable working with them. I did, however, have strong reservations about referring to the process as "group psychotherapy." In fact, the group was little more than a gang of inmates who chose from among themselves those whom they trusted and those who shared similar interests, desires and complaints. In composition, it was not dissimilar to a gang of offenders in the community-at-large, although with less inherent discipline. An interesting fact is that the group encounters somehow produced positive results.

Institutional life during this era was repetitious and generally boring. Seventeen of the twenty-four hours were spent locked in a cell small enough that one had to hook the chain-linked bed to the wall so as to use the toilet facilities. Fifty percent of the total number of cells had no flush toilets. These "bucket cells" were serviced manually. The resident inmate emerged from his cell in the early morning with his filled bucket in one hand and empty tray in the other. The return to the cell was immediately upon exchange for an emptied bucket and a replenished breakfast tray. During the regular workweek the seven-hour day outside the cell was given to five hours in a workshop or at school and two hours of unstructured yard time. Weekends saw yard time stretch the entire seven hours. Institutional personnel allotted all assignments and, as some inmates would say, "they ask you to make two choices, then give you the third." A preferred job was in the kitchen. Apart from the fact that one "got outta the drum earlier" to prepare breakfast, there was the added advantage of eating better as the kitchen crew had direct access to the food and could cook for themselves. They ate in the kitchen rather than within the confines of a cell. An equally important benefit was that the kitchen worker was in an excellent position to devise various profitable schemes from pilfered food.

The official library facilities consisted of a censored list of books and magazines from which the inmate was able to select two of each per week. The institutional librarian and his two inmate helpers carried out the subsequent delivery service as they passed the chosen works through the cell bars on weekly rounds. A more efficient system, however, was the unofficial but highly organized trafficking of the unexpurgated "skin" books and crime tabloids. These were considered contraband, a fact that added greatly to their popularity and value.

Canteen articles were purchased with one's institutional earnings. The canteen list was limited to a few practical items and a very few luxury items, distributed on a bi-monthly basis. A package of tobacco was the number one item, serving as the basic unit of the underground currency. The "deck of weed," in varying amounts, paid debts, procured services and placated enforcers. Furthermore, most inmates smoked and few could afford the luxury of "tailor-mades." Inmate pay, at this time, ranged from the basic daily rate of twenty-five cents, to the executive rate of fifty-five cents per day. A standard portion of this amount was frozen as compulsory savings and given to the inmate upon release. This accumulated amount of money, along with a suit of clothes, formed the basic "release plan" to ease the transition from institutional life to the relative freedom and responsibilities of society.

In summary it is safe to say that the everyday life within the institution was characterized by a pervasive ennui. It was divergence from the prescribed lifestyle, intrigues contrived by the inmates themselves, which allowed for some semblance of individual expression. Unfortunately, most of these machinations were not within the purview of institutional rules and unlucky or betrayed participants were subject to punishment. More important yet, this need to devise methods and strategies for everyday survival, behind a mask of conformity to imposed regulations, increased the psychological and physical chasm between the "we" and "they." The ultimate result of this chaotic lifestyle was a reinforcement of the delinquent values and mechanisms that preclude a healthy post-release adjustment to the community-at-large.

GROUP THERAPY

~ the mob

One could review the theories of personality, explore the schools of psychodynamics and compare treatment techniques to ascertain the basic value of a specific therapeutic group. I believe that the group sessions in St. Vincent de Paul penitentiary, throughout the latter half of the 'sixties, were cathartic and provided an oasis of freedom and humanness in a desert of masquerade, suspicion and violence. In everyday institutional life, the inmates postured and posed in response to the various demands of this unhealthy milieu. Within the group, a different milieu was gradually developed; one in which each individual was encouraged to shed this artificial facade and express oneself freely. This verbal and emotional release is a formidable enough task for most of us who attempt it; it is almost impossible for men within an ambiance of affective repression and constant threat of immediate reprisal.

There was no doubt in my mind then that the primary incentive to form a group, on the part of the inmates, was simply to get out of the institutional routine. There is nothing surprising about this. Daily life is essentially boring and intrinsically unproductive. The authorities, through coercion, orchestrate every activity. Personal responsibility and autonomy are words used as a yardstick to measure how little the individual has progressed, when time comes to refuse transfer to an institution of lesser security or conditional release. In fact, the design of the daily institutional life does not in any way encourage the development of personal responsibility or permit the growth of autonomy. All too often, any form of independence on the part of inmates is perceived as a threat to bureaucratic control, disguised as "the security of the institution." Despite the platitudinous statements that emanate from the upper echelons of the organization today, this is as true now as it was forty years ago.

Participation in this proposed group was to be on a voluntary basis. The novelty of it allured them into this encounter with an unknown goal. The challenge for them would be to test the limits as they embarked on this arcane adventure.

What an adventure it turned out to be for me. Every Friday morning from the autumn of 1965 through the autumn of 1971, the small quarters of the psychology department at St. Vincent de Paul penitentiary echoed to the din of some six to fifteen inmates ventilating their feelings in free expression. Over this span of six years, many different types of offenders came to the group, for varying periods of time. Some left because they were released or transferred from the penitentiary; others departed only to return after a brief regress to the hole, segregation, psychiatry or any combination of the above. The basic criterion for entry into the group: an inability to comply with the rules and regulations of the penitentiary. This intransigence differed among individuals and the causal factors were varied and sundry, but the end result was the same: the individual had been or was about to be the object of some serious disciplinary measure.

I started this group alone but shared it with André Thiffault after September 1966. Although we knew each other well enough, we had never worked together prior to this. He had served his baptism of fire as staff Psychologist at the Pen in the late fifties after graduating from l'Université de Montréal, then worked a few years at the McGill Forensic Clinic. He had just completed a two-year sabbatical in the U.S. and Europe when he came into our group. He fit in like a hand in a glove.

Thiffault was raised in mining country, in the Abitibi region of northern Quebec. He was an intelligent, cultivated man whose interests covered a wide spectrum. He read voraciously, learned quickly and proffered an opinion on most subjects, regardless of whether it had been solicited or not. He radiated self-assurance, a trait that proved to be an irritant to casual acquaintances but a source of support to me. He had an excellent understanding of delinquent dynamics and reactions but the talent that served him best in our field was that of manipulation. He could fend for himself with the best; he could out-con the con and the authorities were never an equal match.

I appreciated working with and learning from this enigmatic individual. I discovered early on that he bore little tolerance for incompetence and was particularly impatient with bureaucrats. Like any good manipulator he had an uncanny ability to spot an opponent's weakness and would immediately run roughshod over his victim. The only defence against this was to take the offensive.

What I am describing above is how I perceived Thiffault in relation to most colleagues, correctional authorities, politicians, etc.; in other words, charming as he could be in a social setting, he frequently turned his world of work into a combat zone. His relationship with the inmates, however, was professional in the best sense of the word. He exhibited a genuine concern for them but was never paternalistic; he would go the whole nine yards for them when he saw that an injustice had been perpetrated but would confront them directly if he sensed a hidden agenda; he was sensitive to their deep-seated needs but would not permit them to wallow in self-pity.

Although the inmates in the group usually chose additional members, we sometimes introduced a new candidate ourselves. Final acceptance or rejection was in the hands of the inmates since they were the ones confined together, twenty-four hours a day. Thiffault was instrumental in extricating an inmate from Segregation and placing him in the group. On the surface, this man was the least likely candidate for any group process. He was dull-witted, chronically anxious and had a speech defect that resulted in one-line outbursts of stuttered speech. He had also developed a psychological addiction to medication, frequently seeking chemical relief through the illicit trade among inmates. He often obtained what he wanted by means of physical threat, a behaviour pattern that resulted in his eventual separation from the general population. As it turned out, he was well known to the other group members and acceptance was immediate.

Marc was the oldest of three siblings, raised in abject poverty in the southeast end of Montreal. His father had abandoned the family early on and the only source of income was a monthly welfare cheque, supplemented by the meagre earnings his mother could obtain by taking in laundry from neighbourhood rooming houses. For a short period of time, a live-in "uncle" was supposed to provide some economic support. As it turned out, his alcoholic intake eclipsed his financial input.

Marc's problems surfaced in the early school years. A multitude of factors, both internal and external, resulted in his inability to cope with the demands of a school structure. The subsequent truancy, fighting and petty thievery led to his appearance in Juvenile Court and consequent placement in various correctional facilities. As a youth, he was big for his age, above average in height and weight. Although intellectually impoverished, he learned quickly that, in this milieu, his size was to his advantage: might was right. He stood over six feet and weighed over 250 pounds when he came into our group.

He was welcomed into the group with the usual backslapping and current handshake. His size immediately earned him the appellation "*le Gros*," a term of respect in this world of muscle and physical dominance. It was not long before the group was taken aback, myself included, by a series of slow, calculated movements on the part of this characteristically impulsive giant. In one hand he held a plastic pouch, the other hand slowly withdrew an object from his jacket pocket. All stared in wonderment, myself with no small measure of relief, as he calmly began to fill a pipe with aromatic tobacco.

"*Colisse, t'a l'air d'un vrai spychologue, le Gros,*" exclaimed Jean-Guy.

The room resounded with laughter. Marc beamed like a pop star responding to the adulation of his fans. He knew he was home. The therapeutic session this morning had begun.

In fact, Thiffault who had been working diligently with him during the three or four months he had been confined in Segregation, was an irrepressible pipe-smoker. He left a telltale trail of tobacco debris, burnt matches and a recognizable stench wherever he had passed. The main goal of his regular visits to Segregation was to help sustain Marc's morale. The oppressive regime there, with its twenty-three hour a day lock-up, took its toll on even the most hardened over a period of time. A psychologically fragile individual, such as this giant, succumbed more quickly. We had observed that extreme deprivation of liberty augmented various symptoms such as anxiety and paranoid thinking; what we now learned was that it could also generate the process of identification.

The original group was composed of five inmates but quickly doubled as the word spread. Here was an opportunity to voice one's opinion on the many injustices of the system: the police, judges, lawyers, administrators, guards; all came under fire. It took little prodding to include significant members of one's past: parents, siblings, teachers, juvenile authorities; all were to blame. The bottom line: everyone, other than one's self, was responsible. I wouldn't want anyone to think that these early sessions were merely bitching bouts. In fact, important issues such as the dominance of "*les Canadiens*" in the NHL and the triumph of the upstart Cassius Clay over Sonny Liston took centre stage at several sessions. No subjects were barred; no limits were placed on verbal and emotional intensity. The psychology department was ensconced in a stone-block structure, so the deafening sounds did not easily escape the building. The interior, however, was something else; the joint really rocked.

André and I would frequently review our overall approach, sometimes in the quiet of a local bar over a noontime liquid sedative. We knew we were on to something, not certain what. Our unruly mob could not be accurately portrayed at any professional conference or congress. They seemingly had no control whatsoever over their verbal or emotional expression. They articulated in the three official languages of the Pen: English, French and profane, often at the same time. A common means of underlining an opinion or simply stating the contrary to what had just been expressed was to jump up, throw out one's chest, and bellow. After all, one had to be heard, to be taken seriously. André and I were of the same opinion: this was not a traditional therapeutic group.

On the other hand, the Mob always disbanded with suitable decorum. They would line up like well-behaved, private school students to have their passes signed by our long-suffering clerk, before leaving at the end of the morning session. The clerk himself, though required to dress in institutional uniform identical to that of a guard, was always treated with respect and increasing familiarity. This, in itself, was an initial but remarkable inroad, given the epoch and the make-up of the inmate participants. More concrete signs of change came in the ensuing months, as verbal reports came to us from various areas of the penitentiary. A number of our group members who had previously been cited regularly with offence reports were somehow more conforming in their adaptation to daily life in the Pen. We were not so naïve as to think we had unravelled the protective blanket of delinquent defiance of authority but . . . maybe we were doing something. Certainly we were learning.

Roger was a young man of twenty-three when he came to the penitentiary in 1963. This was his second sentence, a life sentence for the murder of a man in a tavern. We were later to learn that he had never seen the man before, somewhat of a rarity in murder cases. In fact, Roger felt that the man was surreptitiously speaking about him to his drinking companions. When the man left his table to use the toilet facilities, Roger followed him and without a word, knifed him through the heart. The victim died instantly and Roger experienced a sensation of calm for the first time since his release from the penitentiary some three months prior to this incident. He was arrested an hour later while serenely walking the streets and subsequently sentenced to life in prison. A month after his admission to the penitentiary, his personal demons alighted once again. He attacked a guard in the main cellblock. He was subdued only after having caused partial paralysis in the guard's arm, as he warded off a knife attack to the throat. The result of this attempted murder was a second life sentence.

Roger was the second of two siblings, born and raised in the poverty-stricken section of southeast Montreal. His mother did her best to maintain some semblance of normalcy within the home environment. His father, an Italian immigrant, was a hard-working but basically uncommunicative individual. He spent long hours earning a living as a shoe shiner in the lobby of one of Montreal's major hotels and spent his limited leisure time morosely sipping his homemade wine. His older sister survived this impoverished upbringing by leaving the family as a young adolescent to set up home with a hard-working neighbour.

Roger himself was less fortunate. He showed signs of serious adjustment difficulties during the early school years. Compulsive and indiscriminate stealing, characteristic of the primary delinquent, quickly alienated him from classmates and led to constant fighting. A short attention span and pronounced difficulty in concentration resulted in his doubling grades, truancy and eventual expulsion. His life continued on this downward spiral with juvenile detention and an increasing sense of alienation from others, plummeting to a fateful penitentiary sentence before the age of eighteen.

Roger came to the group on the invitation of Jean-Guy and Marc. Both had known him on his previous sentence and shared some other experiences, in that all three had been raised in the same area of Montreal. What is more important, however, is that inmates are often the best diagnosticians, despite the fact that they are sometimes unable to articulate beyond "he's flipping out" or "he's fuckin' nuts". These epithets are not meant to be derogatory but simply an acknowledgment, often based on fear, that someone is different and needs help. Roger was never able to participate actively in the group, unable to relate to more than one person at a time. I do believe, though, his mere presence among the others gave him much-needed sustenance. In his darker moments he lived under a cloud of sedation, sometimes in the solitary confines of Segregation. Roger's final act of desperation was reflected in his suicide in 1971. A guard in Psychiatry spotted him while making his rounds shortly before midnight one Friday. His lifeless body hung suspended from the top of the barred cell door, his bed sheet twisted around his neck. Roger's tortured life had come to an end at age thirty.

Traditional therapeutic groups are conducted for the benefit of the participating members, under the direction of a qualified supervisor. In the penitentiary, however, the group is as much a learning process for the practitioners as it is for the inmates. If not, it is of no value whatsoever. There are too many uncontrolled variables that impinge upon the life of the incarcerated offender. It is impossible to quantify any significant progress and attribute it to the group process. Subjectively, nevertheless, an astute practitioner may pick up on certain cues, gain new insights and observe subtle changes that may serve well in another context altogether.

In general, what we noticed over the months and years was a growing sense of concern and caring among the group members that surpassed the usual camaraderie. Delicate matters associated with one's personal and family life began to surface spontaneously. On occasion, they were tentatively brought up in a jocular manner, obviously to test the waters. Once accepted, they were discussed in earnest. A genuine sense of security among group members was developing gradually and these budding seeds of trust, foreign to the true delinquent and absent in the overall institutional environment, could eventually have a mediating effect on the behaviour of impulsive individuals.

Roger was in the sixth year of his double life sentence, when his father died suddenly. Up to this point he had spent little time in the general population, effectively unable to respond to the demands of the limited freedom of regular institutional life. For the most part, he oscillated between the isolation of the Segregation block and the sedation of the Psychiatric unit. His presence at our Friday morning groups was often by special dispensation, usually when he was in a less agitated state.

Mr. Brennan, now the Warden, asked if I would accompany Roger to the funeral parlour. In those days, the institutional head had a better handle on everyday happenings. This was a time when experts were not created overnight; people worked with people rather than with files and authority was delegated only to persons, never to positions. Although we had informally discussed his case on occasion, it had never been in depth. Mr. Brennan, however, was aware of our group and obviously cognizant of the possible controlling effect of peer influence.

The visit to the funeral home was arranged. The escorts were handpicked. A senior officer from Psychiatry drove the unmarked institutional car as Roger sat in the rear, between Keeper Landry of Segregation and myself. As we approached our destination, Landry instructed the driver to let us out a half block from the location. He and I walked the remainder with Roger between us. No physical restraints were used. I entered the funeral home alone with Roger.

Gerry Landry was the consummate professional. He had limited formal education but the physical bearing of a natural leader. A man of few words, he remained serene under the most trying circumstances. Despite a gruff exterior highlighted by a deeply resonant voice, he was sensitive toward others, a quality honed through four years of confinement in a prisoner-of-war camp. His personal sense of security allowed him to form the judgment that security measures with inmates, though never one hundred percent certain, were more reliable when based on interpersonal relationships. In this instance, the entire event was carried out successfully. The Warden had chosen personnel who were experienced and knew the inmate. Likewise, the inmate felt that familiar faces surrounded him. I was in the favoured position of being perceived as a positive figure by the inmate and, most important, the influence of the peer group was omnipresent. Our group members had "prepared" Roger with compassion and clarity.

In order to understand the import of this event, it is necessary to see it in true perspective. In Roger's case the year was 1969, the penitentiary was the ancient St. Vincent de Paul fortress and institutional programming was in its infancy. There was no "Mission Statement;" core values" were nowhere enunciated; the "reintegration process" had not as yet been divined. Despite this reality, an inmate serving a double life sentence was temporarily released, under escort, from a maximum-security penitentiary to pay his last respects to his father.

Many years later, on a Monday morning as I was going to my office in the medium security Leclerc penitentiary, I was stopped by John in the hallway.

"Could you call me up this morning, Paul?" I was about to reply that I already had scheduled interviews when I heard ". . . . my mother died yesterday. I'm up tight and I'd like to talk."

I had known John on his previous sentence and had referred him to some community resource centre just prior to his release. I had had little formal contact with him since his return to the penitentiary following a new conviction.

I knew he was serving a relatively short, three-year sentence but was completely taken aback when he told me that he had been "gated." Some years prior to this, a change in the law had given the National Parole Board the power to hold men in the penitentiary, after two-thirds of their sentence had been completed, right up to the end of mandate. The idea behind this had been to prevent the early release of men who were considered dangerous. What lawmakers seem never to realize is that nebulous and impersonal measures like this eventually lead to the inevitable widening of the net. What was originally inspired as a reaction to the repetitive, predatory behaviour of certain sexual offenders was to expand into a series of categories that encompassed the majority of offenders sentenced to the penitentiary. It is not surprising that the original numbers predicted for "gating" had increased exponentially within the first five years.

Along with this attempt to legislate the modification of human behaviour, came certain corollaries. During our morning interview, John mentioned that someone had implied that he might not be able to go to the funeral parlour. I expressed my doubts as to the accuracy of this allegation and told him I would check it out. Several telephone calls later, I was trying to explain an ethically unacceptable position to a grieving man: by law, an inmate who had been "gated" could not be released on temporary absence, other than for medical reasons pertaining to his own person.

The year was 1999, thirty years since Roger had been escorted from maximum security to the funeral home. Progress could now be measured: university-trained personnel were now prevalent in the institutions; offender risk and need scales had been designed; criminogenic factors had been identified; computers compiled the data that formed the basis of a comprehensive correctional plan and regurgitated formal reports to faceless decision-makers. The bottom line: John, serving a three-year sentence in a medium security penitentiary, could not be escorted to the last visit with his mother.

Since the basis for our group in the sixties had been established as that of serious penitentiary maladjustment it comes as no surprise that we had become observers of many a tragic ending. Although a number of men showed significant improvement in their institutional behaviour and eventually were transferred to medium security, others were doomed from the outset because of the length of their sentence, the fragility of their basic psychological make-up or a combination of both. Occasionally, men were invited into the group who adjusted well to the institution but were simply popular with other group members. In fact, this latter type proved helpful as they unwittingly served as a positive barometer for the behaviour of others. It is certainly easier to confront an individual when other members of the peer group are an obvious and realistic measure of institutional adjustment.

Rick was twenty-six years of age when he began his third penitentiary sentence. The first two had been relatively short, compared to the thirty-five years he was now facing. Shortly after his admission to the Pen, he had been placed in Segregation for reasons, which came to light only later. After a brief stay, he was released to the general population and immediately invited into the group.

Rick had never known his father. He was raised briefly by his natural mother and then placed in foster care during the pre-school years. As with many placed, hyperactive children he never had the luxury of stability in home or school placement. By the age of ten he had experienced some seven different living facilities and four schools. This constant bouncing from pillar to post accentuated his sense of abandonment and effectively curbed any development of basic trust. Enuresis was "treated" by his being forced to remain wrapped in his urine-soaked bed sheets while tearfully promising to try and do better. This distorted version of conditioning through negative reinforcement was carried out in an institution run by religious Sisters. Although the bed-wetting eventually extinguished with time, the humiliating experience with was another contributing factor that stunted Rick's psychosexual growth. The strong feelings engendered by this practice surfaced in his phantasy life years later while in the confines of the penitentiary.

Incarceration breeds a culture of its own. Since the inmates are there involuntarily, living in close proximity with all activities controlled by others, specific group dynamics evolve. One of the most common and potentially explosive is the constant vying for control, power and prestige by individuals and groups. The strong become stronger by adding to their group; the weak become stronger by successfully joining a group. This was a basic dynamic of which André and myself had to be aware, so as to maintain some control and avoid dangerous proliferation.

Our Friday morning group was made up of much of the penitentiary muscle. In fact, though, they were only a faction; those whose activities were so out in the open that they were constantly in trouble with the authorities. There were other individuals in the inmate population whose activities and alliances were more covert. These men were less impulsive and subtler in their control of activities and other individuals. In other words, they were better organized, personally, and ultimately less self-destructive. The antipathy between these two types usually remained beneath the surface and did not come to the general attention of the institutional authorities. It was not expressed verbally in the group but André and myself began to get the play when some unlikely characters were invited to the group. One of these was Rick.

Break and Entry (B&E) is often seen as somewhat of a minor crime, one against property. I do not share the view that crime against property is minor per se. When the illegal entry is into a residence where people are present, however, the matter is always considered a serious crime and carries severe penalties. In fact, offenders proficient in B&E will go to pains to ensure that no potential victims are present during the operation. The goal is simply the acquisition of money and valuables; the better organized have ready access to a source, known as a fence, for immediate disposal of the stolen goods at the best possible price.

Rick had been a member of a gang who broke into wealthy homes and business establishments in the Hull/Ottawa area. What brought them to the immediate attention of the police was the element of terror. Certain members of the gang were sexually molesting selected victims of the various break-ins while the others rummaged the premises. As it turned out, Rick was one of the molesters.

This was a little known fact when he was admitted to the penitentiary. The media had made mention of the sexual abuse but inmate access to the media was highly restricted in those days. As well, finger pointing by the various former partners, while jockeying for advantage during court proceedings, further clouded the issue as to who was responsible for what. Rick planned his protective strategy by being openly defiant and threatening toward the guards. This quickly assured him a safe and acceptable haven within Segregation. It also provided him with a passport into our group.

The culture of incarceration reinforces certain judgmental positions regarding behaviour in general and specific crimes in particular, as the strong vie for power over the weak. All sexual crimes are frowned upon and usually result in the ostracizing of the perpetrator. In some instances, the safety of the inmate sentenced for a sexual offence is in great danger. This is not necessarily a clear-cut rule, however. The basic maxim is: survival of the fittest. Those who are able to establish their territory and sphere of influence through physical prowess or by means of intelligent manoeuvring, may well survive. It is not that their behaviour has become acceptable but rather that they have assumed a strategic position of some importance to the others and the original matter is placed on the back burner.

When Rick came into the Friday morning group it served his purpose as well as that of the group. He needed the security of membership in an influential group and the group wanted to augment its strength through additional members. His specific involvement in the crimes that brought him to the penitentiary was unknown to the others as yet. He was aware that if he could establish himself solidly within the group, the ties that would develop should mitigate any later revelations. How much of this was conscious planning on Rick's part is open to question.

Men who have been left to fend for themselves on the streets at a young age develop certain survival skills that become second nature. Similarly, men who come to the penitentiary repeatedly, develop an ability to adapt to changing situations in a manner that astounds the uninitiated and continues to plague correctional planners.

In any case, it was a matter of two years or more before André and myself, after considerable discussion, began to get a more accurate picture. Upon entry into the group Rick fit in immediately. He was affable, witty and charming. He had the right responses and was sometimes the catalyst in having others open up. Some time later things began to change. It was as though the reality of his situation began to weigh on him and he would verbalize fears about the length of his sentence. A burgeoning delusional system emerged and attempts to cope with the future centred on an unrealistic plan for the construction of an intricate living complex. The more he entered into detail, the more bizarre his thinking became. His closer friends became increasingly concerned and reported that he had calmly recounted, but in chilling detail, a recurring phantasy to rape nuns upon release from the Pen.

Rick was subsequently referred to the psychiatric service and hospitalized for some months. He returned to the group while being treated on an outpatient basis. The contrast between his former ebullient self and the new persona was striking and particularly unsettling to the other group members. Rick, "one of the boys" was now a morose shadow of his former self, unable to interact meaningfully with the others. Rick hanged himself in Segregation, just after the holiday season in January 1970. His mother claimed his body.

Marc, Roger, and Rick were not typical members of the group, but were important members of the group. Their pathology was not limited to that of delinquency but rather reflected the superimposed symptomatology of neurosis, chronic psychosis, and acute psychotic reaction. Although delinquency itself is not mono-symptomatic, cases such as the above-mentioned are even more complex. There is a plethora of symptoms and reactions within the general inmate population that warrants constant study and review. The recent identification of criminogenic factors and consequent development of needs and risk scales have a certainly validity but only when understood in the context of the deprivation of liberty. In other words, the actual value of such tools is commensurate with the clinical skill and experience of the person interpreting them. Objective measures such as these are diagnostic aids and must never supplant a highly individualized evaluation. Used alone, they merely create meaningless categories.

If an evaluative summary statement were to be made of our on-going Friday morning group, it would be that it provided a healthy outlet to men living in a highly repressive milieu. The forces weighing on the inmate emanated from the structure of the institutional life and from the peer group. Deprivation of liberty, the cornerstone of incarceration, is more than a physical phenomenon; there are more limitations than the obvious one of mobility. Freedom of expression, a commodity taken for granted in everyday life, is a non-existent luxury during imprisonment. The perceived expectations of the decision-making authorities, defined by their prescribed rules, regulations and policies, are determining factors in curtailing the emotional and intellectual responses of the individual and culminate in tailored behaviour. This circumscribed world also exacerbates the need to respond to the demands of the peer group, further reinforcing the contrived posturing. Self-preservation quickly dissolves into group-identity, as barriers are erected and reinforced between "we" and "they," the watchers and the watched. The dual facets of this environmental pressure are on twenty-four hours a day, seven days a week, year in, year out. The cathartic value of our weekly meetings provided some welcome relief. Primitive steps toward personal initiative were encouraged. Hopefully, the seeds of motivation toward change were being planted.

Many different types of men came to the group over the years, the majority of them in their mid-to-late twenties. The expression of their social skills ranged from the primitive demeanour of the extremely socio-economically deprived victim, through the pathetic posing of the pseudo-intellectual, to the ease of the more refined product of a better educational background. Their criminal activity ran the gamut from the impulsiveness of gratuitous violence to the sophistication of a well-planned operation. This heterogeneous group of men did share one thing in common: all were unwillingly incarcerated in a maximum-security penitentiary.

During these years the physical environment was sparse and the emotional climate was anything but conducive to adjustment to society upon release. Punishment was the principal aim of the sentence, with deterrence as the long-term goal. In fact, the entire process was demeaning and left little room for hope to blossom. The daily routine was set by the authorities and included the few organized activities during leisure hours. Someone, other than the occupant, assigned the living quarters, a cell that served as bedroom, bathroom and dining room. In summary, this stifling environment was an intellectual and emotional desert. We tried to provide the oasis.

The psychology department where we held our weekly meetings was some fifteen feet past the manned gate that separated the administration building from the interior of the penitentiary. Our structure, constructed in cement blocks, was attached to Cell Block One. It had served as a fire station in years past. A heavy wooden, bolted door graced the entrance and the interior was made up of three offices appointed in wood and glass panelling. The furniture was "fifties penitentiary" design which included a lengthy table and several chairs in the largest room where the group did battle.

I arrived some fifteen minutes late one Friday morning, having been delayed by a brief discussion with a guard. As I passed through the gate leading toward our building, my attention perked up to a certain sound. There is constant noise in the penitentiary at all times. I was used to this. This sound, however, was different and I almost immediately identified its source as coming from our offices. What was striking was that there was a certain cadence to the sound. It was similar to counting but I could hear no numbers, simply the muffled sound of several voices shouting in unison. Our group could be raucous but I was only fifteen minutes late, early yet for the verbal participation to reach a crescendo.

As our clerk unlocked the door it was immediately obvious that the place was in bedlam. About eight burly inmates formed a circle. In the centre, held spread-eagled in mid-air by four of the men was André Thiffault. He was being given the fourth "bump" in celebration of a thirty-fourth birthday. I hadn't known it was his birthday. The inmates did. It was our clerk who had tipped off one of the men before Thiffault arrived. They overcame him as he entered the premises. The only part of the tussle he won was that he was successful in convincing them not to remove his trousers. Happy Birthday André!

No doubt there are some who would question our professionalism. Who set the limits? Were there any parameters whatsoever? Did the free-for-all approach not simply reinforce the fact that delinquents do not respect defined limits? The questions are valid. The fact is, however, we were not working in a vacuum; we were not in neutral territory. We were in an arena where the combatants were diametrically opposed. Yet the expectation was that somehow one side was to be motivated to change. The inmates were to learn that their behaviour that brought them into conflict with the law and ultimately to the penitentiary must change so as to avoid their coming back. The basic measures to accomplish this were punishment and discipline, the presumed basis of deterrence. What we realized, with increasing clarity, was that unless the basic opposition of the "we" and "they" was not reduced, the hope for motivation to change was unrealistic. The existing milieu was counterproductive and some breakthrough was needed.

The men had treated Thiffault with friendliness and acceptance, in brief, respect. Their behavioural display, while not characterized by the decorum of an average anniversary celebration, was indicative of the closeness these deprived men felt toward him. Thiffault, himself, never assumed the traditional pose of the psychologist and was accepted by those who count: in this instance, the inmates. In fact, this was the same Thiffault who, in the past, had responded to a middle of the night telephone call at home from an escaped inmate by meeting with him in *Parc Lafontaine*. "*Ti-Guy*" was a lifer with severe mental problems. Thiffault had worked with him over a period of time and had been instrumental in having him transferred to a mental hospital. Shortly after, he panicked and escaped. In a matter of hours, he felt desperate, called Thiffault, and asked for a meeting. André knew it had to be immediate. He met with "ti-Guy" in *Parc Lafontaine* around 2 a.m. He talked "ti-Guy" into returning with him.

Even though we were observing the beginnings of change in attitude and behaviour with some of the men, we became increasingly aware of another reality. The changes were basically tenuous. We were outnumbered; not in head count, but in hours. The positive changes that could be attained during the three-hour, Friday morning sessions were sunk in a morass of negativity the balance of the time. Something more fundamental was needed. One could create a healthier milieu on Friday morning but this was obviously a short span of time when one considers the environmental stimuli of the twenty-four hour, institutional day. Fortunately for me, something within my own milieu was about to change.

I have observed that significant changes in the correctional field are often the result of happenstance rather than of coordinated planning and foresight. For example, prison riots and hostage-takings are inherently destructive and the cause of serious personal grief. On the other hand, the fallout from such events may evolve into a precipitating force for progressive change. This particular sequence of events is unfortunate but, at times, seemingly necessary. When image is of the essence complacency becomes the rule and any proposed change may be perceived as disruptive to a comfortable equilibrium and, thus, subtly prevented.

The unrelated happening, however, need not be innately destructive. The most significant experience in my career was my participation in the creation and maintenance of a Diagnostic and Treatment Centre in New York State. Although much thought, discussion and planning went into the effort, had it not been for a touch of serendipity, the adventure would never have taken place.

THE NEW YORK EXPERIENCE

~ milieu therapy

Prior to 1965, felons convicted under New York State law, who required hospitalization for mental illness, were sent to psychiatric hospitals under the jurisdiction of the state Department of Corrections. Such patients were confined in these hospitals until deemed cured. Many remained indefinitely, even after the end of their original sentence. A court challenge, lodged by a state mental patient, successfully overturned this practice. Thereafter, patients would either be immediately released to the community or transferred to a civil psychiatric hospital at the end of their sentence.

One of the major psychiatric institutions in the state correctional system was the Dannemora State Hospital, located in a small town in the picturesque hills of Clinton County some twelve miles west of Plattsburg, New York. However, the ominous wall of the Clinton State Prison that lined one side of the main street blemished the appearance of this idyllic setting. The prevailing human misery that surreptitiously lurked behind this wall and within the stately confines of the neighbouring hospital was not obvious to the passing tourist.

The effects of the court decision were immediate. The patient population of Dannemora State Hospital was reduced from some 1,400 to approximately 400. This drastic change had direct consequences on the staffing of the institution and on the town of Dannemora itself. The only industry was provided by the State Department of Corrections. It's inhabitants were employees within or retirees from the state prison or hospital; the remainder were relatives. It's motel, restaurant and gas station depended entirely upon these people, as well as the visiting families of inmates and patients. The main source of economic life in the community was now in jeopardy. Clinton County, a staunch

Republican bastion, was under siege. Governor Rockefeller was in power. The political wheels began to turn.

Bruno Cormier was an international figure in forensic psychiatry. In many respects, his voice was more authoritative abroad than at home. A graduate of the Maudsley in London and a trained psychoanalyst, Bruno had returned to his home country and established the Forensic Clinic at McGill University in the mid-fifties. At the time, the Department of Psychiatry was centred on the world-acclaimed Allen Memorial Institute under the control of the later controversial Dr.Ewen Cameron. The Forensic Clinic, though officially within the Dept. of Psychiatry, was an entity unto itself in reality.

Dr.Cormier had the all-too-rare talent of combining clinical practice with research. Although the methodology of his research lacked the rigour usually demanded, it was entrenched in the reality of the daily life of the delinquent, particularly those who were incarcerated. While he established the clinic, he concurrently developed a psychiatric service within the confines of St. Vincent de Paul penitentiary. These two entities were related to the point where they functioned as one. The work in the penitentiary provided treatment for inmates and was a consultative source for penitentiary officials; at the same time, research efforts at the clinic were nourished by the clinical information gleaned from direct, regular contact with the inmates. Interpretation of the clinical material resulted in the many publications. His cornerstone endeavour, from which many future efforts would arise, was the clinical classification of offenders. What made this work particularly insightful was that the interpretation was based on direct observation and longitudinal study of the individual offender. The result was the recognition of delinquency as a process rather than a solitary act. The quality of involvement of the ego in this process, together with the age of onset, allowed for some prognosis as to possible abatement with age. Further study, based on these clinical notions, pointed to the much-maligned concept of motivation and the idea of the "unwilling client" was born.

Bruno Cormier did not work alone but he more than set the pace. He may best be described as a despot, benevolent at times. He was difficult to work with but his intransigence reflected a basic intellectual honesty that, in reality, safeguarded the soul of the Clinic. This paradoxical figure was a true pioneer and, as with many innovators, his brainchild the Forensic Clinic was not to survive his death. Although much of his written work has academic value, the true import of his efforts was revealed through action. This action was really interaction, an inter-action between theoretical interpretation and hands-on clinical practice.

In the spring of 1966, Dr. Cormier called me into his office and spoke of the possibility of setting up a treatment centre in the vicinity of Plattsburg, New York. This resort area, some sixty-five miles from Montreal was well known to me; the content of our meeting, however, was rather vague. Terms such as therapeutic meeting and community milieu were used interchangeably, resulting in total confusion on my part. It was not until some months later, after extensive reading on "Therapeutic Community," and "Milieu Therapy," substantiated by an actual trip to Dannemora, that the pieces began to fall into place. Bruno had never been known for his verbal acuity and I was only one of his colleagues who required a few trips around the block before understanding him. His ideas were evidently clear to him; his problem was enunciating them clearly.

This vague manner of expression had its positive side, nevertheless. Whether used consciously or not, it finally wore down any opposition. I was privy to only one discussion with the New York State officials, the last one before the contract was signed. It was evident by the resigned look on the faces of the State people that Bruno had won. He had insisted on a global contract that gave him sole control of monies paid by the state to McGill for the development of what was eventually called "The Clinton Prison Diagnostic and Treatment Centre." No accounting of how the money was to be spent would be provided to the State. More important yet was his insistence on ultimate veto power in clinical matters. Although he was to work in hand with professionals employed by the State, including the Director of the Dannemora State Hospital, he remained the final authority on all aspects of the program.

This was a stroke of genius and highlighted one of Dr. Cormier's greatest strengths: the ability to anticipate future moves. He would have made an excellent chess player. He quickly realized that several jurisdictions were involved and consequently various interests could come into conflict and obstruct progress. It would take a firm hand

and Bruno was ready. After all, the State had approached him. They were stuck with the problem, basically a political one, to assure the community's stability as to employment. He represented McGill University, the only university within reasonable distance with the expertise and international acclaim to defend such a costly project.

The Centre was to be a Therapeutic Community. One of the basic tenets of therapeutic community is autonomy. In the field of corrections, autonomy is hard to come by and probably explains the ultimate demise of most attempts to establish a true therapeutic community. Many impostors appeared, as the concept became the reigning panacea of the late 'sixties and 'seventies. At Dannemora, the threat of conflicting jurisdictions helped in the demand for autonomy.

The site of the treatment centre was to be a unit within Dannemora State Hospital. The inmate population, however, was to be composed of offenders who were not presently under any psychiatric treatment and had no history of ongoing psychiatric disturbance. Thus by law, they could not be confined in a mental institution. The unit was therefore officially designated as apart from the hospital and subject to the Warden of Clinton Prison. The Warden of the Prison, however, had his hands full with some 1,600 inmates and was not about to complicate his life with a group of "shrinks from Canada." It was almost by default that the needed autonomy for a therapeutic community was established and the clinical prerogative of the McGill team, personified by Dr.Cormier, assured.

Prior to the opening of the Centre, October 3rd 1966, I spent most of the summer months reviewing the literature on Therapeutic Community. This had been at Dr.Cormier's request, which further stipulated that we were to share weekly conferences on the subject matter, in preparing the clinical program. It was in part because of my age that I was selected from the Clinic staff. Realization of the project would eventually entail considerable travel, a factor that could prove more taxing to some of the older staff members. As well, I had considerable experience working with adult delinquents in various settings, despite the fact that I was only in my fifth year in the field.

The review exercise was truly rewarding for me. Although Cormier had little practical experience with milieu therapy as a technique, his intellectual prowess allowed him immediate comprehension and gave substance to our weekly meetings. His ability to integrate this new material into his in-depth understanding of the phenomenon of delinquency was uncanny. The basic concept of Therapeutic Community with its inherent dynamic mechanism of expression, the Community Meeting, took on new meaning when seen in the light of the negative effects of incarceration. The idea of role modification, intrinsic to milieu therapy, gained importance with respect to interpersonal relationships within the target group, persistent offenders, as well as between guards and inmates.

This project was of special interest to me from the outset. I was certainly proud at having been asked to do the spadework to prepare the daily program. There were two more important elements to stimulate me. The first was the fact that the target group had been my principal area of treatment and research to date. One of the underlying dynamics of delinquency is the self-defeating nature of the behaviour. This is even more pronounced with the persistent delinquent; despite the degree of measured intelligence or repeated negative reinforcement through experience, the self-defeating behavioural pattern persists. Thus the challenge to the clinician is greater. The second element lay in the positive manipulation of social forces within the immediate environment, the foundation of milieu therapy. This technique would be new to me but the idea was not a novel one. I had observed that positive results through individual and group work within the penitentiary setting were limited. These limitations were due, at least in part, to the institutional environment. Incarceration is certainly necessary as a neutralizing agent but the manner in which the process enfolds is innately destructive. It reinforces the very mechanisms it purports to correct. A fundamental modification of the immediate environment seemed to be a prerequisite to any meaningful treatment approach.

The conventional roles in a correctional setting are that of the watcher and the watched; the keeper and the kept; the guard as suppressor on, the inmate as the suppressed. These roles are mutually exclusive and transgressors on either side are punished. In the summer of 1966 the framework for a treatment centre in which the pertinent social forces within the milieu would be transformed into positive reinforcers of socially acceptable behaviours, was in preparation. This implied the alteration of traditional roles so as the help break down artificial barriers to change.

Roles are not defined solely by a job description. They are the result of many interrelated factors including the culture and traditions of the particular milieu in which they are acted out. The individual personality reacting to these factors is crucial as well. At Dannemora, we were not to have the luxury of selecting our correctional officers. Some forty men who had been displaced from their former jobs because of the basic changes in the structure and staffing of the State Hospital were suddenly thrust upon the scene during the planning stage of this burgeoning treatment centre. They had been trained for the traditional role of a correctional officer and, as a group, covered a range of fifteen to twenty-five years' experience. We now had to design a training program that would necessarily touch on attitudes and feelings, as well as behaviour, in an attempt to undo some deeply ingrained patterns.

The initial training program that predated the opening of the Centre was in four interrelated phases over a period of some four to six weeks. Without diminishing its importance, it is necessary to state that it was a lead-in to the ongoing training of daily life within the Therapeutic Community. This latter training is better described as a learning process; a process in which each individual, of varying experience and expertise, shares with and benefits from every other individual. A sharing and reinforcing of different areas of expertise supplants the didactic approach of teacher to student.

The first phase of the initial training program was in the form of lectures. This ranged from simple presentation of factual material to a more complex explanation of clinical findings and expectations. The second phase was composed of supportive audio-visual presentations to illustrate what had been offered up in lecture form. The third phase, group sessions, ran concomitantly with the other phases and served as a stimulus to the officers toward free-floating expression of opinions, feelings and attitudes toward this novel material. This entire experience, as later assessed by the officers themselves, had been a challenge that brought about a cathartic experience.

The fourth phase was purely innovative and the creation of Bruno Cormier himself. He had reflected on his original medical internship and its reliance upon supervised contact with patients as an important complement to theoretical study. We were now to be faced with men who had considerable experience working with offenders within a repressive and punitive model. It was obvious that their previous manner of relating to offenders would prove more of a hindrance than help. Up to this point, the training we were providing had been more abstract than practical.

Both Dr.Cormier and myself were actively involved in work with persistent offenders in St. Vincent de Paul penitentiary. As institutional Psychiatrist, he treated all types of mental and emotional illnesses while acknowledging the underlying character disorder in his patients. Some inmates had to be hospitalized within his psychiatric unit. Many whose symptoms were less severe and often reactive, were treated on an "out patient" basis. This gave him direct access to the general inmate population. As for myself, despite the fact that I was working at the Forensic Clinic preparing the daily program for the Treatment Centre, much of my time was spent doing individual and group work inside the penitentiary.

Cormier's idea was simply to have the officers brought to the penitentiary in Montreal so as to observe and participate in clinical sessions. The officers were to be grouped in manageable sizes of ten and interchanged between his psychiatric unit and the psychology department where I did my work. This afforded each officer the opportunity to become involved in clinical techniques as practised by different clinicians. The overall approach stressed the importance of the individual worker's own personality in the treatment process.

This latter point was of the utmost importance since we were dealing with men who had been trained to keep a physical and emotional distance from the inmate. Their principal task had been to ensure that all rules and regulations of the institution be followed. There was little or no room for discretion or initiative. The void this created between officer and inmate was impossible to bridge in the traditional correctional framework. As a consequence, mutual hostility became entrenched and manipulative techniques escalated on both sides.

Our long-term goal was to reshape roles in the creation of a social learning environment. The officer would maintain his essential function as peacekeeper while, at the same time, assuming a new stance whereby he would become both subject and instrument of positive change. This delicate balance could be attained and maintained with a basis in elementary theory and reinforced later through supportive mechanisms built into the total program. As for the inmate, his role would be modified to the extent that, though he remained the explicit subject of the treatment process, his sharing in the development of a constructive milieu would entail new and demanding responsibilities. Our first step then was to prepare the officers for a role that would run contrary to their previous experience and training.

Jean-Guy was an imposing figure as he strutted into the room, fastened into a security harness and accompanied by two guards. He had recently been returned to Segregation and any displacement elsewhere in the penitentiary had to be in the company of guards. His wrists were handcuffed to a thick belt, padlocked at the small of his back. The look of arrogance on his face, characteristic of men escorted in this demeaning fashion, dissipated immediately upon release from the restraints. While the guards were unlocking the cuffs, I noticed one of our trainees step toward the back of the room and affirm in a low voice:

"I'm not getting any danger pay for this".

This type of reaction was perfectly normal, given the circumstances. Here was a muscular inmate, obviously a man who had caused serious problems, being casually freed from the necessary physical restraints. This was a potential threat within close proximity, in an unfamiliar setting. Our trainee was reacting in a manner consistent with his previous training and experience. Hostility and aggression, verbal or physical, were to be met with immediate suppression. The case of Jean-Guy was ideal to illustrate the point of what we had learned; physical controls alone do not correct the problem. In fact they tend to aggravate it over time, as the underlying causes are not addressed.

It was only a matter of minutes, however, before the trainees were obviously at ease. The main reason for this was the relaxed way in which Jean-Guy was able to relate his life experience within the penitentiary and, to some extent, his earlier family life. As I had worked in-depth with Jean-Guy, it was easy enough to guide the interview in a direction that would be more profitable to the trainees. The principal goal was to demonstrate that it was possible to establish a working relationship with an offender, regardless of his behaviour pattern. The implication was that this rapport is imperative if one expects to become engaged in a therapeutic relationship. This element was stressed in subsequent discussions and reinforced through later practical experience. It was rewarding to see that when we were well into operation at the Centre, this lesson had been well learned. Our officers were able to work with the inmates on a continuing basis. The negative bias created by the impersonal approach of treating people as objects was avoided through the constant, intensive association between the two groups.

Throughout the training sessions, the officers were exposed to various inmates individually and in groups. Through encouragement and support, they gradually became more actively involved in verbal communication. It was also interesting to see how easily the inmates were able to relate openly to this group of men whom they knew to be correctional officers. The simple fact that they were participating voluntarily and had been made aware their involvement would be of some value, seemed to alter their usual negative perception of guards; the interaction was evidently genuine on both sides. Engineering the milieu looked promising.

Rob was interesting for many reasons, not the least of which was that we had attended primary school together. Raised in what was then called the "north end", a predominantly Jewish/Irish district in Montreal, we came from similar socio-economic backgrounds. What probably made the difference in our personal outcome was that I was fortunate to have been raised within a solid family unit. Like most families in the neighbourhood, the extras may have been scarce but the basic security was present.

Rob was one of five siblings in a multi-delinquent family. His two sisters graduated from high school, married and raised families, as was the custom of the day. The three boys, however, did not fare so well. The oldest brother had died of the serious pulmonary disease that plagued the entire family, while serving a penitentiary sentence. This had happened some ten years prior to when Rob was haltingly recounting how he had helped carry his brother's body across the penitentiary yard, only to be stopped at the gate where officials from the morgue took over. There was no question of his attending the funeral. This was the 'fifties.

"But he was my brother." Silence momentarily gripped the room as Rob paused to catch his breath. He then went on to relate how his other brother, a few years older than he, had completed three penitentiary sentences. "He's legit now, though. He even works. He drinks too much but visits me whenever he can handle the hangover."

Rob was now serving his third penitentiary sentence, a life sentence for murder committed during a hold-up. He was in the fourth year of a minimum ten years that would have to be served before his parole eligibility date. In fact, he never made it to full parole. At the age of forty, while on day parole, he succumbed to the same congenital disease that had taken his brother.

He had been raised in what is labelled today a mono-parental family. He had little recall of his father, an alcoholic who had abandoned the family several years before. The sole male image was that of his older brothers. All three boys were on the streets at a young age, covertly contributing to the family coffers through the meagre fruits of their petty thievery. Rob's feelings for his mother were stated unabashedly. She was described as a long-suffering woman who had worked feverishly both in and outside the home in an attempt to salvage the family nest. He obviously felt impotent at this juncture in his life to right any wrongs but was determined to do so in the future.

Although he left school after the seventh grade, he improved his knowledge through insatiable reading while incarcerated. During these years, cell time comprised sixteen hours of the twenty-four hour day. Organized programs, other than sports, were non-existent. The inmates used their own initiative to fill the long hours confined in what was no more than a large closet space. Many turned to self-development practices such as reading and playing chess. Rob was one of these and, despite a lack of formal education, became quite articulate. He obviously enjoyed the opportunity to interact with our trainees and later bragged to his peers about "training the screws from the States."

Our trainees were given the opportunity to engage several inmates. During the sessions they became increasingly involved, asking questions and sometimes proffering solutions. The important feature, however, was their growing sensitivity to the inmates as individuals. The work context from where they came did not permit individual interaction other than for disciplinary reasons. They were now seeing and relating to inmates on a person-to-person basis. This was only the beginning but I was elated at the initial results; they bode well for the future.

*   *   *

A Therapeutic Community is designed to maximize the pertinent social forces within the milieu so as to create a social learning setting. Artificial barriers to change are broken down. This involves a modification of traditional roles. In a medical setting, for example, nurses could be expected to practice in clothing other than the standard uniform; doctors would not necessarily be adorned with the usual frock and stethoscope; patients would be encouraged to dress in street attire, rather than the common "johnny-suit." More important than these external changes, however, is the necessary modification of attitudes and self-perception. The traditional doctor/patient and nurse/patient relationships are modified. The doctor remains the principal treatment agent but, just as the patient benefits or learns from the doctor and nurse, they learn from the patient; similarly, with all other inter-personal relationships. Role modification then implies the lessening of artificial barriers, both internal and external, to facilitate affective as well as verbal communication. The fundamental agent of change in this social learning setting is the milieu itself; hence, milieu therapy.

What we were facing in the Dannemora experience was considerably different from a medical setting. At the core were two diametrically opposed groups who came from mutually exclusive camps: guards and inmates. Members of the professional staff were also from diverse sources: those who were employed by the state, directly involved on a full-time basis and those from the Forensic Clinic in Montreal who were present two days a week. There was potential for friction on several levels.

In fact, the transition was surprisingly easy. I give credit to the dynamism of all involved. This was truly a new experience for each one of us. Without minimizing the seriousness and complexity of the challenge, the basic philosophy and dynamics of a therapeutic community did create a forum for frankness and receptivity. This complemented the preparatory work we had initiated with the training program and helped foster an all-encompassing team spirit. The inmates related well to each other despite racial differences, a component accentuated by the unofficially condoned racial segregation of their institutional experience; inmates and correctional officers were able to circumvent the traditional barriers and bridge the gap, some more easily than others; the professional staff, perhaps more slowly than the other groups, showed signs of gradually dropping pretences and shared in the overall learning process.

The inmates came from the various prisons in New York State. The selection criteria were not numerous. It was not a matter of looking for "good candidates." In fact, neither severity of crime nor poor institutional behaviour would annul an individual's acceptance. We wanted inmates who expressed interest in participating in something different; persistent offenders between the age of twenty-five and thirty-five; men who had no continuing history of mental illness and were not presently under psychiatric treatment; finally, those not addicted to narcotics.

There were reasons for each criterion. In summary, the idea was to get men who had been involved in crime over a protracted period, were presently at the height of their criminal career and were not suffering from a specific illness or addiction at the moment. We did not refuse men who had undergone psychiatric treatment in the past, only those who were chronically ill; similarly, drug users were not excluded, only those completely dependent upon their use. In other words, we were prepared to welcome some of the intractable inmates from maximum-security prisons in New York State.

The criteria for acceptance had been sent out to the Service Unit in each institution; files were studied and inmates were interviewed. Those who met the criteria and expressed interest were sent to the Diagnostic and Treatment Centre in Dannemora, New York. The original unit was composed of fifty inmates, a total that was built up gradually over the first month. The men came in batches of four to six at a time. One important element that smoothed the way for incoming inmates was the immediate creation of a Welcoming Committee. This committee was made up of one staff member and four inmates. This served the dual purpose of introducing the latest arrivals to a startlingly different environment by their peers, while giving those on the committee their first taste of joint responsibility.

It must be remembered that these inmates were coming from prisons of one to two thousand inmates. Their transfer was carried out under traditional security procedures. Physical restraints were removed only after they crossed the threshold of the Centre. The sudden change was surprising and, for some, alarming.

As Bobby told me some weeks later, in pronounced Brooklynese,

> "when I got here I couldn't believe my fuckin' eyes . . . I thought I was in annoder woild . . . here was a coupla cons walkin' toward me wit' a hack, 'dey weren't bein brought to me by him . . . it looked like dey was doin' the escortin' . . . ."

The main emphasis of the daily program was the development of basic work habits. Some inmates are good workers in prison; few are able to compete in the work force upon release. Some obviously have no intention of ever working legitimately but those who do, even those who have had previous work experience, encounter considerable difficulty after years of incarceration. The demands of work in penal institutions in no way resemble those in society. In prison, work timetables are frequently haphazard. The absence of a shop monitor may well shut down an entire shop for days on end. Security measures such as searches take precedence over work schedules and may cause regular interruption. Although presence at a particular work-site is mandatory, actual performance is of lesser concern. Visits, schooling, interviews with staff are further disruptions to a continuous workday. Finally, a work environment peopled by those whose presence is due to coercion is not conducive to the development of good work habits.

By design, we had in our Centre only one shop. This was an immediate source of irritation to the inmates. It was a tailor shop. The first complaint was that sewing was "women's work." It did not take long to deflate this trial balloon of resistance; after all, New York City was the centre of the garment trade and was male dominated. Most of our men were from the City and would eventually return.

We had not chosen a tailor shop; we took what was available. In any case, our emphasis was not to be on trade training but the more fundamental issue of work habits: getting to work on time, staying there and completing the required tasks. This seems simple enough. It is anything but. Most of those men would respond to external compelling, they were used to this in prison. Our goal, however, was not to force men to work; what we wanted to do was awaken internal controls and initiatives. They could learn necessary mannerisms by rote; but could they internalize them? After the initial griping that there was no choice of work, they accepted their lot and settled in. They knew they would be able to manoeuvre and manipulate within the shop itself; this was their strong point, wasn't it? What they didn't know was that the most difficult challenge was yet to come.

Society's use of incarceration as the principal response to delinquent behaviour is inherently paradoxical. Anti-social behaviour is basically a refusal or inability to accept personal responsibility with regard to established laws and live within the defined norms of society. The deprivation of liberty, through incarceration, strips away personal responsibility, curtails individual initiative and curbs the growth of inner controls. Upon release, however, the offender is expected to assume the requisite autonomy for socially acceptable adjustment. Despite this dilemma, incarceration remains a necessary reality, if only as a temporary incapacitating measure.

Inherent in the concept of Therapeutic Community is the notion of decision-making by consensus. Diverse groups within the one community share in the daily management. In the best of circumstances this common consent is an ideal to be achieved whenever and wherever possible. It is evident, however, that such democratic fervour must be contained when working with convicted felons; there are obvious limitations issuing from legal realities. Furthermore, the offenders in our Centre had recently come from an institutional regime where decision-making was unilateral. Our immediate task was to create a mechanism whereby they would be exposed to situations where decisions must be taken in consort with staff. This was to be a gradual process, as it would soon lead to confrontation among the peer group. Thus, a dual purpose was to be served: the men would experience a realistic accountability by sharing with staff in the decision-making while, at the same time, creating an authentic situation for the growth of positive, peer-group pressure. What better mechanism than a joint committee? What better area to begin than in the difficult domain of work?

It is important to point out that the committees we developed at the Centre were in no way similar to "inmate committees" evolving in Canadian prisons and penitentiaries. This latter phenomenon was, in great part, a response to the pressures emanating from inmates' rights groups. These committees have developed into a bargaining agent between the power structure among the inmates and the institutional administration. As in any bargaining situation, each side's strength reflects the other side's weakness. For the most part, these committees are perceived by the authorities as a "necessary evil" and are generally treated as such.

What we created was not one committee composed solely of inmates but several committees made up of different members of the total community. Each committee targeted responsibility related to specific activities. The Welcoming Committee was responsible for developing and carrying out a policy and procedure for greeting guests and new inmates; the Housekeeping Committee centred on cleanliness and order on the unit; the Sports Committee arranged the scheduling of various events and coordinated sports activities with the local Community College from Plattsburg. In all, there were six committees, all of which had representation from the inmates and staff alike. These were to be the principal mechanisms by which the inmates shared in structuring the daily life within the Therapeutic Community. They not only experienced the gratification of exercising some measure of control over their living conditions but also benefited from the experience of working in a context that considered the needs and desires of staff as well. On this latter point we, the staff, also had something to learn; consideration of the needs and desires of inmates had rarely been our first consideration.

I became a member of the Shop Committee, along with a shop foreman and four inmates. We immediately established a rotation system whereby one inmate would be replaced every three weeks. Thus, every inmate in the Community would have the opportunity and obligation to serve on the committee. This would also give each inmate a three-month stay and provide for some continuity. Everything was proceeding smoothly. The weekly meetings gave the inmate members an occasion to relate to the shop foreman and myself on an equal footing. This built up confidence and prestige among the participants. The meetings, held during shop hours, also provided some welcome respite from the tedium of everyday work. This secondary reward proved to be a blessing in disguise. It eased the crunch that came when the topic of confrontation was brought to the table.

In prisons and penitentiaries, inmates do not tell other inmates what to do. This is the job of the authority figure, usually the correctional officer. Any demand made by one inmate upon another is perceived as one taking the other "on the muscle". This kind thinking quickly generalizes and is reinforced by the "we/they" phenomenon to the point where in a workshop, for example, an inmate who is too industrious may be cautioned by others, with threats if necessary, to slow down so as not to show up the others. We were insisting that inmate members of the Shop Committee now become the principal catalysts in assuring the development of basic work habits among their peer group.

The Shop Committee, as with the other committees, evolved gradually into a cohesive force. It was a learning experience for all. The presence of the two shop foremen, Ray Casey and Lindon Payne, would alternate on a weekly basis. The two officers had considerable experience in a prison setting but were eager to participate in a new way of working with inmates. They were completely different personality types and presented a dual challenge to the inmates. Within the traditional officer role, individual differences were masked under an authoritarian approach, based on rigidly defined limits. The orders were unidirectional; inmates were accustomed to this. The approach Ray and Lindon were now expected to use was of a more personal nature. The relationship was that of foreman to worker but with allowances for much give and take on both sides, resulting in a more forthright communication at all levels. The goal was not to set up a tailor shop whose success could be measured by production. The idea was to provide a working area in which the inmates would learn to assume personal responsibility and basic work habits. As a stimulus and reinforcement to the growth of personal autonomy, the burden of direct involvement in encouraging and monitoring work habits was increasingly placed on the shoulders of the inmates on the committee.

Ray Casey had the map of Ireland imprinted on his face and the corpulent figure of one who enjoyed the fruits of Bacchus to the full. A family man and father of several teenagers, he was accustomed to rebellion. An individual who possessed few inhibitors to verbal expression, he was cut out for work that promoted close interpersonal contact. There was always the potential for emotional flare-up; there was equally present a noticeable concern for the underprivileged. Lindon Payne was quite the opposite. He was a deeply religious man who left an imprint on others through his honesty and work ethic rather than by any glib proselytising. Seldom to proffer an unsolicited opinion, his responses were well thought out and seemingly devoid of any emotional baggage. Despite this phlegmatic demeanour, Lindon's calm inspired trust and confidence and he quietly became an unofficial counsellor to many an inmate undergoing an unusually difficult time.

These two men were the backbone of the tailor shop. Their daily front-line duty put them in a position to face, head-on, the complaints and manipulations of the inmates. The work area was an arduous one for the inmates, not because of the amount of work or any inordinate demand for speed or accuracy; the necessity to be at work on time, to work consistently throughout the designated hours and to accept all assignments from the shop foreman posed a considerable challenge. The resistance took various forms from outright defiance to subtle manipulations. The shop foremen were the first to become aware of this resistance but didn't have the luxury of resorting to their former prison experience to rectify the ongoing problem. Ray and Lindon, after some immediate confronting, would bring specifics to the weekly Shop Committee meeting. The onus was placed in the hands of the inmate members to correct matters through positive confrontation, not an easy task. The Shop Committee meeting frequently resembled a group therapy session, which in fact it was. Progress was gradual but evident over the long haul. The inmates gradually adapted to this new mode of working and problem solving, each at his own pace. The staff, also at each one's own stride, became more proficient at acquiring new skills by sharing with others on a more equal footing.

The tailor shop, with its Shop Committee as an indispensable component, was the principal mechanism for developing work habits. It must not be seen as an entity unto itself, however. In fact, it was one facet of the total milieu; an integral part of the learning process which encompassed the entire Therapeutic Community. Over time, the benefits gleaned from the learning experience within the work area gradually spilled over into the community as a whole. Problems, some not specifically work-related, would also overflow into our community. A mechanism to deal with situations, which affected everyone, was necessary. One existed.

Joe was the only son in a large, Italian immigrant family. Born and raised in the Bronx, he had manifested learning difficulties and subsequent behaviour problems during the early school years. His constant truancy was an understandable recourse, as the streets provided freedom from the embarrassment of any scholastic challenge. At the same time, he was able to hone specific skills at petty thievery and fighting.

He reached puberty while under detention to the juvenile authorities. Although he never grew taller than five-foot-six, his muscular development was precocious, a factor that served him well in establishing his place among the peer group. His long-time ambition had been to be an accepted member of "the mob" but his criminal career was significantly unsuccessful. He was of little use even to the mob that usually delighted in using strong-arm men of limited intelligence; the problem was, Joe was seldom out of prison. By the time he arrived at our Centre, he had served twenty of his last twenty-three years in prison, including the last nine years straight.

I had met with him on several occasions during his stay at the Centre, mainly to help him integrate more easily into communal life. He was an affable type on a one-to-one basis but had major difficulty in breaking through the inmate/staff syndrome that had been implanted and reinforced over many years of incarceration. Chronic anxiety was evident in his facial expression and clipped verbal responses. He attempted to deal with his emotional life in typical prison fashion, through strenuous exercise and strict compliance to the perceived demands of those in charge. It was obvious that group meetings were his personal purgatory. He attended all required meetings but made every effort to remain in the background. Less obvious were his sexual proclivities.

As it was revealed later, Joe had quite a prison reputation. He was what was described as, in the colourful if not politically correct parlance of the prison world, an "asshole bandit." He was attracted to younger looking inmates and would court them with a three-pronged attack. A combination of gifts, promises of protection and slightly veiled threats usually met with success in the large prison setting. In our Community, however, he had to be more circumspect. He was not sure of the tacit complicity of other inmates. Despite this, he apparently had made some headway with a newcomer.

Dave was somewhat of an anomaly in the Centre. The only child of an upper middle-class couple, he had not displayed any particular problems as a youngster in school or as a teenager. He was somewhat withdrawn and shy. On his own admission, he had never felt "a part of the crowd." Suddenly, at age twenty-two, he committed a series of break-ins with a group of juveniles. Because of the number of offences and the fact that they had been in private homes, he was sentenced to prison. His parents had some political contacts and were able to have him placed in the Centre. At twenty-three years of age, he was somewhat below our lower age limit; as a first offender, he presented a different clinical picture than the others.

The squeaky wheel usually gets the oil and we had plenty of them around. Dave, on the other hand, was an unobtrusive presence in the Centre and escaped our attention in his first few weeks. He did not, however, escape the practised eye of Joe. They complemented each other; the shy and naïve Dave did not make friends easily; the wily and prison-wise Joe quickly sensed a quarry. None of this came to the attention of the staff. I guess we were smitten by a sense of our own success and failed to see the obvious. We were now in our third year; we had much to learn yet, after all we were involved in a learning process, weren't we?

The entire matter came to the fore by pure chance. Another newcomer to the Centre, George, was also attracted by the cherubic appearance of Dave. He was a recent arrival in our midst but was no neophyte to prison and its primitive ways. He saw what he liked and made the appropriate moves. Fortunately, this was carried out in the shop and under the eyes of the committee members who were making their rounds encouraging others in their work. It was not so fortunate, however, when the muscular Joe saw his "territory" being invaded and menacingly confronted George; the latter resorted to a classic prison response by producing a pair of scissors. Other inmates quickly defused the physical encounter, an intervention not that unusual in prison, especially when institutional personnel are present. What was to follow, however, is not seen in prison. The strong feelings engendered by the incident were not allowed to fester. The matter was to be brought up, immediately, at a Community Meeting.

The core of the Therapeutic Community is the Community Meeting. This is the time of day set aside for all staff and all inmates to meet together in an organized fashion and deal with the immediate problems, suggestions and changes that affect the daily life within the community as a whole. In our setting, populated by convicted felons and correctional officers who work on shift, it was necessary to restrict the Community Meeting to some extent. It took place on the five regular workdays of the week. Weekends were a time when the professional component was limited to skeletal staffing. Weekends were also the only adequate time for visitors, most of who came from far off New York City. During the week, the Community Meeting took place on three mornings and two afternoons so as to accommodate the two principal shifts of correctional officers.

The daily fifty minute Community Meeting was followed immediately by a thirty minute Staff Meeting. This latter meeting was an important adjunct as it afforded time to the personnel to deal with issues brought to the floor by inmates but not within the scope of their decision-making. It was also a freewheeling discussion whereby each staff person could benefit from the concrete experience of others with regard to matters of immediate concern. In essence, the Staff Meeting was a natural outgrowth of the Community Meeting, a necessary period of reflection, discussion and integration of ideas and suggestions pertinent to the growth of the community as a whole. Together with the Community Meeting, it was a concrete learning experience for the entire staff and the on-going extension to the original training sessions.

The issues brought out at the Community Meeting were not restricted to specific matters of everyday living in the Centre. This was a diagnostic and treatment centre. The ultimate goal was the evaluation and treatment of the phenomenon of persistent delinquency as expressed in living through a sentence within a Therapeutic Community. The dynamics and reactions of the inmates were monitored and dealt with. In contrast to the suppressive environment of the traditional prison, the Therapeutic Community provided a milieu in which overt expression of feelings was encouraged. The principal arena for this free expression was the Community Meeting.

All inmates in New York State were eventually released under parole supervision. The inmates in our Centre, therefore, were in a preparatory stage for their official parole hearing. At a specific time designated by law, the Parole Board would grant each one a hearing and part of the package presented to the Board would be a written clinical evaluation of the difficulties, conflicts, changes and overall progress the potential parolee had experienced. The Community Meeting was frequently used as an open discussion of particular cases as the time for their hearing came near. The verbal exchange among inmates, correctional officers and professional staff was rewarding. The varying points of view expressed openly to the entire community revealed much about the direction of the Therapeutic Community as a whole and opened up new perspectives with respect to the clinical picture of the individual under discussion.

In any community there are natural leaders. Within a Therapeutic Community, leadership is encouraged but directed to bring out any latent potential that may rest with the less gregarious. In our Community Meetings this reticence was present in some staff and inmates alike. Over time, a more equitable balance was attained as freedom and acceptance of expression began to stimulate the more reserved to assume their place. Obviously, the ease with which some expressed themselves remained superior to others but constant encouragement resulted in most being able to say what they had to say.

Today's Community Meeting, however, was unique. Inmates brought forth the entire subject matter. The principal players in the drama, Joe, George and Dave did not initiate the discussion but were certainly in the limelight. At the outset staff were merely observers, a position that altered almost imperceptibly throughout the entire fifty-minute session. The only concrete information they had was that the shop foremen had witnessed a brief scuffle, quickly squelched by a number of inmates. Within a few minutes, the facts recounted by some three or four inmates made it clear that a love triangle had emerged, an explosive situation had been temporarily defused and that, more important, "we have to solve this problem." There were several elements to this joint presentation, which were eye opening. In the first place, these men came from a background where one does not interfere in the personal matters of others, except by taking sides and resorting to threats. Secondly, they were sending a direct message to the staff that they felt competent in trying to resolve a serious problematic situation, with the support of others but through their own initiative. Finally, they were making it clear to themselves, as well as to the three central figures, that if they were to survive individually while living together as a group, it was necessary that they show the maturity and good sense not simply to neutralize explosive situations but to try and get to the root of the problem and avoid any recurrence.

This Community Meeting that elicited the active participation of the majority of inmates, did not resolve all the issues but it certainly was the catalyst in bringing about a healthier approach to problem-solving. Joe, whose primitive social skills had greatly hampered his verbal participation in the program, was confronted supportively but directly. The tact taken was centred on his difficulty in contributing verbally and only indirectly on his sexual exploits. This latter element was considered a more formal clinical area and better in the hands of the clinicians. In fact, Joe did gradually become more of an active participant in both group and individual therapy sessions. George was castigated, in no uncertain terms, for having resorted to weaponry as a means of protection against the muscular Joe. He was so overwhelmed by the verbal barrage at the meeting that his defence was simply that he was a newcomer and "didn't know the rules of the game." As a result the Welcoming Committee, who had met with him less than two weeks prior to the incident, felt an obligation to renew contact with George in the immediate future. Young Dave did not escape the active attention of the community as well. His role was described as having been the coquette in the affair. One may question the objectivity of some of his inmate detractors but the result was positive. Dave did seem to become more autonomous. Perhaps the vehemence of the verbal assault had a maturing effect.

The ensuing Staff Meeting was equally unique. The immediate reaction was one of shock. It became painfully obvious that our own pretences did not disappear easily. We were surprised at how the inmates tuned into a potentially dangerous situation before we did, dismantled it adequately and, without our knowledge or active help, took the initiative to get to the core of the problem through the appropriate mechanisms at their disposal. It was with some ambivalence, pride in the inmates' mature approach to the episode yet indignant at having been upstaged by them, that the Staff Meeting proceeded. The final verdict: a truly rewarding learning experience.

All facets of a therapeutic community are interconnected; each one feeds into all the others. Issues that arose in the various committees were often exposed to the entire community through the medium of the Community Meeting. Similarly, certain matters brought forth at a particular Community Meeting were later dealt with, in more depth, by the appropriate committee. The purely clinical issues were treated in group and individual therapy sessions and, where appropriate, the concerned individuals were encouraged to put forward certain facts, changes and progress to the larger group. This process would nourish the other groups, involve more people in the ongoing learning process and gradually enhance the sense of trust within the community as a whole.

The staff members who spent the most time with the inmates were the correctional officers. As with any group, some were more talented than others and were better able to integrate elements of their past experience. The conventional role of a correctional officer, given the environment of traditional penal institutions, is appropriate in most respects. An astute and observant officer could learn much about delinquent reactions to and manipulations of the institutional rules, regulations and overall milieu. Their principal task of safeguarding the security of the institution demanded of them to try and stay a step ahead of those they were guarding. We were asking our officers to modify that role fundamentally; perhaps we had neglected to reinforce some of their previously learned qualities. Was this condescension or naiveté on our part? In any case, we were fortunate that our officers brought much talent with them and we "the professionals" learned much from them.

*   *   *

Art Rabideau gave meaning to the expression "diamond in the rough." A native of Cadyville, a hamlet between Plattsburgh and Dannemora, he had entered the Dept. of Corrections officer corps at twenty years of age. Most of his fellow officers were from New York City; undoubtedly, the "kid from the sticks" took his lumps in his early years in the service. Art was nobody's pushover, though. What he may have lacked in formal education was easily offset by a strong drive to learn, a quick wit and basic common sense. His brashness was probably an over-compensation for humble beginnings but with his other innate qualities, combined to produce the most effective leader within our Therapeutic Community.

The inmates were truly ambivalent toward Art. On the one hand, they were frequently stung by the fact that he usually caught them out in their manipulations and would confront them directly. On the other, they silently admired the fact that he showed no trace of vindictiveness. When they were wrong, he let them know in no uncertain terms; his aim was always to try and awaken a sense of responsibility. He was equally forthright with the staff, a reality better accepted by his fellow officers than the professional staff. This left Art undaunted. When he felt someone had mishandled a situation or was less than candid about an issue, he made the most of the Staff Meeting in making his point of view with clarity and no trepidation whatsoever. We had taught Art that a Staff Meeting was for everyone's benefit; he had learned well.

In my third year at Dannemora I left the McGill team and worked full time for the state as the Clinical Coordinator on one of the units. Our community had grown to two units of fifty inmates each, in our second year of operation. As senior officer, Art was my right-hand man. He was now forty years of age and had a good deal of experience. What a blessing; one never had to worry about a hidden agenda. There was nothing hidden about Art.

One morning, about three months into my tenure as Clinical Coordinator, he caught my attention,

"Paul, let's go have a coffee. I've got somethin' to show you." With a grin that cracked his face in two he continued, "I've been conductin' a little research. You should see what these summabitches've been up to."

For about a half hour he narrated his story. He had known that the inmates were following a rotation on each committee but noticed the same names coming back too quickly. His experience put him on alert; he sensed manipulation. We had kept a record that no one ever looked at, except Art. He had perused the files over the past twelve months and found a distinct pattern. There were six committees in the community. Each one was related to specific activities. Not all activities are equally interesting. For example, the Welcoming Committee had among its tasks the responsibility of greeting and escorting visitors through the Centre. Some of these visitors were delightful, young female students from the University, obviously a

71

very popular committee. The Housekeeping Committee, on the other hand, was primarily concerned with the regular wielding of mops and brooms, sometimes in preparation for those charming guests; a less sought-after committee. What Art had uncovered with his research was simply the typical manipulatory behaviour of the delinquent. The popular committees were under a system of rotation, as were the less interesting ones. The problem was, the stronger inmates rotated on the popular committees, the weaker rotated on what was left over. The designations "stronger" and "weaker" did not necessarily refer to physical attributes but rather to a compilation of virtues that placed some inmates higher than others on a hierarchical scale of popularity and influence.

At first blush this seemed to be of minor importance; obviously it had escaped our attention, even those who were on the different committees. In fact, though, it undermined a basic tenet of our milieu therapy. Active participation on a committee was the principal means by which inmates shared in the daily management of the community. It was also instrumental in breaking down the central barrier to social learning and autonomy. The committee placed the inmate in a position to participate in decision-making with others and to accept a portion of the responsibility for the decisions. It was imperative they live through this experience of sharing in areas that were of less interest and in which they were less comfortable. They had been outmanoeuvring us for the past twelve months. The Community Meeting was coming up in about ten minutes. I could feel a quiver of anticipation and it wasn't the coffee.

Art led the charge. As a matter of fact he pretty much choreographed the meeting himself. Some tentative attempts to change the subject by the more articulate inmates were merely brushed aside. He calmly exposed the machinations of the previous year, citing specific names so as to buttress his presentation. His earthy discourse clearly enunciated the underlying value of the committee process and betrayed a genuine concern for those to whom it applied. A number of the more experienced inmates wore a grin of lightly disguised admiration and whispered words to the effect "the sonofabitch got us there".

The ensuing Staff Meeting was of special interest in that there was something for everyone. The officers were duly proud of their leader and expressed their appreciation. The professional staff was gradually coming to terms with the fact that delinquent mechanisms were alive and well. Despite a highly designed therapeutic milieu, supported and reinforced by various group techniques, the ultimately self-defeating patterns of behaviour did not extinguish easily. On the other hand, there was a certain sense of satisfaction in the validity of the therapeutic approach as a whole. The truth of the matter was, a Therapeutic Community is composed of many treatment modalities, applied by individuals of differing background and experience, melded together in a self-contained whole.

*   *   *

Formal case conferences, per se, were not in vogue in our Centre. Each professional provided a service of individual therapy and took responsibility for the written parole report of individuals on a specific caseload. As well, there were bi-weekly group therapy sessions composed of groups of eight inmates, an officer and a group therapist. Apart from the clinical interchange at both the Community Meetings and the Staff Meetings, nourished by individual and smaller group contact, there was sufficient incentive and opportunity for informal discussions ranging from community business to more purely clinical issues.

During my first two years at the Centre, I worked both Monday and Tuesday as a member of the McGill team. Since I stayed in the town of Dannemora overnight and social activities there were pretty much limited to gossiping at the neighbourhood bar, I delayed my social activities until I had spent a few evening hours on the unit. This was a particularly interesting time since the evenings were less structured than the daily schedule. Both the officers and the inmates were in a more relaxed mode. I was pleasantly surprised at the ease with which the two sides related to each other. There were obviously individual differences but, over the two-year period, the gap that characterized the relationship between the two groups in the prison setting was now closing.

I was able to increase my evening time when I became a full time member of the staff after my second year. Since I wanted to maintain contact with the correctional system in Canada, essentially to continue my Friday morning group at St. Vincent de Paul penitentiary, I worked four days and three evenings at the Centre. This left Fridays free to work in Montreal. My work in completely different environments, yet with the same type of offender population, was an excellent learning experience. It reinforced my belief that in the correctional field, much was contingent upon the institutional milieu. Valid clinical treatment and research could be realized only once the principal contaminant had been neutralized. Furthermore, a correctional policy that pays more than lip service to protection of society and rehabilitation of the offender must establish the creation of a healthy institutional milieu as a priority; a milieu in which pro-social attitudes and behaviour are promoted and rewarded.

Evening work on the unit awakened a new reality in me. The role of the officer on the evening shift was fundamentally different from that of the day shift. Beginning at 3 p.m. and finishing at 11:30 p.m. allowed the officers a freer association with the inmates. Apart from the evening meal, most of these hours were unstructured, leisure hours. Sports and social activities were complemented by more individualistic pursuits such as hobby craft and specialized tutoring. The officers monitored and participated in most of the activities. In summary, the officers and inmates developed a social relationship more easily during this shift; what seemed to be missing was contact with other personnel. They had a half-hour meeting with the officers of the previous shift when they were informed of the day's activities and reactions. My informal contact with them during the evening hours, however, revealed a general feeling, and slight resentment, that they were somewhat neglected as real team members. Further discussion uncovered the fact that they felt particularly vulnerable because of the little they knew of the social, family and criminal history of the inmates. This was clearly not a matter of mere curiosity but rather awareness that their co-officers on the day shift had much more access to and involvement in the more clinical aspects of the total program. It was a valid complaint; equally important, it was a healthy request.

What I did was create a mechanism whereby these officers would participate actively in a case conference, on a rotating basis from three-fifteen to four every Wednesday afternoon. The time would accommodate the evening shift and would only slightly interfere with the workshop schedule. I would present a case history in the presence of one or two officers, the concerned inmate and any one or two fellow-inmates he wished to invite. The officers were encouraged to ask questions, proffer opinions and relate observations; the inmate was asked to correct or clarify the information presented; his fellow-inmates were there as observers. Hopefully it would give them an opportunity to know each other more intimately and become better aware of how a clinical portrait developed.

These "Clinical Case Reviews" were explained fully to the entire community at a Community Meeting. I was encouraged by the positive response and eagerness with which both officers and inmates took to the idea. It was evident that all believed the exercise would bring about an increased sense of openness. The Staff Meeting acknowledged the overall acceptance of the initiative and helped work out the logistics. As it turned out, it was considerably more work for me, as I was to prepare the actual review of each inmate's file. On the other hand, the rewards were personally gratifying and evidently helpful to the inmates and staff of the unit.

New York State correctional files were factually complete. All previous arrests, court appearances, convictions and placements, juvenile or adult, were well documented. Pre-sentence and probation reports revealed much concerning family, school and work record. This, together with the information we had gleaned from contact with our community living, provided sufficient information to construct an accurate composite picture. The inmates were well disposed as it was made clear to them that they were invited to their "Clinical Case Review" and could bring along one or two peer observers. The process was explained as an attempt to arrive at the most accurate description of their present status by means of an open discussion among all key players. This was a far cry from the imposed evaluative process to which they were accustomed; an evaluation by persons basically unknown to them and with little or no input allowed on their part. The officers were gratified in that they could now participate more directly in the clinical process. The presentation of the factual material, along with some interpretation, helped them better understand the behavioural dynamics they had been observing. They were encouraged to participate actively by asking questions and relating more current observations. The entire exercise that continued over a period of two and a half years, if judged by the response of inmates and officers alike, was a success. All members of the unit grew in terms of insight and trust. Those responsible for the preparation of individual parole reports were particularly grateful for the wealth of information that came out of these sessions. This gave them an opportunity to collate more material, make further interpretations and verify or modify their recommendations. The officers and inmates also sensed an increased involvement in the actual preparation of each individual for the crucial Parole Board appearance.

$$* \quad * \quad *$$

Although significant gains had been made by the civil rights movement in the U.S., racism was still alive and well in the latter half of the 'sixties. By the time the Diagnostic and Treatment Centre opened in 1966, Malcolm X had been assassinated, the Black Panthers were in full force and the Black Muslims were particularly popular among the Black inmate population. During the lifespan of the Centre, from 1966 to 1972, Martin Luther King was assassinated and Attica Prison, a seething hotbed of racial tension, erupted in a major riot. These two latter incidents brought about temporary lock-ups in the New York State prisons, an attempt to nip in the bud any violent reaction to the tragic events.

Our approach at the Centre was to the contrary. We opened up rather than shut down. As both of these tragedies enfolded, we encouraged dialogue by setting up additional meetings whereby staff and inmates were able to develop mutually supportive mechanisms. The murder of the civil rights leader could have done irreparable damage to the race relations in our Centre; the staff was white, as were approximately fifty percent of the inmates. In fact the openness and sensitivity with which the matter was treated, in all likelihood brought most people closer. Similarly, the Attica riot, which resulted in the death of many inmates and guards, could well have ruptured the ties between inmates and officers in our Centre, ties that had solidified over the previous three years. The reality was that individuals were able to see each other as such and the positive effects of the immediate environment were recognized.

Billy, having emerged directly out of Hell's Kitchen, fought his way in and out of the ring. The product of a large, poor Irish immigrant family, schooling was a luxury for those who showed more promise.

Billy had been a hyperactive child, a behavioural trait that was still in evidence when he sojourned through our Centre for some two years during his mid-thirties.

He had adjusted well enough throughout his three adult prison sentences. He had learned previously, during juvenile placements, that fighting had its down side even when you won and Billy usually won. Although he would win a fight, he still ended up being separated from his friends, losing privileges and doing more time. When he reached the major leagues, he quickly realized that the competition was more serious and the penalties more severe. Although one could never back down when challenged directly, there were ways of avoiding potentially explosive situations: one was by being selective of one's associates, the other was by keeping occupied. The latter measure proved to be easy as he had learned that his chronic tension and anxiety were best kept at bay when working out in the gym or carrying out his duties in the hospital. Both areas provided secondary gains as well. His prowess in the gym, particularly around the punching bag, created and sustained the tough guy image that could provide the necessary survival defences in prison. His hospital work, caring for the sick and injured, softened his image just enough to ward off potential challengers. An added bonus: the occasional provision of pilfered hospital goods to selected, influential inmates. Billy had it made.

His first few weeks in the Centre went by mostly unnoticed, except by close friends and some experienced officers. Billy had completed seven years of his twenty-year sentence for armed robbery. Although he had been doing "good time" working in the prison hospital and maintaining his image through extracurricular activities, he began to get,

"a gnawin' feeling in my stomach that I was wastin' my life." The sensation was particularly difficult to identify, "I thought I was gettin' a little flaky ya' know". He heard some inmates talking about a new program "somewhere upstate" that was for those who had done a lot of time. "When I heard the part about shrinks an' everythin' I says 'whoa', the shrinks I knew were more than a little fuckin' nuts. There was no way I was gettin' on no juice!" It was some weeks later he came across a Service Unit Officer by chance, inquired about the program and "da rest is history."

Billy first approached me after a particularly lively Community Meeting. As Clinical Coordinator, there were times when I had to take unilateral decisions. I would announce them at the Community Meeting. The men knew certain policy measures were outside their domain. When a decision seemed to them to curb certain advantages, however, they never hesitated to protest. We would not censure disagreement; we always encouraged verbal participation. The participation could get hot and heavy but at the end of the day, certain positions had to be maintained. It was not always easy but where does it say it has to be. Billy cornered me immediately after the Staff Meeting.

"Would you come have supper with me?"

I was momentarily taken aback. On occasion, I had had a bite to eat with some of the men while passing through the unit in the early evening. It had always been an informal encounter when a few of them had prepared something special after the regular evening meal. This invitation was more formal; it was only noon hour; I had never spoken alone with Billy as yet.

"Sure, I'll be there. What time are ya' serving?"

When I got to Billy's room, at seven in the evening, the "table" was set. The room was actually a converted cell. Since it was a former hospital cell it was larger than the typical prison cell but would never be mistaken for a dining room. One of us had a chair, the other sat on the bed. The food was quite good, the company more than interesting.

"You're Irish"; a statement, not a question. I hesitated before responding to this unusual and inaccurate greeting.

"Not really. My mother's French Canadian and my Father's from England."

"You're Irish," he reiterated. "You don't understand," he added quickly with a dismissive sweep of the hand, "where I come from that means you're stand up." I sat down, bewildered, hungry, and interested.

Billy had the sparkling blue eyes and flaming red hair that caricature the New York Irish; he also had the bent nose and scarred face that depicts the New York street fighter. He spoke with a pronounced accent and a staccato delivery that required one's undivided attention. Attention was not difficult however. Billy left little open space. When he wasn't chomping on his food, he was checking to see if my meat was tender, my potatoes not overcooked and whether my tea was hot enough.

There was never a lapse in the conversation over the three hours I spent in his "drum." He spoke easily of his family background, an upbringing punctuated by rampant alcoholism, beatings and poverty. Nevertheless, there was no trace of self-pity.

> "I was a pisscutter and deserved everything I got. Anyways, the old man was half outta' his skull with drink when he'd lay a beating on us." The school years were brief; "I spent more time in the gym an' running numbers than in any class. The Sisters couldn't do nuttin' wit' me."

Billy's description of life on the streets was like watching a movie in fast-forward mode. From his turbulent home life, through his frequent juvenile placements and equally frequent absconding from these placements, he painted a clear picture of a youth on the run, going nowhere. Everything came to a standstill when he entered adult prison at nineteen. He had played the street life to the full: car theft, muggings, brawling and a series of B & Es resulted in his first prison sentence. It was a time to reflect and consult. He did and shortly after release was arrested for armed robbery of a service station. New sentence and further consultation with better organized and more experienced offenders; he was subsequently arrested for armed robbery of a loan company; present sentence: twenty years, seven under his belt.

The evening slipped by quickly; I learned more about this man's past in this brief block of time than I would have in a structured series of interviews. Billy was as relaxed as Billy could ever be. We were on his turf; he had called the shot. It was obviously the way the morning Community Meeting had played out that impressed him. He understood there were certain issues that had to be decided upon by staff alone. He also knew that inmates had an obligation, if they were "stand up," to contest. The fact that I held my ground under fire impressed him. Maybe I could be trusted. In any case, to his way of thinking, I had survived a crucial baptism of fire and now became a candidate for his personal rite of passage: I was Irish.

This evening encounter dismantled barriers between Billy and the staff in general. He had been always polite but distant, particularly with the officers. A gradual, increasing accessibility became evident within group meetings. In further contact with him I noticed that, despite a lack of formal education and cultural deprivation, he could converse on various subjects. The verbal presentation was primitive but the ability to integrate factual information was considerable.

His interpersonal relationships were particularly interesting. On observation, his relations with other inmates, regardless of their racial or ethnic background, seemed normal. He worked, played sports and joked with all of them. In individual interviews he categorized others: the Italians were "the guineas;" the Hispanics "the spics;" and the Blacks "the yams." These derogatory terms slipped out with ease and no sign of negative affectivity. The one obvious exception in his relationship with others was that his "table" was white. The phenomenon of establishing a table was a carryover from prison. This was the area where friends of one's choosing would snack, play cards, etc. The tables in our Centre were not as rigidly demarcated as in prison. Men would be seen going from one table to another on occasion or borrowing from one another with ease. I asked Billy at one time why his table was only white.

"I don't eat with the yams," he stated matter-of-factly.

"What if one of the Black guys borrowed a cup or a plate from your table?" I queried. He looked at me with a puzzled expression. It was as though I was asking a question to which I already had the answer.

"I'd t'row it out. I wouldn't do it in front'a de guy . . . I'd do it later" and added, with sincerity "I wouldn't want to insult de guy!"

I knew there was no point in trying to find a rationale here and left the subject for the moment. My idea was to try and uncover more in-depth material over an extended period of time. I never got a clear verbal response from Billy; the response was behavioural.

Harvey passed the Parole Board one Wednesday morning and was granted release. He was to leave the following Monday morning. Wednesday evening he was the centre of attention, not only among his Black Brothers but all inmates and staff alike. It was always a time of joy and hope when a man had been accepted for parole: joy because a guy was getting his freedom and hope because everyone felt he now had a better chance. It was a stimulant for everyone. Inmates could better see some light at the end of their tunnel; staff believed they might have made a contribution.

Harvey, a decidedly reserved person, revelled in the spotlight of the moment. He was the immediate butt of much good-natured kidding, with particular reference to his being overweight.

"Mama likes that lil'extra to hang onto, dont'cha know" he retorted with a grin from ear to ear.

The revelry took a more serious turn suddenly, as he spoke tearfully of his awaiting pre-school children. Harvey, himself, was one of eleven siblings, raised in the Bedford-Stuyvesant ghetto where chances of survival in a competitive society were significantly reduced from the start. He had every reason to be proud. In his own quiet way, He had worked hard on himself while in our community and had helped support his young family with the meagre profits he gleaned from his leisure-time hobby.

I was stunned upon return to the Centre the following Monday morning to discover that Harvey would not be on the bus home. He had collapsed on the basketball floor on Friday evening. Billy had feverishly worked on him with mouth-to-mouth resuscitation, to no avail. Billy never mentioned a word of this to me; I got it from other inmates and staff. I can't remember if he ever referred to the "yams" again; I do remember later seeing Black men eating with him at his table. Therapy is an enigmatic process. It is only our arrogance and condescension, which limit it to the confines of an artificially designed office, appointed with a couch and walls decorated with emblems of self-importance.

*   *   *

I worked at the Clinton Prison Diagnostic and Treatment Centre for five years. It was the most interesting and rewarding experience of my career. The multi-disciplinary team of professionals I worked with, composed of social workers, criminologists, psychiatrists and psychologists, came to the Centre with varying backgrounds and experience. The McGill group worked part-time, an average of two days a week; the state personnel were present the full five-day week. I believe that all, without exception, gave a hundred percent; the climate was infectious. At times there were serious differences of opinion, a healthy sign; no one person or group had the definitive answer. We cultivated a capacity to challenge and confront one another in a spirit of constructive criticism, stimulated in no small way by the dynamism of the inmates. I believe we emerged better persons and more qualified professionals for the effort.

The officers, by their own admission, appreciated their new role. Throughout the lifespan of the Centre as a Therapeutic Community, only one officer found the transition impossible and asked to be transferred back to the prison. His request was granted. It is not platitudinous to state that the officers were the real backbone of the staff; they were always in the front line, regardless of their time shift. It cannot be overemphasized that officers and inmates, given their previous institutional experience, truly personified the watchers and the watched. A Therapeutic Community cannot function without a healthy conversion of these traditional roles. The metamorphosis does not come about overnight but is rather a process that requires support and reinforcement throughout its evolutionary stages.

Mechanisms within a Therapeutic Community, particularly the Community Meeting and consequent Staff Meeting, served as dynamic props to bolster the confidence and hone the transforming expertise of the officers. They often verbalized a distinct satisfaction in their work, a sense of fulfilment in that when they had something to say they were being heard. Informal contact between officers and professional staff over a coffee was a frequent occurrence, as was the occasional social event in the outside community. These associations strengthened personal ties and had a positive effect on the overall work at hand.

We had a guest at a Community Meeting one morning, a senior correctional officer from Clinton Prison next door. This was unusual but there had been some personnel changes at the upper echelons of the prison. This man wanted to see first hand what the neighbours were doing. He was certainly welcome but I for one only hoped that the verbal exchange would not reach a pitch where this delegate from prison would feel uncomfortable. After all, despite his rank or perhaps because of it, he was accustomed to inmates in a subservient role, one in which they said little and usually in token agreement with the authority figure. Our Community Meetings certainly did not reflect this sort of standing. In any case, this meeting was relatively tame, even though it centred on shop matters.

"Hey Ray, I thought you said we were getting that new machine this week?"

"I said we put in the orders for it this week, it'll take a cuppl'a three weeks yet for delivery."

A few other issues were bandied about, nothing to raise the temperature in the room. The most promising feature was that the meeting elicited comments from most of the men, including some of the more reserved. At the Staff Meeting our guest was asked if he had any questions, comments or observations,

"well, this is entirely new to me. I found it interesting but don't know where you're going with it."

Bill Derby, Psychologist and Clinical Coordinator explained in general terms what the Therapeutic Community was about in relation to persistent offenders.

"But aren't you concerned with politeness?" our guest asked. There was a moment of silence as we wondered what we had missed. "I mean those inmates showed no respect to that officer," he said pointing at Ray, "they were calling him Ray!"

"That's because it's my name. Most people call me by my name." I smiled at Ray's immediate response. He continued, "you know, I worked fifteen years in that prison with you and I bet you never knew my name 'till this morning. I think the men here show me real respect."

He left it at that; he felt he had made his point. The officer from the prison looked perplexed. The subject changed.

As I mentioned previously, Dannemora is a small town whose population is completely reliant upon the State Hospital and Prison. All inhabitants of the town know each other; many are related. This brings about a certain closeness and mutual support; it also evokes certain rivalries. When the Centre opened, its newness created some waves in this conservative community. Word got out that a bunch of Canucks were operating in their territory and, worse yet, were mollycoddling prisoners. One wag at the neighbourhood bar referred to "petticoat junction." The catch phrase caught on and spread. Our officers, all local men, bore the brunt of this needling, sometimes friendly kidding and sometimes scantily disguised hostility. They remained above it. Their overall job satisfaction evidently compensated for this paltry irritation.

I hope my enthusiasm over this Therapeutic Community experience doesn't convey the wrong message. I don't believe we unravelled the riddle of delinquency or that we created the ideal milieu for all circumstances. What we set up could not be transposed holus-bolus to the traditional prison setting. Our total inmate population was one hundred at any given time, subdivided into units of fifty. A technique that relies primarily on interpersonal relationships cannot be realistically effective if the numbers are unwieldy. We had the size and, I believe, the attitude. Although our project was based on certain sound premises and principles, it was something novel. We had not handpicked "good candidates" for treatment; we had not selected our officers but placed a heavy emphasis on a training program that continued as a built-in mechanism within the daily life of the community; finally, we had no say as to what kind of workshop we would have but accepted what was available and placed the accent unequivocally upon basic work habits.

In a very real sense, the project was an experiment. We recognized the need for incarceration as a neutralizing agent but, at the same time, acknowledged the deleterious effects of the deprivation of liberty. Thus, we designed a milieu to cope with this paradox. While respecting the notion of restricting certain freedoms, we modified the role of the inmate by augmenting his involvement in the decision-making process. The goal was to instil a realistic sense of personal responsibility.

The problem presented by the principal conflicting forces in prison, embodied in the traditional role of guard and inmate, was met head on. The officers were trained by multiple techniques over a block of time and then immersed in the on-going learning mechanisms built into the total program. The goal was to assist them in the transition from the previously antagonistic role of suppression and control to one of sharing life experiences and skills.

Finally, the professionals representing various disciplines and coming from different work experiences were expected to work in unison. Although Therapeutic Community as a treatment modality allows for eclecticism, checks and balances are needed if there is to be some degree of consistency. In fact, the checks and balances were built into the program itself. The openness to which everyone was exposed and the direct involvement each one had in everyone else's work precluded any loose cannon. Individual therapy fed the various group techniques and vice versa. Likewise, the Community Meeting was particularly revelatory; it was all-inclusive and further refined by the Staff Meeting.

THE RETURN HOME

~ a period of transition

While a group of Montreal practitioners, at the invitation of New York State, were establishing a Centre to study and treat the intricate problem of persistent delinquency, Canadian correctional officials were inaugurating another type of "treatment" centre. The Special Detention Unit (SDU) would undergo several name changes, various Wardens and a surfeit of programs over the years. Its basic philosophy, however, would remain constant: isolation as a means of correcting recalcitrant behaviour. What was not acknowledged was that this very behaviour, at least in part, was a consequence of the process of incarceration itself.

As with any poorly conceived, repressive measure in the correctional field, a result was that the net widened within a short period. Originally, the SDU was created for men who posed an immediate, serious threat to the physical safety of personnel and inmates in maximum security, thus becoming the "super maximum" facility. It would gradually become the dumping ground, a repository of inmates sent for various reasons ranging from overt aggressive behaviour during or before incarceration, to the perceived threat of insurrection and destabilization of the institution. In fact, it was an institutional version of Segregation and, as with Segregation, the basic problem was never dealt with, merely displaced. In some instances, the behavioural problem was exacerbated as the latent emotional content was left to fester in a suppressive milieu of anger, hate and paranoia. Extreme deprivation of liberty would lead to extreme consequences.

The initial idea of the authorities at the time was to build a Special Detention Unit in each of the five regions of the Canadian Penitentiary Service. The outcry against this was so strong, particularly from practitioners and theorists in the Montreal community-based sector, that this pretentious plan was scrapped. Ironically, the construction of the Unit in the Quebec region was well underway. Thus it continued and, upon completion, greeted its first inmates in 1967.

Throughout its lifespan from 1967 through 1972, the original SDU experienced much turbulence including serious assaultive behaviour, auto-mutilation, suicide and two spectacular escapes. Political and bureaucratic "sensitivity" had led to an early name change from Special Detention Unit to Special Correctional Unit (SCU). A more substantial change would have required a dismantling of the fundamental concept of isolation as a means of modifying behaviour.

My first direct contact with the S.C.U. was in 1970. In the summer of that year I became aware, through the grapevine, that Jean-Guy was incarcerated there and asking to see me. The last time I had news from him was by letter from the "penthouse", Segregation in New Westminster penitentiary in British Colombia. It was interesting, but not necessarily comforting, to know that he was back on home turf.

Throughout my years of work in Dannemora I had maintained a presence in St. Vincent de Paul penitentiary. I had continued with the group on Friday mornings and usually followed some inmates on an individual basis in the afternoon. One morning in 1969, our clerk in psychology informed me that the Warden, Mr. Brennan, had called and asked if I would stop by his office before noon. I did and it was decided that we would go to his nearby home for "lunch and a discussion". I knew immediately that my afternoon was a write-off. Lunch with Gerry Brennan was prefaced by a long and strong aperitif.

Mr. Brennan's gruff demeanour led some to believe, mistakenly, that he was abrupt and somewhat distant. What initially looked like a permanent scowl gradually transformed into a smiling countenance, highlighted by bright blue eyes. I believe the initial impression was deliberate and served as a protective facade to mask some insecurity related to his weighty responsibilities as commander-in-chief of the Pen. In fact, he was a genuinely warm and caring man. He and his wife Pierrette had raised twelve children. It was obvious the parental home was still the brood's nest. Those of us who knew him more intimately recognized that his disciplinarian bearing with the inmates belied an authentic concern for the individual.

"We've got to do something with Jean-Guy and I've got an idea", he stated pointedly as he placed a tumbler of amber liquid in front of me.

The ice cubes sparkled in the sunlight piercing through the living-room window. I shifted comfortably on the cushioned armchair, fully aware that the discussion was underway and the weekend break had begun as well.

"I'm sure you do, let's hear it!"

The idea was to transfer Jean-Guy out of the region. Although this had been done before, the plan suggested now was fundamentally different. The previous transfer had been a punitive one that entailed deception on the part of the authorities. The proposal today had the inmate's interest at heart.

"You know he's got more balls than brains" the Irishman stated glibly, "but he sure has made an effort over the past five years or so. I don't think he could ever be released here in Montreal and make it. With his track record inside, they'd never let him alone out there."

I was somewhat surprised at Brennan's candid admission of the vindictiveness of the system. Nevertheless, he saw a window of opportunity and knew that if his plans were to be put into operation he needed me. If Jean-Guy were to be convinced that a penitentiary transfer was for his own good, I was the one who could persuade him.

I had some reservations about the proposal. In the first place, Jean-Guy had been approached some months before with the idea of a possible transfer to the new maximum-security penitentiary, Archambault. I had explained to him at the time, somewhat naïvely, that the new institution was cleaner and that its perimeter, a barbed-wire fence rather than a stone wall, would afford some view of the countryside; the location was in the foothills of the Laurentians. Jean-Guy's immediate response had been a reality check for me:

"what's the difference: same fuckin' inmates, same fuckin' screws", he replied with finality.

Although he would have been unable to articulate the dynamic behind his statement, the basic issue was there: the reality of penitentiary life, interpersonal relationships between and among opposing factions. I was also aware that the stability Jean-Guy had shown in the last few years was due, in great part, to the individual attention we had given him. He had been our cleaner in the psychology department, a job that allowed him direct and regular access to the personnel there. Much of his day was spent in a milieu that tried to reinforce positive behaviour and, when necessary, correct without punishing. It was also rewarding in that he was in a position to refer inmates to us. This augmented his sense of self-worth and gave him an opportunity to develop a positive leadership role among the inmate population. This latter point did not pass unnoticed by penitentiary officials. We both knew a change of venue exposed Jean-Guy to old hazards. Although he would have access to competent help if he so chose, the question remained as to whether he was sufficiently autonomous to make the right choices. Another concern was whether he would be swallowed up by the dominant influences of the penitentiary milieu. In the short term, there could be overwhelming pitfalls. Over the long haul, however, transfer to another region could well afford him a better opportunity to reintegrate into society. In the final analysis, despite reservations, I favoured Brennan's plan.

Jean-Guy accepted the idea of a transfer. He had some reservations but felt that it was worth a try. Mr. Brennan asked whether I was prepared to carry out the escort. This raised some eyebrows among security staff but arrangements were made. This was 1969 and though I was not a regular employee of the Canadian Penitentiary Service my involvement as an escort was not an insurmountable obstacle; there was no "preventive security" department to prevent common sense decision-making; there was not a surplus of directives and law amendments to curb initiative; the fact that I had worked steadily with Jean-Guy over the past seven years was reason enough to believe that the security factor was covered.

In fact, the transfer went without a hitch but with two interesting sidelights. When we arrived at Dorval Airport before six in the morning, we were required to report to the RCMP desk. A bleary-eyed clerk blinked at me when I stated that this was a penitentiary transfer. After a moment's hesitation he blurted out "just a minute" and turned on his heel toward the office in the rear. Jean-Guy and I looked at each other questioningly. We were mutually impressed by our appearance, both suitably attired in shirt and tie. A few minutes later an obviously senior officer emerged and, with a puzzled expression, queried

"which one of you is the inmate?".

The incident was the subject of some good-natured kidding throughout the trip.

"I knew I'm outta shape, t'ings on my mind an all dat, but I hope I don't look like no fuckin psychologist" Jean-Guy exclaimed, bent over in his seat with tears of laughter welling up in his eyes.

The second was during our forty-minute stopover in Winnipeg. As we strolled along the periphery of the airport he exclaimed,

"It's over twelve years since I walked outside wid'out chains. If "dem fuckin" screws could see me now, dey wouldn't believe it!" He was looking into the distance; a hint of freedom. Twenty-nine years of age and the only point of reference in his adult life: the penitentiary.

Jean-Guy arrived at Prince Albert penitentiary in the middle of an institutional lockdown, the result of a prolonged hunger strike. Although anyone who knew him, even casually, knew that he would never willingly go without food. He would support a demonstration but not instigate it. Nevertheless, his institutional file spoke for him. He was placed in Segregation at the end of the strike and subsequently transferred to the notorious "penthouse" in New Westminster penitentiary. It was not long before the circle was completed and he was transferred back to the Quebec Region. Within less than twelve months Jean-Guy had been paraded around the country. Although impelled by the best intentions at the outset, he was withdrawn from the relatively rewarding milieu of the psychology department, through the momentary sensation of freedom while in flight, to the oppressive atmosphere of successive segregation units. He finally ended up in the extreme deprivation of the Special Correctional Unit, having experienced a veritable carousel spinning out of control.

Because of my work schedule, mainly my commitments in New York, I had put off a visit to the S.C.U. for some months. An incident in which Jean-Guy had been stabbed was then brought to my attention. I responded immediately by visiting him in the hospital. Although his torso was completely bandaged, he seemed to express embarrassment more than pain:

> "da little son-of-a-bitch got me from be'ind; de udder cocksucker set me up" he stuttered awkwardly.

He seemed apologetic that he had been taken by surprise; a mode of thinking developed over years of living in an ersatz world of violence and deceit, now magnified within the intense confines of a Special Correctional Unit; certainly special, hardly correctional. The Doctor's prognosis was favourable. He attributed this to Jean-Guy's physical strength and irrepressible determination. In fact, he was released from the hospital within a month and sent back to the S.C.U. His assailants were placed in another wing of the institution. Formal charges are almost impossible to prosecute with success in these circumstances as witnesses are blind and therefore mute.

There was an aftermath to this incident that I consider revealing of certain staff attitudes. I started going to the S.C.U. when time allowed and saw the men in a group. There were six of them whom I knew, all graduates of the Pen. At one of our encounters shortly before Christmas, the men were complaining they were not allowed to send out Christmas cards, other than to those on their visiting list. I knew that in the other institutions there were no restrictions whatsoever on Christmas cards. Jean-Guy wanted to send a card to the surgeon who had operated on him after the stabbing. At the end of our meeting I took his card and promised I would speak to someone about it.

> "I'll give it a try, maybe I can convince them."

The men were locked up twenty-three hours a day, with no natural light or fresh air. It seemed to me that sending a Christmas card might evoke some feelings of humanity in this barren setting. I had the card in my pocket when I went to see the Warden.

"Jean, the guys would like to send some Christmas cards and say they're not allowed."

"We've been through that before. I told them, only those on their visiting list."

"But, what's the problem? Jean, have a little Christmas spirit, I chided kiddingly. I knew Jean, the Warden. He wasn't a bad person just a little constipated.

"I'll bet it's that instigator, Jean-Guy. He's always after something."

I felt my temperature rise but held my cool; "he wants to send a card to his Doctor." "Why does he want to do that?"

I stared at him incredulously, "Maybe because he saved his life."

I knew I was getting nowhere with Jean. He began rambling on about dangerous inmates and security measures that I would know nothing about. I could see that the depressing climate of this tomb-like institution was affecting his judgement. I left. The Doctor received the appropriate Christmas greetings.

It took two major escapes to finally shut down this monstrosity but, unfortunately, the concept lives on. The first escape saw six high-profile inmates climb the wall in the summer of 1972. Five of the six were captured within weeks; the sixth returned to his native country and was later gunned down by French gendarmes. The second escape included the original five of the previous attempt. On this occasion, they actually penetrated the wall of the cellblock, went out into the yard so as to scale the wall. When they realized it was almost time for the official count and their absence would be noticed, they retraced their steps, came in for the count and promptly left a second time. This time they scaled the wall. Their absence came to light about forty-five minutes later when a passing motorist reported seeing a white sheet hanging from the outer wall of the institution. This happened on May 13th 1973, Mother's Day. The guys wanted to pay their respects. There were many red-faced officials; I know, I was one of them.

After the first escape, André Thiffault had jumped at the opportunity to offer his services as a consultant. He had met with the Commissioner of Penitentiaries, Paul Faguy and his senior assistant, John Braithwaite. He knew these two men were open to more progressive ideas than those that resulted in the S.C.U. He proposed that the basic philosophy and structure of the S.C.U. be altered dramatically. Rather than using isolation as a means of managing difficult inmates, the idea would be to involve inmates in the development of a prison that made some sense. The first steps would be to hand pick certain key personnel, garner some funds for construction and keep only those inmates who were willing to attempt this endeavour. The Ottawa officials agreed and Thiffault signed a contract in September 1972. The Warden of the S.C.U. at this time, Pierre Goulem, was a forward-looking criminologist who always had the individual inmate's best interest at heart. He was looking for an assistant. André approached me since we had worked together with the "mob" at St. Vincent de Paul. I had just returned to Montreal and was working full-time in psychiatry at the old Pen, a job that was dreary at best. I thought this new offer could be promising. My fears of resistance on the part of the regional authorities, staunch protectors of the status quo, were allayed by André. He explained to me the support coming from the Ottawa officials and confirmed this later when he obtained a written memorandum, under the Commissioner's signature, acknowledging my transfer to the newly named, Correctional Development Centre (CDC), as Assistant Director. I began January 4th, 1973. What a nightmare.

The title of the senior official in the Quebec Region at the time was Regional Director. When he heard of this new proposal and its backing in Ottawa, he appointed his assistant, Roger Jourdain, as the principal link at the regional level. Jourdain was basically a good man, interested in seeing progress made. Unfortunately, he had no power whatsoever. Any agreements he reached with us carried no weight unless his boss gave the stamp of approval. Although we didn't realize this immediately, it was the perfect set up whereby the Regional Office could delay any real changes interminably. They did just that. After months of delay in construction, we happened to hear that the Commissioner was in the region. He came over to the C.D.C. accompanied by the Regional Director, M.Laferrière. We stated clearly our complaint that certain things were moving too slowly, some not at all. As to the money for construction, the Regional Director looked at us with surprise, "I've set aside twenty thousand dollars as start-up money for this project. You should have access to that immediately." We were relieved to hear this and contacted the Regional Works Officer that same afternoon.

"I don't know what the hell he's talking about" came the startled reply to our question, "he must have a secret account, I don't have a dime for any special project."

This is merely one example of the resistance posed by the Regional Office. After all, we were the interlopers. We were the ones who had dealings with Ottawa over the heads of the regional authorities; a mortal sin, unpardonable in any bureaucracy. The "Jourdain Report", a document that reflected the agreements arrived at, between those of us at the C.D.C. and the regional authorities, was composed of some twenty-one points of accepted change. Eight months after the accord was printed, four minor changes had been effected. The others, including the transfer of certain inmates and members of personnel remained in the realm of wishful thinking.

Thiffault and myself spent the bulk of our time working directly with the inmates. Goulem was fully occupied with the necessary paperwork underlying changes. Our first task was to evaluate the overall inmate population and seek out those who would be willing to embark on a project we believed would be better for all, inmates and personnel alike. It wasn't an easy job; we were dealing with inmates who felt strongly they had been burnt by the system. Trust was not an easy commodity to sell. We had worked with similar types at the old Pen and this was in our favour. Some of them were now incarcerated at the C.D.C. and we were seen as positive figures. What worked against us was the fact that the men distrusted the correctional system as a whole and in reality there was little we could do to change that. Words went only so far, action was needed. We explained our particular approach, a concept that seemed palatable to the men, but over the months were able to show little other than some internal changes. We had the men out of their cells and into the wings and exercise yard as much as possible. Common rooms were in the advanced planning stage. Work opportunity was sparse and consequently the men had too much time on their hands with little or nothing to do; a bad mix in any correctional setting, a particularly dangerous one with a volatile population such as this. It is pure fiction to think that in a penitentiary the observation is unidirectional. In fact, personnel observe eight hours per day; inmates, on the other hand, are observing every waking hour, especially when they have little else to do. In a context such as the C.D.C., where promised change seemed to be little more than words to some, the inmates had plenty of time to observe and plan. Some did and put it into action May 13th. They knew who was working, at what time the guard-towers were unmanned and the exact time of the inmate count.

If there was one positive factor to emerge from the escape, it was that the institution was closed within a week. Inmates and staff were transferred out, a seeming impossibility before the event. Thiffault, Goulem and myself were left behind, under the pretext that we would be able to have the physical changes to the institution completed, unencumbered by the presence of an inmate population. It was not long before our suspicions were confirmed; there would be no more cooperation on the part of the regional authorities now than there had been before. We continued to fight, demanding meetings at the Regional Office and making several trips to Ottawa. We were able to bring about some physical changes such as common rooms, a gym and a larger exercise yard. Every modification took an inordinate amount of time, only after persuasive techniques, bordering on threats. In September 1976, the final nail was driven into our coffin. A riot at St. Vincent de Paul penitentiary gave the Regional Office the excuse it needed. One hundred and five inmates were transferred to the C.D.C. over a weekend. The dream evaporated overnight. Thiffault's contract was not renewed as of September and I was transferred to the Leclerc penitentiary as Psychologist.

Jean-Guy had been transferred back to St. Vincent de Paul penitentiary in 1971, a full year before Thiffault and myself arrived at the former Special Correctional Unit. He was granted a few temporary absences from the Pen, the first two of which I acted as the escort. We visited some members of his family, the most significant his older sister. She and her husband managed a Harvey's restaurant and eventually provided a job placement for Jean-Guy when he was paroled in 1972. He enjoyed the work, especially because he was able to eat there without cost. He met a young woman and fathered a daughter. Their apartment had the evident trappings of penitentiary life; I remember having to step over weight-lifting equipment to get from one room to another. One afternoon after completing his shift at Harvey's, he told his sister that he was going to help out a friend. He never returned. He had gone to help a friend get back a sound system he had loaned out and was having trouble retrieving. Jean-Guy used the only tactic he was familiar with; he demanded it. The response was a shotgun blast that removed the top of his skull. He was unrecognizable to me in the coffin. The only people in attendance at the funeral parlour were his sister, the mother of his child and a nine-month old girl with a handgrip that belied her age and size, a legacy of her father Jean-Guy.

*   *   *

There were some concrete, positive changes that came about in the Canadian correctional field during the 'sixties. Classification and psychological services for inmates were expanded and resulted in some of the better-behaved being transferred to medium and minimum-security facilities. Education and trade-training services increased, giving the released offender a more equitable chance to survive in a competitive society. Corporal punishment, as a means of subduing and deterring seriously disruptive behaviour, was significantly curtailed with the official suspension of "the strap". The parole process had reduced the amount of time to be served within the confines of the penitentiary and those who had been granted parole could now benefit from the assistance provided by a supervisor and complete their sentence in the community. Sensitive, forward-looking individuals within the correctional system brought some of the changes about; other changes were the result of pressures from without. The combined forces, however, lacked integration and tended to encourage a piecemeal approach to correctional problems.

There was a strong movement to enhance the rights of prisoners that began in the 'sixties and accelerated throughout the 'seventies and 'eighties. This was promulgated by well intentioned but sometimes naïve people. Some felt strongly that, because a person had been incarcerated for a particular crime, it did not mean their basic rights should be summarily suspended. Justified as this position is, it fails to take into account the dynamics of the delinquent personality and the detrimental power games that exist in prison. Although the movement has brought about some positive changes over the years, I believe it has also reinforced the piecemeal approach in corrections and unwittingly abetted the neglect to recognize and modify the underlying negative effects of incarceration. Rights are precious and must be safeguarded. However, it is equally important to assure that all inmates live through an experience designed to enhance their chances of eventually assuming the most fundamental of all rights: the right to live in freedom.

Sometime in the late sixties I attended a meeting of the fledgling "L'office des droits des détenus" at the home of Raymond Boyer, a legendary figure at the Forensic Clinic. Raymond, who had personally experienced the rigours of incarceration, was genuinely concerned with the rights of prisoners. Because of his own odyssey through the nightmare of confinement, however, he was well aware that the problem of inmate rights was a complex one and that a solution could not be based on good will alone. He invited me to the meeting because, as he put it, all points of view are necessary. "I want someone there with hands-on experience." As it turned out I did have something to say. A professor from l'école de criminologie, l'Université de Montréal, was making an impassioned plea to right the wrong of a decision imposed upon a certain inmate who had written to him. The man had been transferred from maximum security to the dreaded Special Correctional Unit. As a result, his pay allotment had been automatically reduced from the daily rate of forty-five cents to the basic twenty-five cent level. This was described as a "flagrant abuse of inmate rights". I was somewhat surprised that the issue, as presented, was the automatic nature of the pay reduction with no reference to the institutional transfer. After all, the Special Correctional Unit had been the object of serious dispute since its inception. It was a total institution version of segregation. There was neither natural light nor natural air circulation in the cells where the men were confined twenty-three hours a day. All privileges, including visits, were highly restricted. Constant observation was carried out by means of a security window in the ceiling of the cell. An armed guard paraded on a track above the cell, twenty-four hours a day. If the paranoid thinking, typical of persistent delinquents, was still within the normal range upon entry into the S.C.U., with time served here it became a mental health risk. The inmate's letter said nothing of this but did refer to the pay reduction. He obviously knew which heartstrings to pull on an "inmates rights" advocate.

As soon as Raoul's name was revealed the entire matter was seen in a new light. I had encountered him on several occasions in St. Vincent de Paul penitentiary and knew him as a flamboyant individual who revelled in saving all newspaper accounts and photographs that revealed his escapades while in freedom. Despite his boyish looks, underscored by large brown eyes, curly black hair and cheeks that had never felt a razor blade, a vicious streak lurked just beneath the charming surface. He had been the target of several attempts on his life by rivals. His violent career was later highlighted by several spectacular escapes and a multiple homicide while illegally at large. His destructive pursuits and his life came to an abrupt end at the hands of the police, while ensconced in a Laurentian hideaway during his final period of illegal liberty.

Up to now, however, Raoul's notoriety was pretty much limited to the police and the criminal milieu. He had not, as yet, left his imprint on the correctional scene but was about to begin. He had been informed that a recent arrival to the penitentiary had attempted a "relationship with his woman." His manner of settling this injustice was by stabbing the other inmate in the eye with a pencil. This resulted in his transfer to the S.C.U.; the incident was obviously not mentioned in his letter to the professor. His complaint was simply that he was being punished twice: by the transfer and by the pay cut. His basic sense of justice told him that this double-barrelled punishment was unfair; his basic common sense told him that the least proffered information would guarantee the best results.

At this evening's meeting we had almost been lulled into a situation whereby we would have been attacking a false problem. The real issue was the use of extreme deprivation of liberty as a means of treating violent behaviour. At best, this measure simply displaced the problem temporarily; at worst, it would eventually exacerbate the point at issue. We had almost proceeded with partial information and with no awareness of the circumstances that led up to the situation. Had we taken the matter of automatic pay cut to the authorities as the central issue, we would have been immediately discredited. Ultimately, we would have been reinforcing a system that treats symptoms and avoids causes, one that uses measures to placate institutional tensions in the immediate, at the expense of long-term solutions to fundamental problems.

Over the years, inmate committees have been established in correctional institutions and grievance procedures have been enacted, whereby an inmate may contest an administrative decision. Citizen's committees have been accepted as a means of demonstrating openness to the public. A Correctional Investigator's department, which reports directly to the Solicitor General, stands as an overseer of policies and procedures. Despite these measures or, perhaps because of them, the fundamental malaise that undercuts all constructive steps has never been dealt with. So long as the antagonistic positions of "we/they" are solidly in place, the efficacy of all helping and protective services are seriously undermined. Particularly troubling today is that, through increased dependence upon technocratic devices, an impersonal approach to evaluation and programming has evolved and the gap has widened between "we" and "they". An alarming generalization has now spread to encompass all correctional personnel.

CANADA'S LARGEST PENITENTIARY

~ the seventies / anything goes

Leclerc penitentiary is the largest medium security institution in the Canadian federal correctional system. Located less than a mile from St. Vincent de Paul penitentiary, it was built as a more modern type of accommodation for selected inmates in 1960. The previously constructed Federal Training Centre housed younger inmates serving their first penitentiary sentence; Leclerc was designed for older inmates and compliant recidivists.

The newly developed classification service now came into play. The Classification Officers at St. Vincent de Paul were to assess cases for a Classification Board. Those inmates who met the established criteria were then transferred from the dank fortress of the old Pen to the brightly lit corridors of the new institution. The forty-foot stone wall of the old Pen had limited the inmates' view of the outside world to passing clouds. The perimeter of the new enclosure was a chain-linked fence, overlooking fields dotted with dwellings and a church spire in the distant village, creating a false sense of liberty. Institutional activities were increased and included evening sorties into the main exercise yard. Trade and educational opportunities were now available. Thus, the institution and its daily routine were established; inmates who could fit in were to be selected and transferred there.Fate, however, does not always comply with the best-laid plans. Less than two years after the official opening of Leclerc, St. Vincent de Paul penitentiary erupted in a major riot. The workshops were razed and more than a third of the cell space destroyed. A population of some twelve hundred inmates had to be reduced by a third as quickly as possible. Although an accelerated release process helped diffuse the situation, transfer to another penitentiary became the principal safety valve.

The criteria for admission to Leclerc were necessarily slackened, the result of which set the tone for the institution from then on. Over the years, Leclerc unofficially became a "parking lot." More recidivists, long-term sentences and obstructive inmates would end up there than in other medium-security institutions. Consequently, both internal and external security measures gradually became more stringent. A mind-set resembling that of maximum-security developed among personnel and inmates, thereby increasing restrictive policies and practices.

In the early 'seventies, the latest panacea for corrections in Canada was the living-unit system. The concept was borrowed from the treatment philosophy underlying therapeutic community but did not apply to the total institution. The basic idea was to divide the guards into two groups: those who would attend to static security posts only and those who would handle the dynamic security on the units. This latter group would be living-unit officers dressed in civilian clothes, who would "relate" to the inmates on units of manageable size. Their role would be a hybrid one, counsellor on the one hand and person responsible for discipline and security on the other.

As with most new practices in federal corrections, the living-unit concept was applied across the board. Five medium security institutions opened across Canada in the mid-'sixties and were now targeted as living-unit facilities. Cowansville penitentiary was to be the flagship of the Quebec Region. It had opened in 1965 and was designed in such a manner that, with some alterations, units of a reasonable size could be put together. At least the physical structure was amenable to transformation.By the mid-'seventies, the living-unit concept had spread. This was in great part due to the drive of the labour union that recognized an opportunity for work diversity and consequent personnel increase. More staff positions were always the facile solution to problems and increased union membership as well. Around this time an order came down from on high that Leclerc penitentiary was to be converted into a living-unit institution, in spite of serious reservations of the senior management in Leclerc. The physical plant could not reasonably be converted into independent units. The housing facilities were composed of four floors of cells located at opposite ends of a courtyard. Each floor, divided in two sections by an observational guard post, contained a total of sixty-four cells. Also, the inmate population included a higher percentage of recidivists and long-term sentences than other medium security institutions. Thus, contact between personnel and inmates was tentative and not conducive to a smooth changeover to the living-unit model. The idea of a closer working relationship between living-unit officer and inmate was to prove difficult; a few courses at the Regional Staff College and a change of clothing from uniform to jeans fooled no one. For the most part, inmates and officers knew where each other stood. When I arrived there in February 1977, two positive elements were in place. Firstly, there were no strictly defined tasks for psychologists. We were pretty much left on our own to assume responsibilities as we saw fit; bureaucratic constraints had not been put in place as yet. The second factor was that I would have the pleasure of working with an experienced colleague who had an excellent relationship with the inmate population and was well respected by the personnel. Odette LeCorre had launched her career as Psychologist with the opening of Leclerc. She was therefore the right person to guide me through the daily hazards of this large institution. She had no illusions about the possibilities within such an environment and had no difficulty whatsoever making her opinions known. She also had a particular talent for working with inmates and their families. It was not out of the ordinary to see toddlers scampering about her office, as a teary-eyed mother recounted the woes of a parent left to fend for herself. She was adept at instilling a good dose of reality, with respect to personal responsibility, into the therapeutic relationship with those she was trying to counsel.

As for myself, it was not long before I started a group. As with the formation of previous groups, I would approach one or two compatible individuals and have them select the remaining four to six members. For the next four years, the group met in the cramped quarters of my office on a weekly basis. The central theme of the group remained constant: how the individual offender brought himself to prison and how only he could prevent his own return. The ifs, ands, and buts were merely excuses and acknowledged as such. The allegation that one had to get out of prison before being able to stay out was considered an avoidance mechanism and countered with, "you guys know how to get out better than I do. You're experts at it. You listen to the tune being piped and then dance to it. What you evidently don't know is how to stay out." The group was made up of repeat offenders, an easy target. Apart from the group work I maintained regular, individual counselling sessions with a number of the men.

Gino was one of the first inmates I dealt with at Leclerc. I had known him peripherally at the old Pen some years back. Some time later he was signalled to me because of some threatening behaviour he had shown while in another institution. As it turned out, he had experienced an acute break with reality, a reaction to his lengthy sentence and had subsequently been treated in psychiatry and supposedly stabilized. He was serving a life sentence for a gangland slaying. The day I started at Leclerc, I checked the inmate list for names I might recognize and saw his. Upon inquiry I discovered that he was in Dissociation, the polite name for the hole. It was explained to me that he had been pacing the floor in the workshop, muttering to himself and with a two-by-four in his hands. The inmates as well as the shop instructor were disconcerted. The solution was to place him in isolation; shop problem solved. I went off to the hole.

It was obvious upon seeing him that his problem had not been solved but likely accentuated. He was hallucinating actively. Nevertheless, he recognized me and willingly accompanied me to my office. It is amazing how quickly one can decompress with a simple change of environment. I had no illusions of permanent change but the overt signs of distress had dissipated enough to convince me that the first step was to keep him out of Dissociation. I spoke with some inmates on the wing where Gino had been living and struck a deal: he would return to the wing on condition that I see him in my office on a daily basis. Arrangements were made with the appropriate officials, including the personnel working on the wing, and the deal was sealed. He was back to work in about three weeks. In the interim, a psychiatric interview had been arranged and medication prescribed. A band-aid solution perhaps but at least I was able to maintain some therapeutic contact with him on a regular basis.

About a year and a half later Gino asked to see me one day. He said that his ex-wife and two children were coming in town and he wanted to know if I could arrange a temporary absence for him. I had no decisional power whatsoever but knew the Warden well. He was a young man and at twenty-nine years of age, the youngest penitentiary Warden in Canada. I knew that this could be a good opportunity to start the ball rolling for Gino. There was not a lot to work with. He was labelled a "hit man" for the mob, had previous serious adjustment problems and had little all-round support. He was now in the ninth year of a life sentence, with a minimum parole eligibility date at ten years. He had been eligible for temporary absence since the completion of his seventh year but had not been considered a good risk.

Irving Kulik had worked as a Classification Officer at the notorious Special Correctional Unit for about two years at the outset of his career. Fresh out of University with a Master's degree in Criminology, he had been sent to the pit of hell. Ironically, both sides profited by the experience. Because of an innate sensitivity to human suffering, he brought a genuine sense of compassion to this ill-conceived abode; at the same time, this baptism of fire had placed him in a position where paperwork was at a minimum and contact with the inmate the sole raison d'être for the task on hand. He was an intelligent and organized person as well. These qualities did not pass unnoticed and after a number of years grinding it out, he successfully passed the required competitions and became Warden at Leclerc in late 1977. During our time together we reviewed different issues at several meetings. He made his own decisions but not before listening to the opinion of others, inmates and personnel alike.

I approached Kulik on the matter Gino had brought to me. I explained that because of his institutional difficulties, coupled with a negative police report, Gino would be a hard sell when time came to present his case to the Parole Board. I believed this could be a suitable opportunity to try some initial steps. I had known him since he arrived at the penitentiary some eight years before and had been working with him regularly over the past two years. His ex-wife and two teen-aged children, whom he had not seen but had corresponded with over the past nine years, were in town for a few weeks and staying at his brother's home. As well, his father was seriously ill in the hospital. My proposal was to escort him for an eight-hour temporary absence to his brother's home and during the same block of time, bring him to visit his father in the hospital. My experience was that the men responded well when they felt you were genuinely concerned with personal matters and this reduced security concerns considerably. Kulik agreed with my reasoning and overall plan.

The experience turned out to be profitable for all concerned. Meeting with Gino's family gave me a more complete picture of the family dynamic and opened up vistas for future counselling sessions. Men like this are particularly difficult to work with because their delinquent values are deeply entrenched, after years within a structured criminalized peer group. The clinician must seek out areas that are more socially acceptable and try to direct energies toward those healthier sectors. As for Gino, the simple contact with family, his children in particular, inserted a dose of reality into a drab institutional existence. It was not an easy encounter for him but it did have some beneficial effect. The visit to his father in the hospital was a rude awakening as well. The family had minimized the father's health problems, a situation that was put in true perspective at the visit; in fact, his father was terminally ill.

During this temporary absence, Gino's brother had arranged to have as many of the extended family as possible to come to his home. We shared a lengthy, sumptuous meal together in the finished basement of the home and the event turned out to be a pleasant social encounter for all. It had been a hot summer day so I had hung up my suit coat. When I retrieved it before leaving for the penitentiary, I reached in my pocket for my car keys and came up with a crisp one hundred dollar bill. I knew this had been done with the best intentions; several family members had expressed profuse thanks to me. I went to Gino's brother and made it clear that I was simply doing my job as I saw fit and was suitably paid for doing so. It was an awkward moment, as I was at pains not to be misunderstood. I remained insistent and the matter was resolved, or so I thought.About three weeks later Gino's father passed away. I escorted him to the funeral parlour and once again met with the family, this time under more sombre circumstances. They expressed their gratitude, as though I were the one who exercised such benevolent authority. My contentions seemed to fall on deaf ears as several family members pleaded with me to bring him to the funeral in two days time. I knew that institutional policy was that an inmate could attend either the visitation at the funeral parlour or the funeral; I also knew that a grieving family would not understand the niceties of institutional policy. I promised nothing but said I would speak to the authorities.

The bottom line was that Kulik allowed this third temporary absence. It took some convincing and I understood his delicate position. There was established policy; why the exception? It is important that a decision-maker show no favouritism. My argument boiled down to the fact that Gino, himself, was an exception. I was able to convince Kulik of this and also that it would give me further leverage to work with this complicated case.

After the church service and funeral procession to the gravesite, we returned once again to his brother's home. The entire family was seated at a lengthy table. After a moment of silence Gino's brother rose from his chair. I had my head bowed, expecting a brief prayer on this solemn occasion, when I heard "*Il professore* Williams . . ." I immediately looked up and faced the outstretched hand of Gino's brother, offering me a gift-wrapped box. The applause from those around the table added to my embarrassment. I accepted with some ambivalence what was being offered as a token of gratitude, wondering to myself how I could politely decline. Upon opening the box I knew I had been snookered: it contained a gold cross and chain. For the sake of the purists, I can only say there must be some sort of poetic justice. Approximately six months later, my home was broken into and among the items stolen were my gold cross and chain. No miracles were worked with Gino but I believe these temporary absences did noticeably open up communication. Much is made, officially, of the success of the temporary absence program, usually measured by the fact that the offender did not abscond. Theoretically, it is supposed to be a bridge between the institution and the community. Unless it is highly personalized, however, I believe it can become a bridge between an institutional lifestyle and a delinquent lifestyle in the community. As with all "successful" programs, they become a "one size fits all" part of progressive release; consequently, their true import is diluted.

The work I did with Gino helped me prepare his case for presentation to the Parole Board. I was able to comment on his mental and emotional state, his behavioural adaptations both in and outside the penitentiary and describe the familial resources. Nevertheless, he didn't instil confidence easily but we worked with what we had. The National Parole Board had not as yet been strangled by policy guidelines that would inevitably become written in stone. In addition, the proliferation of amendments to the law that would eventually curb clinical interpretation and innovative decision-making, had not been promulgated either. Thus, it was still possible to explain certain nuances of human behaviour. The hearings had not as yet become the dry forum of bureaucratic procedure, highlighted by lawyers pompously strutting across an unfamiliar stage, posturing as clinicians.

In fact, Gino was released on full parole. He had been incarcerated twelve years. He was to remain in freedom for over two years. A return to the penitentiary was for a relatively minor offence, seen in the light of his heavily laden past. He has continued a marginal adjustment in the community for several years now. Given his previous life pattern over a substantial period, his present adaptation to the demands of liberty is just short of remarkable and may certainly be considered successful.

The group sessions I had in my office at Leclerc over the four-year span included several interesting figures. Since this was a medium-security institution the turnover in inmate population was more so than in St. Vincent de Paul; inmates were more quickly transferred to lesser security or released to the community on parole. Institutional policies were less stringent than in later years, an example being the numerous temporary absences allowed. This was before case management strategy was introduced; classification officers, psychologists and living-unit officers dealt directly with inmates, rather than "managed their cases." Regular interviews, family contact, temporary absence escorting, etc., all brought about constant contact between institutional personnel and offender. This was to dissipate gradually to the point where, from the mid-eighties onwards, the approach in corrections became increasingly impersonal, characterized by scale-type evaluations based on categories of inmates rather than on individuals and interpreted in the light of computer-fed information.

Ralph, a group member, had been raised in the lower west end of Montreal. The product of a multi-problem family wracked with alcoholism, he was placed in the care of the social services of the day. Three of his brothers were chronic alcoholics, two of whom supplemented their marginal lifestyle through petty thievery. Ralph, himself, presented a more serious picture. As a hyperactive child with no real roots in family or social life, learning difficulties and behavioural problems came to the fore early. Constant truancy, fighting and petty thievery resulted in his placement in Shawbridge Boys Farm and subsequent absconding and general disruptive behaviour led to brief sentences served in Bordeaux Jail. All of this paved the way for a criminal career culminating in penitentiary incarceration.

At twenty-six years of age he was sentenced to hang for a murder committed during an armed robbery. He and two others knew that the local grocer made a night deposit every Saturday, immediately after closing his store. They approached him on the street; Ralph was armed; a tussle occurred and a shot fired. The three fled the scene empty-handed as the victim slumped lifeless to the ground. Within half an hour the three were arrested and Ralph charged with murder.

After conviction, he spent close to a year on "death watch", the isolation wing for those awaiting capital punishment, in Bordeaux Jail. His sentence was commuted to life imprisonment some twelve hours before his appointment with destiny. It would seem that the need to maintain the image of being cool throughout incarceration was of the utmost importance; the only recollection of "death watch" he admitted to, was of the inmates he had met there. Ralph's first years of incarceration on the life sentence were turbulent. He had fathered two children while at liberty, one of whom he had helped raise for a while. Upon his conviction for murder, however, the mother of his infant daughter had expressed a desire to get on with her life and raise their daughter alone. This was of little significance to Ralph while he faced the hangman's noose but became a central issue once his sentence was commuted. He was now facing a long stretch inside and could not visualize it without the support of wife and daughter. Words led to arguments, then to threats. The institution became aware of the situation and overheard the threats and an alleged plan to escape. The immediate solution to serious problems in the early 'sixties was transfer; he was transferred to Kingston penitentiary where he remained for the next six years, then transferred back to St. Vincent de Paul in 1966 where he remained until released on parole in 1971. He was at liberty for approximately eighteen months and then revoked for possession of a gun and a stolen car. Re-incarcerated in 1973 at Archambault penitentiary, he was transferred to medium-security Leclerc in 1976, where he became a founding member of our group and instrumental in introducing new members.

I had encountered Ralph while he was at St. Vincent de Paul in the mid-'sixties. He would appear now and then at various meetings and occasionally asked to be seen individually. At the time, I was still connected with the McGill Forensic Clinic and Miriam Kennedy, the Senior Social Worker, spoke to me at length about Ralph and his family. She had been a Social Worker with Youth Protection and had dealt with him when he was a child. The information and clinical impressions she was able to give me were of great help and instrumental in opening the door to Ralph. He remembered her well and considered me OK, on this term alone.

He had mellowed considerably over the years and by the time he came into the group at Leclerc he was like an elder statesman. He was now forty-five years of age, the oldest in the group. He was serving a third penitentiary sentence and had been released and re-admitted during this present sentence. He had taken several courses through the Dawson College program at Archambault and continued his educational journey while at Leclerc. He was known by every inmate who had been in for more than ten minutes, not only because he had been in the system a long time but, more so, because he liked to preach to everyone, relating everything to his own story. He was a member of A.A., had learned the approach well and never let up. Those who knew him well had devised a technique whereby they could avoid the sermon. When they would see him coming in the yard, for example, they would grab any new inmate and say to Ralph,

"Hey, Ralphie, this guy's a fuckin' greenhorn fill 'im in will ya". He fell for it every time. He appreciated that he could "help" someone.

In the regular group, the men were able to exercise the verbal controls to prevent Ralph's sermonizing. When it came near his parole date in 1979, the men were merciless. They cautioned him in no uncertain terms to say as little as possible and only what is necessary.

"Bite your fuckin' tongue. You don't, you put them to sleep, they wake up an' you're doin' another bit!"

Ralph went to his hearing alone and emerged with a full parole. The guys were delirious: happy for him but scratching their heads as to what happened. No one ever established whether he had mesmerized the Board Members with his long-winded stories and they paroled him to get rid of him or that they actually believed he could make it. This was 1979 when Parole Members tried to evaluate an individual's progress and determine whether he would now be able to comply with conditions. Were the same case to be presented today I don't believe he would be released, certainly not on full parole. At best, six months to a year of escorted temporary absences; likely to be followed by a period of unescorted temporary absences along with work in the community; then sent for a stretch in a halfway house. Only after these steps had been completed would full parole be considered. After all, the public must be protected: this is a "notorious case," third penitentiary sentence, life for murder, revoked with new charges after eighteen months on parole; "have all the criminogenic factors been dealt with?"; "is this an assumable risk?" In fact, Ralph did very well. Upon release, he occupied much of his time with A.A. meetings. It is doubtful that he could ever have been classified as a true alcoholic. He had spent so little time in freedom that he really never had the time to develop this debilitating habit. In any case, he liked to tell his story and seemed to benefit from the experience. He had found a truly attentive audience as well, since he was able to attend a different group almost every night of the week. Within a month or so he met Sylvia, a barmaid who had not had a drink in the past three years. They were married within a year, built a home together and set up a business as well. Things were not always easy but they never gave up. Even when Ralph put his idea to "help" into practice and it seemed to backfire, they did not get discouraged but merely tried again. He believed that with his life experience he would be able to help some juvenile delinquents. He started with one and never got a second. The story goes that the youth had spent two days at Ralph's home before absconding.

> "This guy's worse than any worker I ever had at Shawbridge.
> He never stops talkin' and givin' me fuckin' orders!"

His career as a counsellor was short-lived but he plodded on. Eventually he and Sylvia set up a flea market and did exceptionally well. He lived with Sylvia, crime-free for fifteen years. I had attended their wedding and met with them occasionally over the years. The last time I saw him was the night before he died. He was lying in a hospital bed with terminal lung cancer. Some months later we spread his ashes on a property he and Sylvia had bought in the Laurentians.

Ralph had been a persistent offender, a Primary Delinquent who manifested behavioural difficulties during the early school years, throughout adolescence and well into adulthood. The compulsive stealing and difficulty relating to the peer group in his pre-puberty years led to placement. The teen-age years began with suspension from school and the continuing turmoil resulted in juvenile and young adult detention. He began his third penitentiary sentence, the life sentence, during his mid-twenties. In summary, Ralph showed all the signs of an individual whose criminal career would abate late, if ever. For reasons difficult to identify, he was able to assume a crime-free lifestyle in late middle age, despite the poor prognosis.

$$* \quad * \quad *$$

The decision to release a man on parole is always chancy. There are many factors to consider, the major one being whether the offender has undergone some sort of change that would lead us to believe he is willing and able to live in freedom in a socially-acceptable manner; basically, will he be able to complete his sentence in the community under conditions and remain crime-free. What makes this a particularly difficult judgement is that the institutional experience does not prepare the individual to live in freedom. It is directed toward acceptable institutional behaviour. If the inmate does not behave as required, he does not benefit from the amenities meted out by the correctional system. Transfer to lesser security, temporary absence, private family visits, etc. are all contingent upon acceptable institutional behaviour and all play in the decision regarding conditional release.

The basic fallacy is that acceptable institutional behaviour is indicative of good post-release adjustment. In the last twenty years, or so, a shift in thinking has come about with respect to this. Less emphasis is now placed on satisfactory institutional behaviour. The converse, however, does not apply; although good institutional behaviour is considered less of a positive factor in parole decision-making today, poor institutional adjustment still weighs heavily against a favourable parole decision. In reality, poor institutional adjustment may be a normal reaction to incarceration; it might even be a sign of increased personal autonomy. The only manner in which this may be determined is through an intimate knowledge and evaluation of the individual offender. The parole decision does not change the length of the sentence but the manner in which a portion of it is to be served. The judgement as to whether an offender is able to complete his sentence under supervision in the community is basically a clinical one. This does not mean a clinician need make the decision. Evidently, parole decision-makers cannot know each offender encountered at a parole hearing. If they are to be in a position, however, to assess the information presented to them, they should be sufficiently knowledgeable in three fundamental areas: delinquent dynamics and defences; the effects of incarceration; and the appropriate, supportive resources in the community. Thus, the selection and training of parole decision-makers is of primary importance, if their role is to be one of value and not solely of prestige. They must bring with them some relevant expertise and be able to demonstrate this in a decision-making setting. Perhaps a probationary period while in actual practice would be a viable way to evaluate this power of discernment. Finally, they must be free of political ties. During deliberations many factors are to be considered including the severity of the crime and the repetitiveness of the behaviour but the fundamental issue centres on an analysis and interpretation of individual dynamics that may indicate behavioural change. Are the internal and external circumstances that led to the delinquent acting-out sufficiently altered so as to assure compliant behaviour upon conditional release? The entire issue of parole decision-making is crucial today mainly because of the direction in which the parole process has evolved. The one hundredth anniversary of conditional release was celebrated in 1999 and much of its history has been documented. Significant figures have been noted and their contributions acknowledged, along with the advancements that have been made. Less in evidence are the misunderstandings and distortions that have plagued the parole issue, on occasion forcing the proponents to make questionable compromises. The loudest voices of critical opinion, at either extreme of the continuum, have brought about concessions that at first blush may have seemed acceptable but with the scrutiny of time proved to compound matters. Those who claim that too many offenders are released conditionally have had the effect of creating artificial obstacles unrelated to the reintegration of offenders into society. Those who believe that all offenders should be released conditionally have unwittingly contributed to the development of a release system that blurs the fundamental difference between a bi-lateral agreement and unilaterally imposed restrictions, between parole supervision and mandatory supervision.

In the early 'seventies the law was modified so that all offenders would be released under supervision. Those who successfully passed their parole hearing were released at the third of their sentence under parole supervision; those refused parole were released after completion of two-thirds of the sentence and placed on mandatory supervision. The same basic conditions applied to the two groups and the same authority, the parole officer, carried out the supervision. In effect, those who had been assessed by the Parole Board and adjudged unable to be released conditionally at the third of the sentence were released at the two-thirds mark with identical conditions, imposed unilaterally. This proved to be the thin edge of the wedge in determining a crucial change in the direction of the Parole Board. Within a brief period of time, special conditions were added to certain cases released on mandatory supervision. When these did not have the intended effect, the Parole Board was eventually empowered in law to keep men incarcerated until completion of the sentence. Despite political assurances that this extreme measure was to be used only in extreme cases, the early years of this legislation witnessed the inevitable widening of the net. The National Parole Board had now gone beyond the pale. What had originally been designed as a releasing mechanism, now assumed the guise of a detention board; what had been designed as a relatively simple procedure to deal with a difficult problem had become a complex system that has altered objectives and lost sight of the goal. The ultimate goal is reintegration of the offender into the community in a socially acceptable manner so as to provide realistic, long-term protection for society.

*   *   *

I completed almost four years at Leclerc penitentiary, from February 1977 to September 1980. In those days, the role of the institutional Psychologist was defined pretty much by the individual working in the position. At the outset we were three Psychologists, a number reduced to two within my first year there. The inmate population held steady at about four hundred and fifty. I always believed that the inmates were the best source of referrals. Since they lived in such proximity they were well aware of each other's needs and also knew various pressure situations inherent in institutional life. If psychologists don't hide out in their office, and we didn't, the word as to their availability, spreads quickly.

I ran two groups at this time, the second of which emerged about a year into my stay at Leclerc. It required a different approach, simply because it was made up of six offenders and their wives. The men were all recidivists, so the wives knew the score. We would meet every Wednesday from six to eight-thirty in the evening. The effort was somewhat radical for the 'seventies; there was no private family visiting program as yet. The idea for this particular group came from the inmates themselves. They selected their own members, set down the ground rules and then approached me with their proposal. The visits were to be held in the Socio-Cultural department, a large room set aside for various inmate activities that often included guests from the community. The format would be a meal prepared by the inmate group members followed by a group session from seven-thirty to eight-thirty. The proposal included a special evening, once a month, when their children would participate. I was surprised at the organizational ability shown by the men; they had seemingly covered every aspect of the proposal. My only question was to how the selection of inmates had been made. Once again, they had done their homework. Each individual was serving a sentence of at least ten years. There were no obvious restrictions as to age, crime or number of previous sentences. In other words, the selection seemed representative of the inmate population serving lengthy sentences. The rationale was that these men had been separated from their families for a lengthy period and efforts should be made to maintain familial ties. The appropriate permission was obtained and the group started in the autumn of 1978.

It was obvious from the outset that there would be no control problems. There had been one selection criterion left unsaid; this was evidently a group of personally, well-organized inmates who had established tacit, but clear, limits. They knew they had a good thing that was worth protecting. They also shared duties in preparing and serving the food, as well as the clean up prior to the discussion.

As with other groups I had in the penitentiary, the inmate interest did not come from some deep-seated awareness to express and deal with problems. The motivation was closer to the surface than that. The delinquent, by definition, tends to centre the world around himself; immediate gratification is the order of the day and difficult life situations are seen as the result of external factors, rectified by manipulating relevant events, issues and people. Over years of incarceration family ties become increasingly tenuous, a direct threat to the offender who gradually perceives himself in the role of victim, as opposed to aggressor. The mate in freedom holds the true reins of power; personal autonomy appears to be slowly eroding. This, however, seldom emerges in the conscious life of the inmate but rather as an amorphous sense of discomfort. Life in a correctional institution is not geared toward introspection and self-awareness. It is a day-by-day existence characterized by ongoing attempts to extricate oneself from external oppression and control with little or no recognition of one's own responsibility for the predicament.

Thus, these group meetings were to be different from any I had previously experienced. In other groups, individual differences were acknowledged, even highlighted on occasion so as to rebuild a sense of personal identity, an element under continuous siege throughout the institutional experience. The one constant theme was that each and every individual remains responsible for his present situation: the commonly shared reality of incarceration.

The presence of wives, however, altered this basic dynamic. They introduced relationships that went in a myriad of directions. Apart from her own individuality, each wife experienced her own quality of relationship with her particular mate. The extent to which she becomes the "silent partner" has a considerable effect upon the lifestyle of the offender both while in the community and throughout incarceration. The supportive and unquestioning presence of the wife when money is available to pay bills and the family lifestyle is comfortable, takes on a different guise when the provider is no longer present. Variables such as the amount of time the couple shared at home, the number of children, the economic status and the support of the extended family weighed in the balance as well. Despite these variables, the central issue remained constant: the offender's responsibility at having placed himself in his present predicament and that only he can take the means to avoid doing so in the future. The presence of the wives accentuated the negative effects brought on the family, an issue of importance to them and a source of bewilderment to the husbands. The process of incarceration reinforces the self-centredness inherent in the delinquent make-up as the needs and demands of institutional life are exacerbated while the reality of life in the community is increasingly shut out. Thus the problems and concerns of family life become gradually but steadily more remote. The inmate becomes wrapped up in his artificial world while his mate becomes the sole provider of emotional and material sustenance to the family.

The entire project was an overall success for the inmates, their wives and me. I was able to gain considerable insight into the dynamic of a couple where one partner is involuntarily institutionalized. The overflowing effects of the deprivation of liberty on family life were also exposed. Wives and children of inmates are often the long-term victims of delinquent acting-out, although seldom recognized as such. Both the inmates and their wives profited from an increasingly open discussion of pertinent matters common to all. This latter point is of particular importance, given the innate suppression and overt denial of family problems in this repressive milieu. The moments of shared intimacy between individual couples played no small part in reducing the sterility of the institutional experience and contributed directly to a reawakening of the realities of home living. The monthly presence of the children reinforced the notion of parental responsibility as the men assumed the role of providers and supervisors of the evening meal, now compounded by the reality of several boisterous children. These family evenings were a respite for the wives and an observational treat for myself. The men, however, returned to their cells immediately upon completion of each monthly soirée, physically and emotionally vanquished.

The relevance of these weekly sessions can be seen and understood only in the context of the times. Although the correctional authorities in the seventies coined the phrase "the Opportunities Model," the number of available programs was minimal in comparison to today's standards. They were fewer in quantity but, as today, were handed out piecemeal rather than as an integral part of a comprehensive approach. On the positive side, there was a greater tolerance for diversity of opinion and practice than in later years. Psychologists and

Classification Officers were not restricted to a role that would later be designed, bureaucratically, to support and carry out a "one size fits all" approach to the multifaceted problem of delinquency. The services of psychology and classification were helping services in the 'seventies, a provision of assistance to the inmate to carry out his sentence with a view to eventual release; the subsequent supervision in the community was also geared to helping the offender adjust.

If one were to take time to read the lengthy and elaborate description of current institutional programs, one may indeed be impressed. The reality, however, is something else. Although many programs are valid per se, the manner in which they are presented and the global milieu in which they are ensconced, seriously diminish their relevance. The success or failure of any agent of change is contingent upon the receptivity of the subject. The true delinquent, by definition, does not perceive a need for internal change and the penitentiary milieu is not designed to awaken this awareness. Punishment, repression and control, the basic tenets of the correctional system, are counter-productive with respect to self-awareness and behavioural change. Motivation, then, becomes the problem to be addressed and not a sine qua non to acceptance in a particular program. One of the most intriguing aspects of the phenomenon of delinquency, and certainly its most intransigent obstacle to treatment, is this basic absence of genuine motivation to change. Regardless of the havoc wreaked upon one's life and family, the behavioural pattern persists. Despite the fact that the measured intelligence quotient of the offender population is commensurate with that of the general population, the incongruity of the delinquent's cognitive process remains manifest. The only gambit that I have found helpful to pierce this carapace is through direct confrontation in a caring atmosphere. One must be perceived as compassionate and trustworthy, a sizeable challenge in a setting imbued with cunning and deceit. Nevertheless, it is imperative to maintain a clear-cut standard of socially acceptable attitudes and demeanour.

The group work I was involved in during the seventies was somewhat different from that of the sixties. The barren atmosphere of the maximum security St. Vincent de Paul penitentiary instilled a general sense of hopelessness. The lengthy sentences, coupled with the spectre of violence that drifted incessantly just beneath the surface, produced an ambience of fear and suspicion touching both inmates and personnel alike. The group, at that time, was devised to provide an oasis of comfort and a semblance of personal freedom whose cathartic value was to exercise a positive influence upon the institutional adjustment of its participants. Little emphasis was placed on the realities of life in the community-at-large, past or future. The immediate threat to be contended with was the ominous present.

The Leclerc experience was basically different. This medium security institution was relatively comfortable and held out some hope, as one could see the light at the end of the tunnel. Inmates who were generally compliant and could present some credible release plan had a reasonable chance at early release. They could be released on Day Parole into a halfway house for a period of time and subsequently placed on Full Parole. This latter status meant that they were to complete their sentence in the community-at-large, subject to specified conditions that included reporting to a Parole Office on a regular, determined basis. Thus, the group could contend with the question of personal responsibility for one's life situation. I always took the position, particularly with the persistent offenders, that they were responsible for putting themselves in prison. They made choices, some bad from the outset, others that looked good in the short term but were evidently disastrous in the long run: the ultimate result, incarceration. This technique of direct confrontation can be used only once a climate of trust has been created. It must be clear to the participating inmates that this challenge to their attitudes and behavioural pattern is done in good faith. They must participate willingly; if their presence is the result of mere coercion, they will respond accordingly, either by withdrawal or play-acting. If there is one principal factor that stimulates a group in the traditional correctional setting, it is a genuine openness: "cut the bullshit," is the maxim, an adage that must apply to inmate and personnel alike.

*　　*　　*

Another release mechanism that gained popularity and was used to excess in the seventies was the Temporary Absence (TA). At the time, it was under the jurisdiction of the Warden. A TA could be granted with or without escort for a period of time not exceeding three days. The most frequently granted at Leclerc was the TA with escort, usually from eight to fifteen hours. Cases would be studied by a committee and forwarded to the Warden for the final decision. The living-unit officers usually handled the escort duty. However, a psychologist or classification officer who followed an inmate regularly would sometimes accompany that inmate. Group TAs with five inmates or less were granted on certain occasions and for special events.

In my four years at Leclerc, I escorted several inmates, usually to their family and many of them on more than one occasion. I found that it was a great help in my work as I got a more complete picture of the inmate and how he relates to persons and circumstances in his immediate environment. I believe that the TA, when carried out by interested and competent staff, can add a modicum of reality to the evaluation and treatment of the delinquent whose daily life is artificial and non-productive. Unfortunately, the TA quickly became commonplace and ultimately a "right" to a reward for acceptable institutional behaviour, rather than a diagnostic and treatment tool.

Although most TAs were successful, there were some inmates who absconded, even while under escort. This was always the main concern of the escort since the institutional authorities could respond heavy-handedly with the staff member should the inmate be declared illegally-at-large. I never faced that problem myself. In great part, this was due to sheer luck, as I believe that any inmate could take off from an escort if he set his mind to it. On the other hand, I believe that my major safeguard was that I usually knew the one I was escorting quite well. Oftentimes I was acquainted with the family he was to visit. In those rare instances where I would accompany someone I didn't really know I would first obtain the assurances of those inmates who did know him. In a penitentiary setting, this type of assurance is as close to a guarantee one can obtain.

George came to see me in my office one morning. He was a member of both my groups and very influential among the inmate population. He was a member of that now extinct breed of bank robbers who contributed to the dubious distinction of Montreal as the "bank hold-up capital" of North America, during the sixties and early seventies. He was currently serving a life sentence and was now completing his seventh year incarcerated. He approached me in his usual up-beat way.

"Paul, how're you doing? We need your services." George always deferred to the royal "we."

"What's up now?" I asked, feigning frustration.

"You know that little guy, Johnny, the one who delivers the papers up front here, he needs to get out."

I stared.

"No one wants to escort him."

I knew immediately that every issue had been covered. Johnny was obviously eligible for a TA; his situation would have been scrutinized thoroughly, and he would pose no problem since he would have been an integral part of his own "evaluation." George, if anything, was thorough.

"I know who you mean 'cause I've seen him pass by here with the newspapers . . . but I don't know who the hell he is . . . I've never said a word to him" I protested. "No problem. He knows you!"

This was stated with an air of finality. He knew who I was, so everything was O.K. I told George I would think about it and to tell Johnny to stop by my office. In the meantime, I would review his file so as to have an idea who I would be meeting.

"No one wants to escort him." The words echoed in my head as I perused Johnny's file. No kidding! No one wanted to escort him because no one was crazy enough to put his job in jeopardy because some inmate "needs to get out." Johnny had begun a four-year sentence some twelve years ago. His sentence had since increased to twenty-four years, the result of a number of armed robberies committed while at-large on two consecutive escapes from custody.

George was back in my office moments after I had him paged, grinning from ear to ear.

"I know what you're thinkin'; there's no need to get gun shy; he'll come back with you; you can take that to the bank." This was stated so quickly that George's metaphorical speech pattern was lost on me for the moment.

"But he's done nothing but escape. This can never be sold to Kulik!"

"Leave Kulik to me" George stated confidently. "This guy's got twelve in straight and will never see the light of day if we don't help him." There was that damn "we" again!

"If he's ever to get a shot at the Board, he has to offer somethin'. If you take him out, it'll give him somethin' to work with."

As it turned out, George had spoken to Warden Kulik prior to approaching me. Kulik's initial reaction had been identical to mine.

"This guy's track record is really impressive," Kulik said sarcastically, "he sure is fast on his feet." George was always persuasive, however.

"If you send him with Williams, Mr. Kulik, I guarantee he'll be back."

"Does Williams know something I don't? Or do you think he can out run this guy?" Kulik retorted with a self-satisfied grin. Kulik promised he would study the case. It was a day or two later that he called me to his office and recounted his meeting with George.

"I'm half tempted to let him go. What do you think? Would you take him?"

I knew then Kulik was ready to agree. I had pondered the matter myself and thought it was worth the risk. The brief encounter with Johnny had revealed little. He gave the expected promises to comply which, alone, meant little. I have never met an inmate who was stupid enough to tell his potential escort that he was planning to take off. What persuaded both Kulik and myself, separately, was the confidence we had in George. If he gave his word, you couldn't ask for more. He would have done his homework and would have "instructed" Johnny in the dos and don'ts, with clarity. George was solid. The only real matter for discussion was the known impulsivity of Johnny and whether this TA was worth the risk. I believed it could be of value to the three of us: Johnny, Kulik and myself. Kulik's decision was in the affirmative.

The destination was the flat of Johnny's girlfriend, on St. Denis Street; the time allotment was eight hours. Both his mother and sister were present, a godsend for me as I was able to glean much information on the family history and early development of this unknown individual.

It also accommodated him as he renewed his acquaintance with Jeannette in the boudoir. The TA was successful from the institution's point of view as Johnny returned safe and sound at the appointed hour. I made the best of a seemingly long day by mentally compiling a developmental history of my most recent client, an exercise that helped me engage him in regular counselling over the ensuing months. The only incident that I left unreported, for fear of misinterpretation at a later date, happened as we were driving back to the institution.

We were due back for 5:30 p.m. and so were in the bumper-to-bumper traffic along Pie IX Boulevard in the height of rush hour. We were about third in line at a red light when Johnny said to me in a strained voice,

> "You don't know how hard it is for me to return to the pen. I want to jump out and run for it."

His statement had come out of the blue, following a period of complete silence while we were in the car. It all happened so suddenly that I had no time to panic. When I turned toward him, he looked at me and must have read in my eyes what I only remember feeling later: a realization that if he wanted to go, there was absolutely nothing I could do. Here we were, hemmed in on one of Montreal's main arteries, at rush hour. If he runs, I wave.

> "I'm not going anywhere. I just wanted to let you know how I feel. George told me you're a psychologist and that I should express my feelings. I'm sorry!"

I breathed an audible sigh of relief. I would have to speak to George. This "psychologist" shit was getting out of hand. My nerves couldn't take it.

There were many TAs I participated in over these four years; some were of obvious value, others less so. All were interesting. George had asked me whether I would escort an individual whose penitentiary moniker was "the Beard." His jet-black growth reached down to the top of his chest, giving him the appearance of a Latin dictator.

"I know you don't know him well but he asked for you. He doesn't trust anyone in the joint. He's been in ten years now and wants to see his family."

Further questioning revealed that his family meant an ailing father and an awaiting girlfriend. "I'm game if you can clear it with the boss." Arrangements were made and we set out on our two-targeted sojourn. We were to be gone for seven hours, from four in the afternoon to eleven at night. Not all TAs could be during day hours, mainly because of working families; not all personnel cared to escort during evening hours. I presumed that these were the main reasons I had been approached.

Not so. The Beard's father, presently at home on sick leave, was a guard at Bordeaux Jail. He had not seen his own son in ten years. Since his main duty had been transporting the accused to court and the convicted to the penitentiary, both father and son realized that penitentiary visits were out of the question. He would be recognized and this would eventually lead to trouble. This evening's encounter was an opportunity for the two of them to touch base.

Over the next four hours, the three of us shared a meal and I was privy to the expressed sadness, guilt and gloom of the tormented past life of this family. Parental rupture, alcoholism and poverty had taken its toll and the father's illness was now admittedly more severe than previously surmised. The duration of the visit proceeded under a cloud of unpromising finality.

The second part of the TA was spent at the apartment of the Beard's girlfriend, a place well appointed in furniture covered with imitation animal skin and walls adorned with selections of penitentiary art. After hurried introductions, at which Gigi excused herself profusely for not having had the time to change from her work attire, they immediately repaired to the bedroom. "The Beard" was able to assuage his depressive feelings elicited in the first part of this excursion from the penitentiary, while I somewhat morosely babysat the television in the living-room of this three room abode. We were back at Leclerc at the appointed hour. "The Beard" was quiet in the car, as most men are upon return to confinement. A murmured "*merci, pour ton temps*" helped me over the general sense of futility at this exercise. Maybe, just maybe, a few hours in disorganized freedom were, in the long run, healthier than over-organized external control.I was mildly surprised, about a month later, when I overheard that "the Beard" was going out on another escorted TA in a day or so. It was not that I particularly wanted to repeat my previous experience but it would have been customary to approach me the second time since the first had been considered O.K. I became aware a short time later that "the Beard" absconded during his second escorted TA. Protection takes many forms in this shadowy milieu.

There was a group TA I was involved in that was probably more interesting by the way it came about than the actual outing itself. Some five inmates, four of whom I worked with on a regular basis, had been training for long-distance running. Their goal was to obtain permission to enter the Montreal Marathon. When I got wind of this I chuckled to myself and gloatingly thought of a real issue I could confront my group with at our next session, as three of the five runners attended the Friday morning session.

It has always been my belief that the delinquent usually has trouble carrying out a task from beginning to end. There are various reasons for this, many of them reinforced through correctional institutional living. Lack of internal discipline and control, as well as a need for immediate gratification, are some of the dynamics which propel the delinquent to begin a task without necessarily considering certain basic prerequisites, only to abandon the task before its completion. I knew little about long-distance running but was certain that it involved meticulous training on a gradual basis, over an extended period. Theoretically, an excellent challenge for the delinquent: the freedom of the eventual run would provide the stimulus; the long-term commitment would be the insurmountable task.

Friday morning began with the usual banter. The group was in its usual good mood at the outset. This was the end of their work-week, a phenomenon that in no way resembled a work pattern in the community but had a similar euphoric effect because of the impending break.

> "I heard about the project to register for the marathon. Do you think you'll get permission for a TA just to hand out refreshments to the passing runners?"
>
> "No, three of us are . . . O.K., I get it. You're breaking our balls! What's the pitch now?"

"I'll be serious. How many are you trainin', five?" I questioned.

"Yeh, an' fuckin' hard too." replied Willie with insistence.

"Don't waste your time," I quipped, "not one of you will finish . . . and I mean, even the training."

The general murmuring was laced with mocked derision, "Listen, wise guy, you couldn't run haffa' mile."

"That's beside the point. I'll bet not one of you will complete the marathon," I said offhandedly.

In a moment I realized the die had been cast. Although I couldn't see them responding to a figure of speech, "I'll bet not one . . ." they could, and did. Amid the mingled comments of bravura and feigned hurt feelings, the voice of George rose above the others.

"Now about this bet. The five of us will finish. When we do, you take us to the Stadium see the Expos."

"And if you don't?"

"We will. And we'll go one better. We get the tickets, you just take us."

This Friday morning's meeting never did get any more serious; the office resembled a miniature tavern, without the beer but with as much gusto and macho exaggeration as to the prowess of the Expos, long-distance runners and the fact that all bets must eventually be paid.In fact, the five completed the Montreal International Marathon; two of the five ran it under three hours. This was an astonishing feat for men who had never competed in long-distance running before. The fact that their running facilities and dietary control were less than international calibre made it more impressive yet. As for my theory on the dynamics of delinquency, well, back to the drawing board.The bet was paid. After some finagling with penitentiary authorities, the inmates were able to present an acceptable project to get permission for a group TA. The Expos were a serious team that year but they lost this one to the front running Pirates two to one. Almost sixty thousand fans watched as another nail was hammered into the Expos coffin in this September stretch. Among the crowd were five serious offenders and one humbled psychologist. The main consolation for the latter was that this group activity was decidedly healthier than the usual plotting of the various groups in the penitentiary yard.

*   *   *

There was a further development in my career midway through my stay at Leclerc. *La Commission québécoise des libérations conditionnelles* (CQLC) was created in law in April 1979. I was appointed one of several *commissaires communautaires* (CC), the appointment made by the provincial *Ministre de la Justice,* precursor to the *Ministre de la Sécurité Publique.* A CC was, in fact, a part-time member of the Parole Board. The term "community member" was to imply that the individual in some way represented the community from which he or she came. This appellation was more pertinent to those who came from communities outside the large metropolitan areas of Montreal or Quebec City. The "community member" from Rimouski or Sorel, for example, could quite likely be thoroughly familiar with the material and personal resources of their respective community. This did not have the same relevance in the more diverse metropolitan communities.

The CQLC was mandated to hold parole hearings for those in provincial prisons. These offenders were serving sentences of less than two years; those serving a sentence of six months or more were entitled to a parole hearing at the third of the sentence. The federal Parole Act was the judicial basis for the new Board and Quebec became the third Canadian province to have its own Parole Board, along with Ontario and British Columbia.It was to be an interesting experience, enriching yet intimidating, in the sense that I was to be in the position of decision-maker with respect to someone's freedom. Evidently, these offenders presented less of a problem than those in the penitentiary. Generally, their crimes were less severe. Nevertheless, the repetitiveness of their delinquent behaviour was characteristic of many.

Parole is a frequently misunderstood concept. It is mistakenly perceived as a shortening of the sentence, a distortion of the Court's intention and a simple reward for good institutional behaviour. In fact parole is an integral part of the sentencing process. The Judge is well aware that the offender may be conditionally released at a certain point in the sentence when meting out the term. The Judge determines the length of sentence and another body under law, the Parole Board, decides how a portion of that sentence is to be served; law sets the dates for parole eligibility and the Parole Board, after considering many factors, reaches a decision. The basic question is: is the offender capable of completing the sentence in the community, under specific conditions? The paramount condition is that of remaining crime-free. The seriousness of the original crime is taken into consideration but, more important than the crime, is the offender. Is the offender likely, or not, to re-offend? When emphasis on the crime takes precedence over evaluation of the offender, the fundamental meaning of parole is distorted. It becomes a reward or punishment rather than an assessment of the offender's ability and willingness to profit from supervised release into the community-at-large. The *raison d'être* of this entire process is the reintegration of the offender into society so as to provide realistic, long-term protection to the public. Despite the misrepresentation of facts sometimes put forth by the media, usually the knee-jerk reaction to one spectacular failure, the parole process is an overall success. Recidivism while under parole supervision remains significantly lower than when the offender is released with no comprehensive and relevant assistance.

A CC was contracted for two years, a mandate that could be renewed only once consecutively. With bureaucratic delays, my tenure as CC was from 1979 to 1984. During this five-year period, I was able to gain valuable experience and learn the delicate balance between the negative effects of incarceration and the need to maintain imprisonment as a neutralizing agent. Timing was of the essence. My experience in having worked with serious offenders was really a double-edged sword. On the one hand, I could be less threatened by the repetitive but relatively innocuous behaviour of some offenders I came across in the provincial system. Thus, I was sometimes able to assuage the fears of colleagues with a different experiential background. On the other, however, I sometimes had to be held in check by more temperate minds and convinced to refuse parole to individuals I would have released, simply because they were becoming more entrenched in their delinquent ways while incarcerated. An extreme example comes to mind.

Ron was a nineteen-year old serving eighteen months for a series of break and entry charges, as well as car theft. This was his first adult sentence but he had a heavily charged history as a juvenile offender. I saw him as potential penitentiary fodder if nothing were to be done. During the deliberation phase of the hearing, I discussed the matter heatedly with my colleague Paul Picard. Paul was a lawyer with some twenty-five years of practice in criminal law; he was also very intelligent.

"Williams, you must be nuts. This guy won't last a week on parole. There's no way I'll vote to release him."

"What I'm suggesting Paul, is not to send him home but get him in a half-way house. If not, this kid's going to end up in the Pen," I retorted.

"He has no release plan whatsoever . . . he should have contacted a half-way house himself and that's not our job."

"Look, Paul, we can put off our decision 'till next week. In the meantime I'll contact Terry. If he accepts him, we can send him to Decision House for a month or two."

Picard looked at me askance, "Williams, you're getting soft. This guy won't make it but if Terry's ready to take him, I'll go along with it."

Terry Batten was a no-nonsense, street worker who graduated from the school of hard knocks. He ran his halfway house with an iron will and, I suspect, sometimes with an iron bar. I contacted him by 'phone, described Ron's background and the situation. He agreed to take him and Ron was released to the halfway house the following week.

The next I heard of Ron was through the news media the following week. I had just sat down at my desk in Bordeaux Jail, ready to begin a day of parole hearings. The clerk came in as I was getting my files ready, "Paul Picard said to give you today's paper. He just called from Orsainville," he stated and quickly retreated. The *Journal de Montréal* headline referred to "*un hold-up spectaculaire en Arthabaska*"; page three told the story, under a photo of Ron.

Some days later I spoke with Terry Batten. "You sent me a live one that time. The bastard lasted ten minutes," he stated.

"What happened?" I queried.

"He arrived at the house around two in the afternoon. I interviewed him about ten minutes and told him I'd talk to him at length after supper. I had a full afternoon so I told him I'd see him at seven sharp. 'den he asks me if he could go jogging while he's looking across the street at the park. I gave him the OK and that's the last I seen of him. The little fucker must've jogged all the way to Arthabaska."

This was an important learning experience for me. It is easy to judge others and yet fail to see the vulnerability in oneself. I had previously noticed that the prior experience of others, whether police officer, lawyer or any other background, occasionally predisposed them to decision-making that was less than objective. I had failed to see the same susceptibility in myself. The friendly kidding I got from my colleagues, particularly my friend Paul Picard, helped me turn this debacle into an exercise in self-education.

The CQLC was created in law and passed through *l'Assemblée nationale and,* after *le Cabinet* had accepted the nominations, le Ministre appointed its first members. Thus, parole board members are political appointments. This is pretty much a necessity in a democratic society. The Criminal Justice System touches all, belongs to all; its administration, at least theoretically, is best in the hands of our elected officials and there's the rub. The primary goal of elected officials is to get elected, then re-elected. One of the means of better assuring this is to curry favour whenever possible. This must be done responsibly.At the outset, the permanent members of the CQLC were selected diligently. There were five members whose professional experience covered the spectrum since all five had careers directly related to criminal justice. One was a trained clinician whose work experience had been at various levels of administration in criminal justice; another had twenty years of police work, attaining the position of Chief of Police; a third was a career defence lawyer; the fourth, a clinical criminologist with extensive experience with the mentally ill who had come into contact with the law; finally, the fifth a clinical psychologist with vast experience in the correctional field in various jurisdictions. The strongest point of this make-up, however, was the openness among them that allowed each individual to share his or her knowledge and experience with the others, so that all could learn. Clinical and administrative meetings were held weekly. All members, including the President and Vice-President, were directly involved in the parole hearings. Bureaucracy was kept to a minimum and the administrative staff was there simply to provide a service to facilitate decision-making. These early years were characterized by a camaraderie and enthusiasm that inspired hope for change, an eagerness that spilled over into the ranks of the part-time members of the Board.

Thus, the combination of overall expertise and experience among the members, both permanent and part-time, placed this newly arrived organization at the vanguard of correctional development. Most of the provincial prisons were antiquated; overpopulated dungeons from a past era, too often harbouring a surplus of social misfits who could be under helpful supervision in the community. What better opportunity than a new, dynamic organization to forge ahead and help uncover the precipitating causes of crime and delinquency while, at the same time, rooting out the elements that reinforce delinquent behaviour through incarceration?

This early euphoria gradually dissipated. The oppressive milieu of century-old Bordeaux Jail, no less a stone and steel fortress than St. Vincent de Paul penitentiary, drained one's hope for meaningful change. A heavy shawl of lethargy hung over the daily routine of personnel and prisoners alike. Just as the underlying anger and hostility in the penitentiary produced a climate of impending aggression, so the rapid inmate turnover of the provincial prison created a behavioural automatism among the personnel. Despite this we plodded on. Hearings were held and suggestions for change were made. However, professional jealousy between the "old guard" and the new paroling authority eventually won the day and substantial change failed to become a reality. I consider my first five years with the CQLC as more of a learning experience than anything else. There is only one criminal justice system but it is composed of various parts. The principal sections of the Judiciary, Corrections and Parole are independent, yet interdependent. If the complete system is to function as one, each of these sections must work in unison to achieve the ultimate goal: justice. This is easier said than done. The internal jealousies and power plays to maintain the upper hand, further complicated by an overriding political agenda, tend to cloud basic issues and obfuscate the end game. In the long run, I believe that much honest effort and genuine expertise is sacrificed to the maintenance of the established power structure, bureaucratic and political.

It is written in law and also a regularly preached homily at all congresses on criminal justice, that incarceration is to be employed as a last means and that, when incarceration is necessary, it is to be applied in its least restrictive form. Many examples of failure to adhere to this maxim can be cited.

M.Genest was a sixty-seven year old offender serving six months for failure to report income. Non-compliance to pay the stipulated fine resulted in his incarceration. He was a first-time offender, a retired chartered accountant now sixty-five years of age. The procedure we followed at parole hearings was to peruse the applicant's institutional file, prior to the interview. This file recorded the basic information that identified the individual, the general nature of the offence and the length of sentence. Any outstanding reports of hostile attitude or aggressive acting-out were in immediate evidence. Rarely were there any detailed accounts of the individual's life that would lead one to believe that someone in the institution actually knew him. In fact, as I soon found out, none of the inmates were really known; some could be identified in part, by different members of personnel, usually those who had come into conflict with them. In summary, the parole applicant in the teeming Bordeaux Jail was pretty much an unknown quantity as he walked into the room for his parole hearing.

I was taken aback at M.Genest's appearance. He certainly looked more like an accountant than a condemned offender. He had certainly broken the law. He had continued to practice his profession after official retirement by providing help to demystify the encrypted income tax forms provided by the government. This, in itself, is not a crime but rather a blessing that deserves reward. He was rewarded; he received payment. What he did not do was declare this income. This is a crime, usually punishable by restitution, with interest, plus a fine. M.Genest was initially unable to pay the lump sum; tarried in making gradual payments and eventually, when brought before the Court again, was sentenced to six months by an obviously overly taxed Judge.

Two major problems that are brought to the public's attention constantly are the high cost of incarceration and prison overcrowding. These are usually explained away by the declaration that prisoners are treated luxuriously and that there is a perennial crime wave; neither reason resembles the truth. In any case, I wonder why a pre-sentence report didn't suggest that community work might be more appropriate in this instance than incarceration. I'm certain that there are community-based, non-profit organizations that could have benefited from the services of an accountant, without cost. I'm reasonably sure that M.Genest would have better understood the import of his anti-social behaviour with such a sanction. Finally, I would even hazard a guess that the protection of society, that much touted maxim of self-important bureaucrats and politicians, would have been properly served without resorting to imprisonment.

The overall experience of my first five years with CQLC was a positive one. The role of decision-maker was decidedly different from that of treatment person. The various excuses, rationalizations and general manipulations the inmates brought forth were familiar but at times I found it necessary to bite my tongue so as not to respond in a confrontational manner. It was a novel twist simply to make an assessment rather than challenge and attempt to modify the delinquent defences. As well, it was rewarding to work with others who carried the same responsibility but came from a different experiential background. Hearings were composed of a CC and a permanent member. Thus I had a weekly opportunity to share experience with five professionals of different backgrounds, on a rotating basis. Although the permanent member usually initiated the hearing, there was always sufficient space for my input.

I returned to the CQLC for a second double mandate in the 'nineties and discovered that some discouraging changes had come about. I was able to sense the inroads that political powers had made. This never touched the decision-making itself. I want to make it clear that I never had any indication there ever was political pressure in an individual case. Political interference, however, may be much more subtle. Various inequalities in our society are a reality and certainly must be dealt with. Our politicians are aware of this, if only because well-intentioned people, downtrodden or otherwise, put pressure on them. The problem is, how are these inequalities to be rectified?

I believe Parole is a valid concept and the process should be simple. The subject matter, however, is complex. Theoretically, the parole hearing is an evaluation of any change that indicates the parole applicant is able to complete his sentence in the community, under supervised conditions. It is presumed the individual was responsible for the behaviour that resulted in his incarceration and some change would be expected if one were to think that the behaviour would not be repeated. Punishment alone does not necessarily alter behaviour in a positive manner. Therefore the institutional experience the parole applicant has lived through becomes an important factor. Finally, since the applicant is being evaluated with a view to returning to the community, it is important to know and understand the milieu into which he is to be released. In other words, there are three important elements that the parole member must be cognizant of: the dynamics of delinquent behaviour, the effects of the deprivation of liberty and the validity of personal and material resources available in the community. In the best of worlds, all parole members would be so endowed; in a less perfect setting, a parole member should be expert in at least one area and possess a willingness and ability to gain expertise in all three.

Upon my return to the CQLC I was under the distinct impression that the above-mentioned elements had taken second place, at best. Factors such as establishing a gender and ethnic balance seemed to have taken priority. I believe it is important to rectify all inequalities in our criminal justice system, indeed in our society as a whole. Nevertheless, I strongly believe it is a disservice to any minority to resort to any form of tokenism. The basic criteria for selection of parole members are important. The selection process must be inclusive and open to all, all who fit these criteria.

The importance inherent in the role of the parole member rests not only in decision-making. Since the evaluation depends directly upon the three elements mentioned above, the parole member is in a key position to recognize the areas where change is needed. Has the sentence been a productive means of dealing with problems presented by this particular offender? What effect has incarceration had, good or bad, on this specific individual? Are the resources in the community realistic and valid, so as to aid the individual reintegrate into the community-at-large? These are key questions to be addressed by all who are active in criminal justice if the entire process is to develop in a positive direction. The role of the parole member is one that has too often been left untapped in this respect. The important caveat, however, is that their selection be on clear-cut criteria; their training remain on an ongoing basis; their decision-making remain autonomous, yet interrelated with sentencing and correctional practices.

THE OFFENDER IN THE COMMUNITY

~ the John Howard Society of Quebec

Josh Zambrowsky was a criminologist who had worked as a therapist in the Diagnostic and Treatment Centre in New York. He had been part of the McGill team. Although we were on different units, we were familiar with each other's work. By 1980, Josh had been at the John Howard Society of Quebec (JHSQ) for the past four or five years and was now its Executive Director. He was an bright man, witty and very demanding of his staff. He telephoned me at Leclerc one morning and invited me out to lunch.

> "If you're looking for an administrator, frankly, you've got the wrong guy." I had heard his assistant had recently resigned.
> "No, I would handle the administrative end of it. I would like you to come on board because of your clinical skill," he clarified.

My knowledge of the John Howard Society was quite limited at this point. Early in my career, as staff psychologist at St. Vincent de Paul, I had met their workers who visited inmates on a weekly basis. At the time, I didn't know what they were actually doing but their regularity was noticeable. In those days, services provided by the community were sparse, officially divided along linguistic and religious lines. Although the John Howard Society was for English-speaking Protestant inmates, most inmates were bi-lingual and few had any strong religious affiliation. Thus, the organizations did not adhere strictly to the artificial delineation.In fact, today there are John Howard societies in the ten provinces and two territories of Canada. Some provincial societies are composed of several branches in various regions of the specific province. The largest John Howard representation is in Ontario where there are some sixteen branches. In all, John Howard societies range from coast to coast affording a veritable national presence. Although each Society is autonomous, administered by its proper Board of Directors, together they make up the John Howard Society of Canada (JHSC) governed by a Board of Directors comprised of board members from the provincial and territorial societies.

Thus our Society in Quebec is a self-governing, non-profit corporation with its own Board. The first of the agency's five principal objectives, the successful reintegration of adult offenders into the community-at-large, is a self-sustaining cornerstone and clearly articulates the basic *raison d'être* of the organization. While the other objectives are significant in themselves, they also bolster this primary objective. The promotion of constructive change in criminal justice, the clarification of both the correctional and the parole process, the safeguarding of basic rights and public education with respect to existing systems, all are intrinsically important. They assume a more profound meaning, however, when seen in the light of the restoration of the offender to the community. This reintegration process provides a long-term benefit to society in the form of realistic input towards the prevention and control of crime and delinquency.

The JHSQ realizes these objectives in consort with others. The networking is carried out at various levels with government agencies as well as community-based organizations, on both a provincial and a national basis. The purpose is to profit from the expertise of others while sharing certain acumen gleaned from its own experience. Issues perceived from a local point of view usually take on new meaning and importance when observed from another perspective. The combined approach of learning and teaching is designed to sharpen the tools of the craft for all concerned.Most provincial John Howard societies have several branches, each with its own Board from the immediate community. In these provinces, the provincial Board of Directors has representatives from the various local branches, lending some unity to the entire operation. Some John Howard societies date back to the late eighteenth century. In later years, John Howard Society of Canada was formed and has been, in reality, an association of the various John Howard societies with its Board of Directors composed of representatives from the several provincial member societies.

Nevertheless, the history of the John Howard in Quebec is unique. Although traditionally an anglophone organization, it has provided services to offenders and their families in both official languages of Canada and has often served as a referral centre for linguistic, ethnic and racial minorities who have come into contact with the Canadian criminal justice system. It began as a community-based, non-profit corporation like all other John Howard societies. However, in 1974, a change in provincial law brought adult services under the umbrella of the social service network and what the JHSQ gained in financial security, it lost in organizational independence. It became a Service Unit within the Ville Marie Social Service Centre (VMSSC) and the provincial government assumed staff salaries. At the same time, however, its Board of Directors was reduced to the status of an Advisory Board, effectively eliminating its decision-making power and ultimately distancing the organization from its roots in the community.

It was to undergo further significant changes over the ensuing twenty years, hitting a peak of involvement and relevance in the latter half of the 'eighties, only to decline steadily in the 'nineties. Changes in law, political priorities and bureaucratic bullying were active in the fate of the organization. From the pinnacle of two offices, comprised of a total of some twenty-seven employees, it finally reached the abyss of an organization whose doors were open two days a week and staffed by a minute number of part-time, contractual personnel. At the time of this writing, the JHSQ is fighting for its survival as a viable, community-based resource in criminal justice, particularly in the correctional field. Because of its unorthodox history, having been politically and bureaucratically flipped from private organization to para-public status and back, it has been exasperatingly difficult to establish a modicum of stability. Its anglophone tradition in an overwhelmingly francophone milieu has not made its plight any easier. The provision of services in the two official languages of Canada has, to some extent, proven to be a double edged sword.

I decided to take up Josh's offer and began a new phase in my career in September 1980. I was still a part-time member of the CQLC that allowed me to keep my hand in where the action is; my new duties were mainly doing clinical supervision of the JHSQ staff. Most of the workers had social work training and experience and several were graduates of the McGill University School of Social Work. The few who had less scholastic training, including two ex-offenders, had considerable practical experience.

I worked as his assistant for approximately one year. During this time, he showed me the ins and outs of the VMSSC system. In effect, we were a fairly autonomous outfit, mainly because the type of clientele we dealt with kept the Ville Marie bureaucrats at bay. They believed we worked with a highly volatile population and I learned that it was to our advantage not to discourage this skewed perception. We had our hands full preventing Correctional Services Canada from interfering with our work; we didn't need further bureaucratic control. Josh had always been interested in the clinical aspect of criminology and had profited from the experience of hands-on practice while working for McGill in Dannemora, N.Y. However, his real strength lay elsewhere. His sharp intelligence brought him quickly to the core of intricate problems in criminal justice. He had also completed his schooling in law. He was therefore particularly insightful as to the necessity of meaningful legislation while, at the same time, the dangers of over-legislation. Shortly after he left JHSQ he became Executive Director of the Canadian Association for the Prevention of Crime. In fact, it was under his aegis that the organization altered its title and became more inclusive as the Canadian Criminal Justice Association (CCJA). He remained there some five years, never shirking the responsibility to point an accusing finger at those whose agenda was less than forthright. He never "picked his shots" and in the end paid for his honesty. He eventually left the CCJA, passed his Bar exams and practiced law out of a Kingston office until retirement. His feistiness in the Courts has won him the respect of adversaries, particularly in the area of penal law. He has frequently challenged the power and might of government agencies in an attempt to rectify wrongs for the underdog, always bearing in mind the true nature of the problem with an expertise nurtured by previous clinical experience.

I decided immediately upon assuming my duties as Executive Director that I would not limit myself to administrative work and working with the staff. This was a matter of personal interest and concern. My main interest in the field had always been to maintain direct contact with the offender. I see this relationship, whether in group or on an individual basis, not only as necessary to any real clinical intervention but also as a prime source of information and learning. My chief concern was that the more I distanced myself from personal contact, the more remote my thinking would become with respect to the realities of the phenomenon of delinquency. I had seen other practitioners unwittingly lose touch with the fundamentals of corrections as they assumed more senior administrative positions, remote from the basics of everyday practice; their overall clinical acumen had suffered. It had happened to others, would I not be vulnerable?

*   *   *

My initial contact with Harry centred on his covert request to remove "the Bug" from Segregation back in 1962. In the mid-sixties he was co-founder of my first group in the old Pen. We kept contact over the ensuing years both while he was in the penitentiary and during his brief stays in the community. He would keep in touch by 'phone when on the outside; periods that rarely exceeded a few months at a time. It was much later I learned that while in the "milieu" Harry always made his presence felt.

Harry was the second of four siblings raised, as he put it, "on the corner of Guy and Notre Dame." This was a low socio-economic / high delinquency area in the 'forties. Although to outward appearances the family was intact, closer scrutiny would have revealed a constant current of hostility between the parents seething barely beneath the surface. The father, an uncommunicative man, was nevertheless steadily employed at one of the larger breweries and provided for the basic, material needs of the family. His presence in the home was seemingly limited to the evening meal after which he absconded to the comforts of his drinking companions. The mother, described as hard working if somewhat disorganized around the home, was subject to sporadic outbursts of temper. At the end of a day confined in the home she encircled herself with neighbourhood friends, all well provided with a supply of the brewery's product. Behavioural limits were poorly defined and disciplinary measures inconsistent.

This depressing, unstructured home environment directly affected all four siblings. Both girls had serious behavioural problems during their adolescent years. The older survived by leaving the home before age twenty, to raise a family with a long-time neighbourhood acquaintance; the younger, less fortunate, experienced problems with the law well into her twenties. Harry's younger brother, the youngest of the family, was sentenced to the penitentiary once, then adapted marginally throughout life, always on the periphery of petty crime.

Harry was special. Compulsive stealing, truancy and fighting marked his early school years. One of his earliest memories of the unstructured home environment was when his father was away from the home in the armed forces:

> "I must've been t'ree or four, my mudder's out wit' some of her friends drinkin'. She would never leave us alone, me an' Joanie, so I remember dis ole broad from the neighbourhood mindin' us. I woke up in the middle of the night 'cause I hafta piss. The bat'room's across the kitchen an' the ole broad's snorin' on a chair, half naked an' really ugly. She was always wantin' to kiss me, so I was scared but I had to piss, ya know. So I shoot across the room an' I must've hit somethin' 'cause she wakes up an' tries to grab me. I spin back aroun' into my room an' jump under the covers. Nex' morning I wake up an' I'd pissed the bed. I get a fuckin' beatin' for pissin' the bed. How's dat grab ya, Mr. Williams?"

There was little trace of affect in his monologue; it had become matter-of-fact long ago. The few and erratic familial controls had no impact whatsoever on Harry. He was on the street all hours of the night and into petty thievery well before puberty. An attention span deficit, coupled with serious behavioural problems within the school setting, precluded any academic advancement. Placed in Shawbridge Boy's Farm at the age of ten, the next several years proved turbulent at all levels and reached a peak with his first penitentiary sentence at seventeen years of age. By this time, Harry had adopted certain social graces, behaviours and attitudes that ingratiated him with the delinquent peer group. He gained popularity with his peers similar to the respect accorded in the adult criminal milieu. The basic ingredient was a hint of violence that communicates at a gut level. The penitentiary officials of the 'fifties were sensitive to this even though there were no refined diagnostic tools. The physical proximity of institutional life bred a certain primitive awareness on the part of the inmates. Harry was assigned to the infamous "stone shed" early on, a measure designed to control his youthful, impulsive aggressiveness by the presence of more experienced, older toughs. The intended effect would not be realized.

On one occasion, Harry got into a fight with another young inmate who outweighed him by some twenty pounds. He was getting the worst of it when other inmates separated the two. Butch, one of Harry's friends was helping to hold him.

"O.K. man, is it over?"
"Shake me loose, it's forgotten."

The moment the two combatants were let loose and had shaken hands, Harry calmly reached for a nearby rake and, not so calmly, beat his opponent senseless. "I was wrong. I guess it wasn't over. It is now!" Harry sauntered away. The others followed. He was establishing his place. "Fuck wit' me will ya?" he murmured, as much a reassurance to himself, it was not lost on Butch and the others nearby.

Harry married Sally in 1969 upon completion of his fourth penitentiary sentence and stayed out for almost two years. I was invited to the wedding but unable to attend. My commitments in New York provided me with a convenient reason to decline the invitation. In fact, I was becoming more aware of his impulsive and increasingly violent behaviour. His paranoid thinking pattern, a necessary survival mechanism in the treacherous criminal underworld, would take unpredictable turns at times. Although I had never become the object of its focus, I knew that there were no guarantees. What I'm saying is that I was not devastated at not being able to fit Harry's wedding into my social calendar.

Nevertheless, I was able to visit him some few weeks later. Sally was away at work. He explained their routine as such: Sally worked evenings at a club on Cote de Liesse and Harry would drive her there for six in the evening and pick her up around two in the morning. I knew, by the name of the place, that it was not considered to be a trouble spot, but definitely connected. Well, what else?

As it turned out, I was not to meet Sally until Harry returned to the Pen some two years later. I certainly heard about her in the intervening months, however. The most memorable time was about a year after their wedding when Harry contacted me by 'phone; he sounded uncharacteristically perturbed.

"Mr. Williams," Harry was always deferential. "Sally's gone an' shot herself . . . the fuckin' bulls t'ink it's me. How could I do somethin' like 'dat, ya know?" The question hung in the air momentarily. "She put a rifle in her mout' an' pulled the trigger. I don't even own no fuckin' rifle!"

The problem was obvious; the heat was on Harry. It was only after several minutes that I was able to pose a direct question and ascertain that Sally, though seriously hurt, was expected to survive. It was only years later that I was able to piece together what had happened.

At the time, a war was on in the west end. It was not a major confrontation, numerically, but certainly serious in its violence. As frequently happens, there had been a perceived double-cross among gang members. I say perceived because it is impossible to establish who is responsible for what in these disputes. Considerable gunfire had been recorded in the newspapers on several occasions but the adversaries had never been arrested. Police had, no doubt, some idea but little evidence and limited interest. This was simply a "settling of accounts among known criminals," as the media euphemistically put it. The veneer of concern for public safety comes to the fore only when "honest citizens" are touched, physically or otherwise.

One newspaper account had referred to the fact that, "citizens were awakened to gunshots at 2 in the morning and unidentified assailants were peering over snow banks along Madison Avenue in an attempt to pick off their adversary across the street." Nothing was printed in the following days. Obviously, peace had been restored to assure the restful repose of the local inhabitants. The most significant recorded happening, however, was reserved for a later date.

Justin crawled to a taxi stand at Dorval airport early one morning. Through swollen lips, he mumbled a plea to be taken to a hospital. He had six bullet wounds including two in the facial area. He had been left in the trunk of a car at the airport parking lot. The six shots had been assurance enough for those responsible to dispose of the body hurriedly and, as a consequence, not close the trunk properly. Only a higher power could explain the rest. The best the medical profession could proffer was that the sub-zero temperatures of this winter night had helped congeal the blood and stave off death. The victim survived and insisted he could not identify his assailants. Despite this attempt to maintain some sense of "honour", he was later chased into the protective unit of the Pen. This murky world of deceit, violence and greed protects itself by refusing to forgive or forget.

Harry had been a major player in these brutal skirmishes. Not only did he see fit to be "packing" whenever he went out from his apartment but, as the violence escalated, he deemed it necessary to sleep with a loaded gun under his pillow. This procedure had its downside and caused some inconveniences; relieving himself in the middle of the night, for example, proved cumbersome. He would release the safety catch on his forty-five and crawl, in total darkness, across any space not enclosed by a solid wall. These antics, precipitated as much by increasing paranoia as by the reality of his lifestyle, did keep him alive. By the same token, they had a decidedly unsettling effect on his marital union. Sally, no neophyte in the game, nonetheless was increasingly distressed by the situation. She was frequently confined alone in the apartment, forbidden to go out to work. The resultant arguments were short-lived, brought to an abrupt end with curt threats. The increasing anxiety, punctuated by panic attacks when interned alone, finally proved to be too much for her. She chose her own protective weapon, the rifle leaning by the front door. Her choice actually saved her life; the length of the barrel prevented an accurate aim. She blew out her cheek on one side but survived.

It was not until Harry was back in the Pen that Sally decided to leave for the United States. A postscript to this relationship was that she remained in written contact with Harry and even came back to Montreal for a week. She visited him in the Pen three times and it was on one of these visits that I was invited to meet her. She was an attractive, well-spoken young woman, the portrait of an up-and-coming, dynamic go-getter. She phoned me before leaving town to thank me,

> "for all you've done for Harry, he really respects you."
> "How about yourself now, Sally, how're you doing?" I enquired politely.
> "Things are really great now, Mr. Williams, I've turned my life around. I've got a good job in this club in Phoenix, Arizona; the tips are super!" I hesitated momentarily, "Well, I'll take care of Harry. You take care of yourself now, Sally."

I hung up the 'phone with a tightening sensation in my throat; there were many "Harrys" out there. They tended to cluster in a specific milieu. I envisaged this young woman continuing along her self-destructive path.

I made mention earlier of Harry's paranoid thinking being an asset to him. In the particular world in which he was living, a certain amount of suspicion and mistrust is necessary for survival. When it increases and gets beyond control, the mechanism becomes a symptom of psychosis. The delineation that separates mental health from insanity is a harrowingly thin line for men who are mired in this surreal world. I had witnessed Harry cross over the line on occasion, while incarcerated. He would become increasingly paranoid and lose contact with reality, manifesting ideation of self-reference on the road to complete disintegration. At such times he would become suicidal. On one occasion, while incarcerated at Archambault maximum-security penitentiary, his self-destructive streak reached a pitch. His auto-mutilation began with increasingly severe lacerations to various parts of the body and culminated in an attempt to hang himself with his belt. It was only when an inmate in the next cell noticed blood coming from under Harry's cell door and shouted for the guard that he was saved. He was taken to the institutional hospital, duly stitched up and then transferred to the psychiatric unit in St. Vincent de Paul penitentiary the following day. It was during this recuperative phase that Harry's artistic talents resurfaced. During healthy periods of incarceration he painted sporadically. While mentally ill and during recovery, his production increased and one could observe his artistic productions go from the macabre to the more normal. These self-destructive, psychotic episodes occurred intermittently and, to my knowledge, only during incarceration. While in freedom, Harry's demons assumed another guise. His paranoid thinking served as a protective mechanism; his hostility was rarely expressed verbally, thus creating a semblance of normalcy. His superficial charm was disarming, masking a viciousness that was ultimately homicidal.

Ross was basically a loner who had made a name for himself in the seedier clubs in the west end of Montreal. He was seen by the connected crowd as a mooch who lived off others and was despised as such. He was seen by others as someone to be feared. His menacing comportment and brazen insistence on drinking on someone else's tab had created the desired image. In fact, Ross placed somewhere in between. He needed no arm-twisting to participate in any sneaky endeavour and had learned, some years previously, that taking someone's life was relatively easy and could be profitable. At first, the profit came from the mark's pocket, usually someone from out of town who had inadvertently flashed a wad of bills while paying a round. The victim would be followed upon leaving the club and attacked at some advantageous spot such as an unlighted parking lot. Later in his career, Ross realized his talents could be hired out. Greed finally got the best of him and he made a fatal mistake. Sean had pulled off a profitable score. Safety deposit boxes had been ransacked over a long weekend. The police had their suspicions, the "boys downtown" were more certain. Ross knew Sean casually and had no problem gaining entry into the affable Irishman's home under some innocuous pretext. The decomposing bodies of Sean and his girlfriend were discovered some days later, after neighbours complained of strong odours emanating from the residence. The backlash was immediate. The milieu usually does its own investigative work and metes out its own justice, for one of its own. The retributive action is basically one of self-protection.

It was only a matter of time before Harry was asked to "investigate." He knew Ross and his principal hangout, a bar on Upper Lachine Road in the heart of the west end. Harry sauntered in one Saturday afternoon to make enquiries since Ross had not been seen recently in his other habitual haunts. As it turned out, he was in the bar, inebriated and armed, a dangerous combination. Harry was simply on a "sightseeing tour" and unarmed; he couldn't just leave without arousing suspicion so he sidled up to the other end of the bar. In moments Ross lurched up to him, brandishing his weapon and grumbled,

"I know what the fuck y're here for, ya wanna take me off the fuckin' board."

Harry turned slowly toward him, looked him straight in the eyes and said in a low, clear voice, "You're fuckin' nuts man, put away that piece. I've no beef wit' you!" He slowly opened his coat with both hands, "Take it easy man, you're stressed out for Chrissakes!"

Ross was momentarily taken off balance but continued, "I know you're out to get me!"

Harry knew he had to call his bluff. It was a coin toss but he had little choice, "Do what ya hafta do, but stop fuckin' yellin'."

Ross stumbled up to him and put his hand on his shoulder. "I'm sorry man, I've had too much to drink, I don't know what I'm sayin'," he mumbled in a lowered tone.

"An' you don't know what you're doin'," Harry said under his breath.

Approximately a month later, Ross was sipping a drink in a Club on St. Catherine Street. He had moderated his alcohol consumption considerably but, after all, this was a day of celebration. The St. Patrick's parade had just passed. The crowd would be coming in any minute now to continue the boisterous festivities. Two masked men entered by the rear door. Ross' last visual contact was with the eyes of one of his killers. Eyewitnesses claimed that one of the gunmen had lifted his mask partially before the fusillade.

I was not aware of most of these events when Harry came to report to us at the John Howard, late in 1981. Many of the pieces fell together with information that came to light after his death. I was well aware, however, that we did not have an easy case for supervision. Harry was highly unpredictable but his basic lifestyle would not and could not change. He was now in his early forties. He presented the classic portrait of the Primary Delinquent, having manifested attitudinal and behavioural problems in the early school years, continued with a distinctly delinquent adaptation throughout adolescence and persisted in his criminality throughout his adult life. Change was not possible; some control could be hoped for. It would depend upon a relationship; Harry did not respond well to coercion. We also maintained an open door policy at JHSQ, never refusing a case. We tried to continue with those we had followed through their incarceration and were usually able to do so. There were some exceptions to this since Correctional Service Canada had the final say in assigning cases for supervision. At that time, our contract limited us to a maximum of fifty cases for supervision, as well. Harry had been released from Archambault penitentiary after having completed two thirds of his ten-year sentence. Thus, he was on mandatory supervision (MS), not parole. The conditions are identical to those of parole but they are unilaterally imposed on MS. This is not a bi-lateral contract; the individual has already been assessed, at the third of his sentence, as unable to be released to the community under supervision. Nevertheless, at the two-thirds mark, he is released with identical conditions, now decreed. Thus, a man on MS is usually a client who is less than motivated to comply with anything other than basic reporting; a reporting often punctuated with the words, "Here, sign my paper!"

Harry had been arrested in Ottawa for attempted armed robbery, sentenced in Ontario and incarcerated in Kingston penitentiary. About two years into his sentence I was in Kingston at a psychologist convention and took the time to stop in and visit him. He spoke about wanting to transfer elsewhere and I suggested Dorchester penitentiary in New Brunswick. My only reason was that I believed the criminality on the east coast was less severe than in many other areas of Canada. This was somewhat naive in that Harry would obviously gravitate toward those with whom he was most comfortable; but you worked with what you had.

He did transfer to Dorchester and expressed in one of his letters that he would like to try and settle in Halifax upon release. I knew there was no magic solution but any place was better than Montreal. I contacted Vince MacDonald, the talented head of parole supervision in the area. Vince was unorthodox. He related well to offenders in general and had a wealth of street experience, never intimidated by an offender or bureaucrat. He made the initial enquiries only to find out that the Halifax police would not tolerate "any organized crime figures from Montreal." I chuckled at that one, wondering what movies they had been watching. Harry was completing his sixth penitentiary sentence; talk about organized.He reported to us for almost two years. During this time he would come to the office as required, every two weeks for the first six months and on a three-week rhythm afterwards. There was little that could be done. He had never worked legitimately in his life and now, in his mid-forties, was less equipped than at any time in the past. Always pleasant and polite, he was a favourite of the secretaries. The most obvious instability lay in his living conditions. Most of his adult life had been in the penitentiary. His longest stay in the community, the two-year period at the end of the sixties, had been hectic with criminal involvement but his home life had some modicum of stability, due entirely to Sally's organizational ability. That was more than ten years past and Harry was now alone with no steady partner. He passed brief periods with one or another casual girlfriend. Our record sheet of his residences read like that of a true itinerant.

One morning he phoned me at the office, "Mr. Williams, I had an accident with my motorcycle last week and have been laid up since. I can't come in today, could you come over to my place?" This was not an unusual request in that several of our workers carried out some supervision at the parolee's place of work or home. Circumstances were quite different with Harry; no place of work and no fixed home.

"Where are you staying right now?"

"I'm at the Cavalier, I got a room here. Just ask for me at the desk."

I held my breath for a moment before replying, "I'll be there about two p.m." This promised to be an experience. The Cavalier, known also as "the Zoo", was the main meeting place of the West End Gang, the media-generated moniker for a group of English-speaking criminals in the west end of Montreal. The boys used to say that it generated more heat than a steam bath; in English, it was under regular police surveillance.

"I'm here to see Harry."

The desk clerk was unimpressed. "Harry who?" he questioned suspiciously. I suppose the only unknown "suits" who appeared here were detectives.

"Just tell him Mr. Williams is here."

I had said the magic word. I was ushered into a darkened, smoky motel room. Three or four figures sat by the wall. On the double bed lay Harry, in skivvies and a bandaged knee.

"Guys, this is Mr. Williams, my parole officer". Harry, ever polite, gestured toward the seated figures.

*　　*　　*

I have mentioned previously that I believe incarceration is necessary as a means of neutralizing dangerous or repetitive criminal behaviour. It is imperative to stress this because community-based organizations, including JHSQ, are sometimes incorrectly perceived as prison abolitionists and blind defenders of inmates' rights. There are individuals who hold to this simplistic position, a malady due more to a soft head than a soft heart. Nevertheless, this extreme position is print-worthy and unfairly used as a basis of criticism of the entire community-based sector. This unscrupulous judgement misrepresents a cogent philosophy and undermines an efficacious approach to criminal justice issues.

Incarceration is indispensable but must be used prudently. Canada has the second highest incarceration rate in the western hemisphere. This is patently unacceptable. We must adopt a more mature approach to the intricate problem of crime and delinquency and avoid the knee-jerk reaction, "lock 'em up!" I believe our high incarceration rate is more a reaction to media hype, than a result of informed public opinion and more a bureaucratic response to police and political pressure, than a proposed solution to an alleged soaring crime rate. In point of fact, the last twenty years of the twentieth century showed a continuing decline in the crime rate, including violent crime. In order to reduce the rate of incarceration, both the judiciary and the correctional services must make more use of existing community resources and encourage the development of further resources. Strident attention rather than mere lip service must be paid to the spirit of the law and stated correctional policy that incarceration is to be employed as a last resort.

More than ninety-five percent of offenders in federal penitentiaries are released under some form of supervision, thus completing their sentence in the community. I insist on making the distinction between release on parole and statutory release. In the first instance, the offender has been evaluated and considered capable of completing his sentence in the community under conditions that include supervision. This decision, made by members of the National Parole Board (NPB), comes after an exhaustive study of the case and an in-depth hearing with the inmate and other concerned parties. Should parole be granted, a bi-lateral contract is signed and the offender is released to the community to complete his sentence with specific conditions and under the supervision of a parole officer. Both the parolee and the parole officer are fully cognizant of the conditions imposed by the Board and agreed to by the offender. Statutory Release, on the other hand, is the automatic release at completion of two-thirds of the sentence and includes a mandatory supervision.

The assumption underlying release on parole is that the individual has undergone some change during incarceration and is now able to complete the sentence while living in the community. The release then is seen as a gradual, supervised re-entry into the community. The role of the parole officer is that of a helping agent who assures that the conditions of parole are respected and provides the necessary aid and support to the parolee. The sentence has not been changed; however, the manner in which a portion of it is to be served has been re-defined. These are two phases of one process, the ultimate goal being the reintegration of the individual offender back into the community, thereby enhancing the protection of the public on a long-term basis. In theory, the validity of parole as a viable concept of early release is contingent upon the efficacy of the institutional experience as a catalyst to change. Prior to incarceration, the offender was unable or unwilling to cope with the demands of law-abiding living in freedom. If one is to assume that the same offender, upon return to the community, is better able to contend with these exigencies, then some basic change has occurred and been recognized. Thus, the institutional experience must be more than a mere separation of the offender from society so as to satisfy some primitive need for revenge. It must be designed in such a way as to stimulate inner change. This cannot be emphasized too strongly. Important as it is that incarceration be used judiciously, the nature of the institutional experience, as precipitous to positive change, is of equal consequence.

Unfortunately, since incarceration has become the primary de facto response to delinquent behaviour, the very nature of the process is seldom discussed in depth. I am surprised that terms such as punishment and retribution are still bandied about as though they contained some inherent positive value. In truth, these catchwords rear up less often than before depending upon the political climate within a specific locale. However, their meaning is now couched in the politically correct euphemisms of deterrence and denunciation. In either instance, the phrasing mirrors the talents of political wordsmiths and spin-doctors more than any genuine reflection upon the *raison d'être* of incarceration and its long-term effects.

Deprivation of liberty is a serious matter and must be treated as such. The neutralization of unacceptable behaviour by such means is sometimes necessary but the negative consequences must be weighed as well. The simple removal of someone from society rarely solves the problem. It certainly displaces the problem, temporarily. Whether anything is ultimately resolved or not will depend, in great part, upon what takes place in the interim. If the final goal is truly the reintegration of the individual offender into the community-at-large, then the period of incarceration and the re-entry into the community must be seen as two linked phases of one process. Thus, the process neither begins nor ends upon release from prison. The period of incarceration must be fashioned in such a way that the offender may gain some insight into personal responsibility for his own life situation, learn that internal change is possible and develop a desire and willingness to bring about this change. The re-entry phase then takes on a new reality as a completion of the total reintegration process. The role of the parole officer must be defined as principally that of a helping agent. If meaningful support with a view to successful reintegration into society is to be provided by the supervisor, an understanding of delinquent dynamics and an acknowledgement of the effects of the deprivation of liberty are prerequisites.

There have been identifiable reforms, over the years, with respect to correctional institutions. Some have been merely cosmetic, others of more significance. The 'sixties witnessed the introduction of a system of classifying inmates for placement at various security levels. A growth in psychological services complemented the psychiatric service in pinpointing emotional and mental disturbance. The medieval practice of employing the strap as a means of punishing aggressive institutional behaviour was abolished midway through this decade.

The 'seventies began with some promise as the living unit system was inaugurated. Five medium security penitentiaries were to be subdivided into various units, staffed with living-unit officers who would be responsible for the internal dynamic security as well as the daily counselling of inmates. A blue ribbon committee with national representation presented an exhaustive report to the Solicitor General of Canada, Hon. Jean-Pierre Goyer. The "Design of federal maximum security institutions" addressed many issues and made several recommendations; the underlying thesis centred on the

unhealthysubculture within the existing institutional milieu. One of
the principal recommendations was that the size of the institution
should be limited to one hundred and fifty inmates and the living units
should not exceed a capacity of twelve inmates. Furthermore, since
the emphasis was to be on dynamic security and human relationships,
the selection of personnel must necessarily stress personality qualities.
The aim of the correctional process was defined as the preparation of
the offender for return to the community. In this respect, members of
the community-at-large were seen as an integral part of institutional
programming and it was further suggested that community services,
provided on a contractual basis, be expanded.

This working group, composed of correctional experts from
both the government sector and the private sector had made incisive
recommendations based on an in-depth study of the correctional
system of the time. They referred to the need for fundamental change,
including the closing of certain penitentiaries where the institutional
milieu was devastating and the overwhelming malaise irreparable.
Unfortunately, as with many reports and recommendations, they were
generally ignored and eventually shelved.

As it turned out, the 'seventies were an enigmatic time. The decade
that had begun with some refreshing air of hope, deteriorated into a
nightmare of despair. The tragedy at New Westminster penitentiary,
where the forces attempting to save a hostage accidentally killed her,
was followed some two years later by the murder of a young penitentiary
warden outside his home in Montreal. The institutional violence spilled
over into the next decade when in 1982 three correctional officers were
tortured and murdered during a riot at Archambault penitentiary.
There is no one factor that accounts for such brutality but the failure
to explore and transform the unhealthy and potentially explosive
institutional milieu remains a basic issue to this day. The major incident
at the Kingston Prison for Women, in the 'nineties clearly attests to
this.The 'eighties saw an increase in the number of penitentiaries and a
proliferation of institutional programs. The most significant feature of
the new penitentiaries, however, was their location. It was obvious that
overt political gain was the driving force behind the decision as to their
placement. The most glaring example of political patronage is cited
to illustrate the point. With no concern for realistic services, staffing
needs and travel hardship for visitors, the Port Cartier penitentiary was

constructed. The arrogance of political might stood steadfastly in the face of concerned opposition, oblivious to any semblance of common sense. It continues to be an embarrassment, years later.

The incremental growth of institutional programs continued throughout the 'eighties and well into the 'nineties. Educational, vocational, leisure time and specialized treatment programs were the order of the day. Numerous ideas for these programs arose from sources outside the government sector and professionals from the community implemented them. Thus the community itself was introduced into the daily institutional life, helping to mitigate the oppressive nature of the milieu and eliciting a more positive response from the inmate population. Unfortunately, this advantage was not recognized and within a short period of time institutional personnel administered many of the programs.

A simultaneous outburst in the use of technological methods, highlighted by the computerization of information, allowed for a more extensive database and led to the development of predictive scales and grids. These objective measures would serve as evaluative tools in the quest for certainty with respect to the prediction of risk. The ensuing glut of administered programs, related to needs and criminogenic factors as portrayed by the objective measures, created and reinforced a comfortable mind-set of managing cases as opposed to working with individuals. The personal factor was being gradually undermined; the concretization of inmate categories was taking prominence.

This piecemeal approach to correctional philosophy and practice ignored the basic forces that play within the institutional milieu; forces that shape the roles of both inmates and staff and ultimately define the fundamental value system therein. The beneficial effects accrued through positive programming, supposedly designed to develop autonomy and personal accountability, dissipated through exposure to an authoritative setting that demands adaptation to repressive control. The increasing use of technological methods contributed directly to a withdrawal, physical as well as emotional, upon the part of the front-line staff. The buffer between inmate and decision-maker, personified in the past by the Classification Officer, was now disappearing with the emergence of a case manager. As a consequence, the former antithetical position of inmate vs. guard, rather than being dealt with, was now generalizing to encompass all personnel. Correctional institutions were becoming more manageable, as were their inmates. Was this increasingly impersonalized approach, however, consistent with the stated aim of preparing individuals for a return to society with a view to long-term protection of the public?

There are many factors in the evolution of the Canadian correctional system that have unwittingly worked to hinder the development of a constructive release process. The introduction of mandatory supervision at the completion of two thirds of the sentence surreptitiously undermined the concept of parole supervision. The automatic nature of the release, coupled with the imposed supervision, tended to subvert the idea of offender incentive toward guided self-help. Since the supervision was to be carried out by traditional parole officers, the distinction between the two release modes became blurred and the role of helping agent became mitigated by this emphasis on control. The nature of this forced relationship engendered a contumacious spirit on the part of many offenders released on mandatory supervision who felt that, upon release from the penitentiary, their debt had been paid. This in turn reinforced a dynamic of external restraint over inner control, a basic shift in the relationship between the parole officer and the supervised offender. The entire concept of conditional release was fundamentally altered and the door was now ajar, open to further repressive measures later characterized by a multitude of special conditions, intensive supervision, assigned residency and the ultimate paradoxical situation: detention to expiration of sentence.

I believe, however, that a critical change that affected the reintegration process negatively was the politico-bureaucratic decision to join together the Canadian Penitentiary Service and the National Parole Service in the mid-seventies. Theoretically, this amalgamation should have been a good move. The institutional phase of the sentence should flow naturally into the post-release phase; the former should be a preparation for the latter; the two should be perceived and carried out as separate but related services along a continuum. The theoretical underpinning here, however, would be that treatment of the offender is inherent in the sentence. This implies the provision of a planned environment conducive to social learning. The institutional milieu must be designed to recognize and deal with delinquent traits and reactions while at the same time reinforcing pro-social values and attitudes. This fundamental change in correctional philosophy and practice would then replace retribution with an institutional milieu structured to allow for the implementation of therapeutic techniques and the reinforcement of constructive results. Newly acquired behaviours could later be supported and strengthened through the help and guidance of the supervising parole officer throughout an integrated post-release phase.

In fact, no such treatment paradigm existed. Correctional institutions remained basically warehouses where offenders do their time. By the time the parole service and the penitentiary service were combined, institutional programs had increased considerably and the "Opportunities Model" was in vogue. Inmates were offered a plethora of programs, the belief being that simple exposure to this buffet of delights would somehow inspire the incarcerated offender to enlist in a process that would lead to behavioural change. Many did enlist, often driven by the possible reward of early release rather than through an awareness of a need for substantial inner change. What did happen with the uniting of the two services was the gradual emergence of a monolithic, government bureaucracy: Correctional Service Canada (CSC). The Canadian Penitentiary Service, the larger of the two, absorbed the personnel of the National Parole Service and dominated the correctional policy and practice from the outset. Although some senior officials of the National Parole Service were incorporated into the new organization at senior levels, their lack of experience in the institutional setting limited their influence in basic planning. Naturally, because of their own professional competence and standing they vied for input. One of the results was a significant increase in paperwork, highlighted by the development of static measures of evaluation, eventually leading to a depersonalized approach to the assessment and treatment of the offender.

These developments did not happen overnight. The amalgamation of these two major services occurred officially in 1976. The effects, however, were felt throughout the balance of the century and continue today. This centralization of government correctional services increasingly monopolized the policy, practice and thinking within the field. The community-based sector, formerly a vibrant source of innovative practice, was virtually emasculated. Relegated to a consultative position, usually after the fact, it became ever more dependent upon the government agency for funding. This subordinate rank affected the services provided by and within the community, reducing them to a mere cloning of the CSC dictum. Both sides lost out because of this.

*   *   *

It was in the early 'eighties, however, when we had Harry on mandatory supervision. The full concentration of power in the correctional field was not completely in the hands of CSC as yet. Halfway houses operated by community-based organizations, officially designated as Community Residential Centres, still maintained a degree of autonomy. They were able to select their clients and manage their residential program with limited interference. The parole and mandatory supervision carried out by private agencies was likewise able to proceed with some independence. Although the basic rules and procedures were defined by the government agency and were applied to all, there remained a margin of manoeuvrability that left some room for clinical judgement and essential innovation.

At the JHSQ, for example, we differentiated between those on parole and those on mandatory supervision. Frequently more time was spent with those on MS, particularly at the outset of their supervision. They had previously been refused parole and thus more clearly personified the unwilling client. Their reluctance to comply was acknowledged; they were reporting under duress. For many, they had done their time and owed "nuthin' to nobody." What helped us with many of these cases, however, was the fact that they knew us. Several had been followed on a voluntary basis throughout their incarceration; some over years through various sentences. Although they reported to us unwillingly, we were not perceived as the bad guy. Thus, it was easier to secure their compliance and develop a positive relationship over time. The increasing trust that ensued allowed us to dig a little deeper and occasionally prompted the individual to open up previously restricted areas. Cases were not assigned haphazardly. The staff member most familiar with the case generally carried out the supervision. Cases which presented a more pronounced history of intransigent delinquent behaviour, or whose psychosocial profile was more intricate, were assigned to the more experienced personnel. Individual supervisors, however, did not work in a vacuum. There were weekly case conferences where supervisors made presentations on a rotating basis. These clinical sessions allowed the presenters to hone their particular skills through discussion and constructive criticism. At the same time, these sessions provided valuable, ongoing information sharing within the context of a training forum for all concerned. Ultimately, I believe both the supervised offender and those of us at the JHSQ benefited. The community-at-large was also better served in the long run.

The CSC parole officers were in a less favourable position than we were. They owed allegiance to an organization, a corporate body that was becoming increasingly more centralist and burdened by an accretion of policy and procedure directives designed to ensure orthodoxy. Although the more talented parole officers struggled valiantly to maintain professional autonomy, the tidewater of peer pressure gradually dragged them in the undertow of blind conformity. As a consequence, velleity steadily supplanted initiative and the over-legislation of the ensuing years would bolster a pervasive mental inertia. A dynamic course of action linking the joint phases of incarceration and post-release, tailored to the individual offender, was quickly becoming a "one size fits all" approach to the intricate process of reintegration. The role of the supervising parole officer formerly that of a dynamic aid to reparation and reinstatement, now paled to that of an anaemic surrogate, subject to the vagaries of political priorities and acquiescent to bureaucratic convenience.

What we were trying to do with Harry was simply to exercise some maintenance work. He was unable to adjust to society in a normal fashion. Legitimate work was out of the question. He had never ingested any basic tenets of the work ethic. In fact, the many years of incarceration had ingrained in him the worst work habits, effectively precluding legitimate employment had he been so intentioned. Likewise, his associations were and had always been solely criminal. From early abandonment to the streets of southwest Montreal during his pre-puberty years, through the more structured environments of juvenile detention, provincial jail and federal penitentiary, Harry had been exposed to and expected to contend with the demands of the delinquent milieu. We were attempting to provide a non-criminal haven within the JHSQ, a minuscule sanctuary in his tempestuous world.

Prisons are actually for men like Harry. The repetitive anti-social behaviour of the persistent delinquent, whether directed against person or property, must eventually be curtailed. In the short term, incarceration does effectively contain the behaviour. By the same token, this same course of action is counter-productive over the long term. The very attitudes and values that sustain the prevailing behaviour pattern in freedom are strengthened by the manner in which the process of incarceration is realized. The cultural milieu of the penitentiary is a highly concentrated microcosm of the criminal world outside. The proximity and automatism of institutional living, buttressed by the inherent mechanisms of suppression and control, intensify the peer-group influences and demands upon the individual. The process is a ceaseless reinforcement of the basic attitudes and value system that need to be altered if behavioural change is to be anticipated. When Harry came to the JHSQ in September of 1981, he had recently turned forty-four years of age. He had just completed more than six consecutive years in maximum security, having promenaded from Kingston, through Dorchester and finally to Archambault penitentiary for the final six months prior to release. Upon release he leaped from the institution into the freedom of society equipped with some three hundred dollars, no home, no legitimate means of income but plenty of friends. He had spent more than eighty-five percent of his life incarcerated, since his first admission to the penitentiary at seventeen years of age. Our job now was to monitor him as best we could, provide encouragement and support and hopefully maintain him within the community-at-large. Our strongest ally, in reality our only one, was a semblance of trust that had built up over the past twenty years. He had been followed throughout the long periods of confinement and during the brief stays outside. We knew his severe limitations to cope appropriately with the demands of freedom. We were equally cognizant of the fact that additional incarceration would simply incapacitate him further. Short of abetting overt criminal behaviour, we were prepared to try anything and everything to help maintain him in the community.

The visit to the Cavalier Motel where Harry proudly introduced me to his friends proved to be a learning experience in itself. Although I was aware that this particular environment was not ideal, I was realistic enough to acknowledge that his comfort in these surroundings had been conditioned over a lifelong experience. Any change in this respect would be a long-term proposition and not simply the result of an edict. The problem of reintegration into the community-at-large, particularly for the persistent delinquent, was obviously more abstruse than the jejune approach espoused by armchair social scientists.

What the visit to the "the Zoo" did, was sensitize a certain portion of the criminal milieu to the work of the JHSQ. This kind of publicity is seemingly the subject of some misinterpretation. Interestingly enough, in my experience, the questioning has always come from the direction of supposed colleagues, never from the side of the criminal element. JHSQ is in the business of working with adult offenders, sometimes called criminals. We have defended them, confronted them, socialized with them and even hired them. We do not however, commit crimes with them. They know this and usually are appreciative of the fact that we are able to maintain affability, while at the same time knowing where to draw the line: neither approval of nor complicity in criminal behaviour.

Harry continued to report regularly. His mental health remained stable though fragile. He was able to relate easily enough to the staff members but reserved the deep-rooted fears and paranoid interpretations of his personal netherworld for the privacy of my office. Occasionally he would appear unannounced at the office, usually a few days before or after a scheduled appointment. It would be obvious that his sense of time was askew. I would make the interview short and reschedule for the next day or so, simply to ascertain whether there were any further signs of mental deterioration.

It was unlike Harry to miss an appointment entirely, without telephoning within a few days. At one time, however, it came to my attention that Harry had missed his last scheduled appointment. More than a week had passed and I was called on the intercom from our reception desk.

"Mr. Williams there are two gentlemen here to see you . . . one is Mr. Dooney."

Although I had met him only once casually, I knew who Dooney was, the "main man" in the West End. His reputation was phenomenal. According to the police, he was one of the biggest drug traffickers in Canada; according to the word on the street, he was a stand-up guy you didn't cross but was also considered the most generous among the bosses.

"How are you Mr. Williams? I'd like you to meet Alan," he stated with outstretched hand. After the initial handshakes and pleasantries, "Have you heard from Harry lately, he doesn't seem to be around?"

"I haven't heard from him recently . . . I'm becoming concerned. It's not like him, he's overdue and hasn't even called."

Dooney's speech pattern switched to street vernacular, "I'll be frank, he's actin' strange lately. He keeps talkin' about bein' watched. I think he's loosin' it!"

"Well, it's not like him to miss an appointment and not call," I reiterated.

Dooney spoke directly, "are the fuzz lookin' for 'im? I think that's wat's bodderin' 'im."

"If the police were looking for him we would be advised," I admitted. "No, as far as I'm concerned there's nothing on him."

"That's it then! He's fuckin' flipped out again!" he said with some agitation, yet some relief. He turned to Alan who had not said a word, "see I tol' ya! It's all in his head. He's done nuthin' or he would've tol' me."

He turned quickly back to me, "Mr. Williams when do you want him in?"

"Like yesterday!"

"He'll be here tomorrow first thing. OK?"

"Right on."

"Thanks a lot. Sorry to bother you. He'll be here tomorrow, I promise."

The three of us shook hands. The interview was over. Harry was at the reception desk when I arrived the next morning.

*   *   *

Treatment of the offender, particularly the Persistent Offender, is always problematic. This may be said equally of treatment during incarceration as well as in the community. The basic personality structure of the true delinquent is not open to a traditional therapeutic approach with its underlying premise of motivation. At the basis of this aversion is the fact that the delinquent does not perceive the source of his problematic life situation as emanating from within. The resultant projection upon external sources such as police, courts, guards and parole boards effectively precludes any genuine motivation towards internal change. What frequently occurs is a certain cerebral acknowledgment of proposed solutions. What remains lacking, however, is the requisite affective acceptance, which would allow for internalization of these same tenets. Treatment programs that do not address the problem of motivation and simply use its absence as a reason for exclusion play directly into this dynamic. The brighter or better-organized delinquent quickly learns the necessity to comply with prescribed programs, not because of any insight into the need for internal change, but simply as another manipulation of the external environment so as to gratify immediate needs.

Apart from the difficulties reflected in the personality structure of the delinquent, the goal of the treatment itself presents a dilemma for the clinician. During the incarceration phase of the sentence the problem lies in maintaining a balance between conflicting treatment directions. On the one hand, there is a thrust towards the development of new coping mechanisms for post-release adjustment. At the same time, certain adaptive devices to respond to the pressures and demands of the daily institutional life must be maintained. As the individual learns to become more autonomous and integrates new patterns of behaviour compatible with living in freedom, he runs the risk of jeopardizing a suitable harmonization with the prevailing institutional milieu. The rising conflict, due directly to the process of incarceration as it currently plays out, is obviously exacerbated for those serving a long sentence and those who have completed several sentences.

Post-release treatment of the offender is more arduous yet. As an unwilling client, his simple presence on a regular basis is difficult to obtain other than by outright coercion. Compulsory measures are hardly a foundation for any therapeutic technique. Under present circumstances, the initial stage of any work with the released offender is the task of dismantling learned attitudes and behaviours, which have been shored up throughout the period of incarceration.

As in any learning process, mistakes will be made, obstacles are encountered and regression to more comfortable attitudes and behaviours is to be expected. However, this usually constitutes an abrogation of one or more conditions of release. Since the treatment is generally related to the supervision, the judgment call is whether or not the offender is to be returned to the correctional institution for breach of condition. If a return to prison is effected the chances of reinforcing the very elements one has been attempting to modify are greatly augmented. The question then arises as to whether there is any realistic hope the released offender can be helped reach some insight and learn new attitudes and behaviours conducive to living in freedom.

In the final analysis, the sole viable manner in which treatment of the offender can be efficacious is through the implementation of a course of action lasting throughout incarceration and continuing upon release. This implies a fundamental change in the structure, staffing and philosophy of corrections in general and the correctional institution in particular. This basic alteration would transform the process of incarceration into a vehicle of personal growth for staff and inmates alike. The thrust would be in the direction of adjustment to living in freedom rather than adaptation to institutional life. Thus a veritable process of reintegration becomes a possibility. Harry is an example of a decidedly difficult case. Although above average in intelligence, he was never able to use this tool other than in a manner that was ultimately self-defeating. He had manifested serious behavioural problems in the early school years, unresolved issues that continued through adolescence and endured throughout his adult life. This intractable persistence is characteristic of the Primary Delinquent, the most disheartening prognosis in the field. In his case the syndrome was further convoluted with an overlay of mental illness.

However, Harry is simply one of many who wind their way through the prison and penitentiary system and spend the better part of their life therein. Those of us who have chosen to work with the adult delinquent, particularly the Persistent Delinquent, are well aware of the serious disadvantage of attempting clinical intervention at the pinnacle of a delinquent process. We work with what we have, strive to reduce contributing factors and endeavour to create a context within which conditions will be favourable to positive change.

We put Harry on a weekly schedule so as to monitor his mental state more closely. He seemed to be somewhat relieved that first morning back after his brief absence. Although neither of us mentioned Dooney's visit it was simply understood that we were both aware of what had transpired.

"T'ings have been rough ya' know, Mr. Williams," he said as he rubbed the back of his scalp. The gesture brought back to mind his recounting to me, while in the Pen some years back, that he sometimes felt as though some object inside his skull was moving around at times. He continued, "I kept t'inking someone's watchin' me an' it's drivin' me fuckin' nuts, ya' know!" then, after a momentary pause, "but t'ings are much better now."

"Why don't you pop in the office once a week for awhile, we could shoot the shit?"

"You got the time, it's OK wit' me"

The next few months witnessed Harry barely maintaining an even keel. What was troubling for me was that I realized his paranoid thinking, as all paranoia, was to some extent based in reality. His particular demons dated back many years and surfaced when he was under stress. Stressful stimuli in the Pen were one thing, the triggering mechanisms in his murky world on the street, however, were more ominous.

One morning I was expecting Harry at the office for ten o'clock. Around nine-thirty he 'phoned.

"Mr. Williams I won't be able to report today, I gotta' get outta' town. I'll be gone by noon."

Judging by his voice and knowing his precarious mental state, I was not about to insist on his coming to the office. "That's cool Harry, but maybe we could meet somewhere, you pick a restaurant an' I'll join you wherever." If this was a resurgence of his paranoid thinking I didn't want to spook him further; the suggestion of a neutral ground would be less threatening.

"Yeh! Maybe we could meet around eleven-thirty. I'll call ya' back." The line went dead.

Around eleven o'clock Harry called again.

"I can't make it Mr. Williams . . . I gotta' beat it right away, t'anks for everythin'

"O.K. Harry . . . but listen, watch your back."

Those were the last words I ever said to him. I was completely in the dark as to what was going on but knew Harry well enough and was sufficiently acquainted with his milieu to guess that the road ahead would not likely be smooth. Violence and treachery are commonplace in the criminal world and inherent mechanisms are in place to deal with both. The unpredictability of mental illness causes fear and anxiety and the tolerance level dips to its lowest point.

Harry's body and that of his current girlfriend were found in a shallow grave in Nova Scotia the following year. They had been murdered some six months prior to the discovery. The police had been tipped off and the alleged assassin hanged himself in a cell at Dorchester penitentiary upon hearing that the bodies had been uncovered. The story was that Harry had been sent away to Nova Scotia so as to relieve police pressure on the West End crew. As it turned out, the individual who was to provide the hospitality for him out east eventually became his executioner. He apparently thought Harry had been sent to remove him from action; thus, the labyrinthine ways of this netherworld of fear and suspicion.

About a month after his body was discovered, I was contacted by Harry's family and asked to attend a memorial service. Apart from his brother and two sisters, the remaining immediate family, I stood with a young woman whom I had met as a visitor for Harry at the Pen some years before. The silence in the chapel was deafening; not one of the "friends" who had been so eager to greet him upon release from the Pen was present. Harry would no longer make his presence felt in the "milieu."

ATTEMPTING TO INFLUENCE CORRECTIONAL POLICY

~ the dangerous offender

Late in 1980, the Solicitor General of Canada, at the urging of community-based organizations, decided to strike a consultative committee to look into the problem of institutional violence in federal penitentiaries. There had been a significant increase in major disruptions in various regions of the federal correctional system over the previous eight or nine years. Archambault penitentiary had experienced an inmate revolt, which had halted institutional operations for an extended period of time. The tension rose significantly and was not to dissipate for some years. New Westminster penitentiary in British Columbia had been a seething hotbed of turbulence that culminated in a hostage taking in which a staff member had been killed. The unrest was known to be contagious and threatened to spread throughout the five regions of CSC.

Although the federal correctional system had its "super maximum" security facilities, now labelled Special Handling Units (SHU), there was much concern over this means of dealing with the problem. In the first place, it was seen as closing the barn door after the horse had left and, secondly, the extreme isolation inherent in these handling units may well exacerbate rather than correct the problem. Thus the Dangerous Offenders Consultation Committee (DOCC) was set up and met on a basis of four meetings a year from 1982 to 1985. It was composed of fourteen members and a permanent recording secretary. Equally represented by government and community, the committee was also considered to be nationally representative. It was with some pride and hope that I embarked on this journey, feelings that remained throughout the many meetings and into the preparation and submission of the final report in June 1985.

The meetings were conducted in an atmosphere of camaraderie. The composition of the committee was diverse as to background, priorities and experience of the sitting members. Despite this we worked as a team, cognizant of the fact that we were faced with a complex problem that demanded some resolution. It was acknowledged early on that frankness in dialogue and acceptance of different points of view were indispensable if any headway were to be made. The National Parole Board, Correctional Service Canada, the Solicitor General Secretariat and the Union of Solicitor General Employees represented the government sector; the community had representatives from Police, the Citizen's Committee and various community-based organizations. The players were in place; the game had now to be decided.

The original mandate was to monitor the SHU program and provide recommendations for dealing with dangerous offenders. The after-care agencies, however, proved instrumental in assuring an expansion of the terms of reference. Eventually they were to include an examination of critical issues in relation to dangerous offenders and a review of CSC efforts to improve their identification and handling in order to reduce institutional violence. Furthermore, an effort was to be made to coordinate the contributions of all groups and individuals on this topic and advise the Solicitor General with respect to policy matters and program development.

Our work over this three and a half year period was not restricted to discussion and debate. We had several field trips, which resulted in on-the-spot visits to the handling units. An interim report that targeted an evaluation of the SHU at Millhaven penitentiary in the Ontario region and the Correctional Development Centre in the Quebec region helped to close the two facilities. My initial euphoria at the announcement of these closings was short-lived. It was soon evident that, despite the closing of the specific physical plants, the basic treatment philosophy was alive and well. Two new SHUs were opened: one at the Regional Reception Centre in Quebec, the other at Saskatchewan penitentiary. The facilities were more up-to-date, modern dungeons where isolation masks as a viable means of treating disruptive and dangerous behaviour.

Our second and final report was on alternatives to Special Handling Units and was submitted to the powers that be in June 1985. There were twenty recommendations, many of which were directed towards existing correctional institutions, as preventive measures. Ongoing training for all personnel, as well as a more specific conflict management and prevention training directed at front-line staff, were suggested. A program of crisis intervention that would solicit the active assistance of inmates was also proposed. The size of future institutions was to be limited to two hundred inmates and the recommendation that existing facilities be sub-divided into semi-autonomous units, not in excess of fifty inmates, was put forth. It was also urged that Wardens and their senior assistants assume a high visibility role as a means of increasing interpersonal contact between inmates and principal decision-makers.

Apart from several recommendations designed to alter the existing institutional system, a number of us pushed for more fundamental change. We felt strongly that much of the disruptive behaviour was reactive; patterns that were symptomatic of the suppressive nature of the daily institutional life. This had to be demonstrated operationally. After many sessions of intense discussion and heated debate, a majority finally accepted the principal recommendation of the final report, that a Social Development Community be established within Correctional Service Canada. The idea of coping with crime and delinquency, principally through social development, was not new with respect to work in the community-at-large. What was innovative in this proposal was bringing the concept to the institutional level. This was certainly a more radical recommendation than the others, in that it struck at the heart of the correctional system: the penitentiary. It proposed a totally new entity, from bureaucratic procedures, through staff role definition, into inmate participation in circumscribed decision-making. It was a proposal that went deeper than the modification of an existing phenomenon. There was certainly no unanimity reached within the committee but the lengthy debate resulted in winning over a majority of the participants to the idea. The basic argument favouring the proposition was that the existing means of dealing with disruptive and dangerous behaviour was primarily through isolation, which undoubtedly subdued the behaviour temporarily but did not address the precipitating causes. There was little reason to believe that simply quashing the acting-out through external restraints would have any effect once these restraints were removed. In fact, there was good reason to speculate that the long-term effects of the isolation could produce more serious results. The extreme deprivation of liberty was known to engender frightening consequences. The suggestion to introduce specific programs into the SHU was countered with the allegation that it was too little too late.

One of the participants on the committee was my former colleague Josh Zambrowski. He was now Executive Director of the Canadian Criminal Justice Association. Both of us had experienced the merits of milieu therapy in the past and knew that this was an opportunity to introduce the technique into an exceptional arena. Thus we agreed to write up a description of a program, which would necessarily encompass the total institution and serve as the blueprint for a Social Development Community (SDC). The written proposal was submitted under our names jointly, as an Annex to the Final Report to the Solicitor General, in June 1985, on Alternatives to Special Handling Units.

The underlying treatment philosophy of the Social Development Community was to be the direct antithesis of the Special Handling Unit. Whereas isolation, a process of dissociation of inmate from inmate and inmate from staff, formed a basis of the SHU approach, increased association was a principle inherent in the proposed SDC; a course of action fashioned to develop inner controls rather than an attempt to elicit a positive response to external control. The pertinent social forces within the immediate milieu were to be altered by means of an increase in personal involvement, principally through shared responsibility. The goal was to create an ambiance diametrically opposed to that of existing correctional institutions. The void created by the dichotomy of the watchers and the watched was perceived as the constant that precludes the implementation and maintenance of viable therapeutic techniques. This gap was to be bridged.

From the outset, we considered the term "Dangerous Offender" somewhat of a misnomer. The issue at hand referred to inmates who presented serious management problems because of their disruptive behaviour. Dangerous Offender is a label that encompasses those whose crime was designated dangerous but whose institutional behaviour may well be exemplary. Furthermore, the labelling creates a category that tends to obscure individual differences. In this instance, the label also fails to acknowledge the reactive nature of the behaviour. We perceived institutional behaviour patterns, disruptive or otherwise, as symptomatic of the deprivation of liberty.

It was important to acknowledge the SDC as a pilot project and, as such, one that required some time to evolve. The undertaking was not to entail a full-scale transposition of the existing SHU population but, rather, was to be the development of a milieu within a total institution; a milieu designed to deal with delinquent mechanisms and reactions, including those characteristic of the SHU population. The elements of shared responsibility and accountability in decision-making are not brought about overnight but the result of an ongoing learning process. Therefore, certain prerequisites would have to be enunciated and accepted if the concept were to be realized.

The stipulation that a total institution was required must be underscored. The fundamental nature of the changes at all levels necessitated complete autonomy. Evidently, as an integral part of the criminal justice system, the institution would be subject to the laws of the time embodied in the Penitentiary Act, the Parole Act, the Criminal Code and the Charter of Rights. The sentence of the Court was to be carried out. On the other hand, we wanted to be free of inhibitors to realistic innovation. The myriad directives, instructions, guidelines, etc., frequently emanating from sources far removed from the field of action, were seen to be an obstruction to creativity. Maximum flexibility, rather than blind acceptance of written decrees would be required of the staff. Insubordination and minor acting-out by inmates, for example, would be dealt with through the combined efforts of staff together with the inmate peer group. The purpose would be to elicit the causes of the behaviour and apply appropriate remedies as an integral part of a comprehensive learning process.

Apart from institutional authorities, the line of command would be limited to a direct link with the Commissioner of Corrections or one of his designated senior assistants. That person would necessarily be knowledgeable of the project, convinced of its validity and prepared to assist in dissuading detractors. We knew from experience that opposition could arise from any quarter and be generated by any motive; the resistance of the Quebec Regional Office, to substantial change at the Correctional Development Centre, was within recent memory.

The primary objective of the proposal was to create an institutional setting that would eventually render the SHU program unnecessary. The belief was that we could demonstrate that institutional violence can be substantially reduced through the development of a milieu characterized by diminished external suppression and the gradual supplanting of the delinquent sub-culture with socially acceptable values and behaviour. The implications for change were significant, targeting basic issues such as the bureaucratic structure of the institution and methods of staff selection and training. Emphasis was to be on quality rather than quantity; the number of staff was important, as many as necessary but as few as possible. An openness to change, an interest in innovative methods and a willingness to learn were attributes sought after. These qualities were considered crucial in fostering a daily decision-making process, which would include inmate participation.

Senior management of the total institution was to be reduced to a minimum. Clarity of role definition was to take precedence over the number of managers. The governance of the entire facility was to rest ultimately in the hands of a Director supported by three assistants: the A/D Security would be responsible for static security on the perimeter, as well as security escorting outside the institution. Patrol, guard towers and any other device deemed necessary to ensure external security were also within his sphere. The A/D Administration would be primarily a service provider, a guarantor that material necessities for the operation of the total institution were in place and within budgetary limits. If one Assistant Director were to be first among equals, it would be the A/D Program; herein rests the authority obligated to ensure the direction of the program in light of the primary objective of the proposal. The individual occupying this position would be charged with the responsibility for everything that occurs and everyone who works inside the institution. Internal security and discipline, an integral component of the daily living, falls within his purview. However, a most important consideration regarding these three role definitions is that, though they are interdependent, they must remain mutually exclusive. Their interdependence is defined by their ultimate accountability to the total institution; their exclusiveness lies in their differing spheres of activity.

The ultimate authority for the total institution is the Director. His principal task herein is to ensure that the primary objective of the proposal is carried forward through the coordination and smooth functioning of the three activity areas of his assistants. It is imperative that the role of each Assistant Director, especially that of A/D Security and A/D Program, remain mutually exclusive. In traditional correctional settings the terms "security" and "discipline" are used interchangeably and are employed as a means of control. What we were proposing, indeed insisting upon, was that the A/D Security and his staff were to make sure that no person or object enter or exit from the institution illegally. The demarcation line was the perimeter and their field of activity extended from the perimeter outwards. Direct contact with inmates was to be limited to security escort duties.

The rationale behind this work containment arose from the fact that the role of A/D Program, along with that of his entire personnel, was to be anchored in a close working relationship with the inmate population. Freedom of verbal and affective expression was to be encouraged rather than suppressed. The inhibitors to expression, characteristic of the correctional setting, emanate as much from the inmate sub-culture as from the submissive nature of incarceration. This overall quashing of basic self-assertion is often a triggering mechanism to sudden eruptions of violence. Our aim was also to develop a practical sense of shared responsibility and accountability, a practice that would ultimately encroach upon the sensitive area of discipline. Obviously this was to be a formidable enterprise for both personnel and inmates; neither faction had experienced this before, as it goes contrary to the basic code of either side within the framework of their traditional roles.

The initial step, one of foremost importance, lies in the selection of staff. The principal criterion revolves around interest and ability. We acknowledged that not everyone is suited to any and all type of work. Those interested in and able to demonstrate some aptitude for working with incarcerated delinquents on a regular, intensive basis, would be considered for work within the institution; those whose abilities were more in line with the expert manipulation of tangible security devices and who expressed a preference for work apart from the inmate population, would be deemed more apt for duties on and outside the perimeter. The delineation of the field of action underscores the importance of basic, distinct comfort zones in potential personnel, a crucial factor underlying motivation. This approach to staff selection purported to help avoid unrealistic demands and expectations in the workplace. The final selection would be effected only after assessment within a practical training period.

The role of A/D Administration, like that of the other assistants, is ultimately to focus on the implementation and maintenance of the overall program. Along with the provision of a service, particularly with respect to material needs and clerical matters, this Assistant Director is to ensure that bureaucratic procedures are kept to a minimum. In a milieu where shared decision-making is to be encouraged and gradually expanded, it is imperative that the customary self-feeding bureaucratic process be constantly monitored and contained. The inmate involvement in decision-making is clearly circumscribed and never unilateral; it is to be a dynamic course of action whose growth is commensurate with the ascending maturity level of the community as a whole.

In summary, the proposal was to create a therapeutic milieu within a total institution. All roles were to be modified so as to enhance social learning. The milieu would be designed in such a manner as to allow for the identification of delinquent mechanisms related to the various forms of acting-out. The experience of increasing shared responsibility is concomitant with the evolving peer group influence and pressure towards new modes of socially acceptable behaviour.

A thorough understanding of the ultimate goal of the program is essential to bring about role modification successfully. Thus, the basic training program was not to be limited to a certain segment of the staff; it would apply to all. Although the initial sessions would necessarily be didactic in nature, so that the fundamental principles of milieu therapy are clearly enunciated, the more important phase would be interactive and ongoing. Everyone brings a certain knowledge and dexterity from their previous experience and shares with everyone else. In a spirit of transparency, one and all are capable of contributing to and learning from each other. It is essential that this learning process be incorporated into the daily life of the institution with the active participation of staff and inmates.

The Annex to the Final Report on Alternatives to Special Handling Units went into greater detail with respect to the daily structure of the overall program. Specific mechanisms designed to encourage and reinforce active inmate participation, as well as their mounting involvement in shared decision-making, were described. The ongoing training program, inherent in the daily schedule, was clearly outlined and its importance accentuated. The need for meaningful work was argued but the main emphasis was placed on the necessity to develop basic work habits consistent with those required in the workplace outside.

The value in fostering positive peer group pressure was stressed. In all strata of society, peer group expectancies and demands play a key role in defining and mobilizing attitudes, values and behaviour patterns. This is especially evident among groups who perceive themselves as apart from the mainstream. In the traditional correctional setting, however, identification with the delinquent peer group stems more from a need to close ranks against rather than unify towards a common goal. The rudimentary dichotomy, "we" vs. "they", precludes the growth of healthy peer group influence.

Although this proposal for a Social Development Community was presented as an alternative to the rationale underlying and methods employed by the Special Handling Units, it was made patently clear that a wholesale transfer of the SHU population to this new venue was not possible and that such a move would simply invite disaster. The implementation of a healthy milieu is a developmental process, based on interpersonal relationships and requires time to evolve. What was suggested was an institution of limited size that would gradually incorporate dangerous and highly disruptive inmates. Those who use physical aggression as their principal method of problem solving would necessarily be in the minority if the primary mechanism of change were to be effected through peer pressure. Thus their number would be contingent upon the maturity level of the SDC at any given time.

A time frame of some eighteen to thirty-six months, a range based on previous experience, was suggested as appropriate for meaningful participation. Some basic acceptance criteria were put forth, mainly to exclude identified police informers and those with chronic mental illness that required psychiatric intervention. Behavioural difficulties of any gravity would not serve as a basis for refusal. It was also pointed out that a large complement of social science professionals was unnecessary. The crucial issue regarding staffing was to engage front-line correctional personnel who were motivated to embark on an innovative endeavour. They would then take part in an ongoing social learning process built into the overall program. The cost of the entire project, in monetary as well as human terms, was demonstrably less than the cost of building and maintaining a Special Handing Unit.

Thus, the proposal for a Social Development Community was forwarded to the powers that be in the Solicitor General's office in 1985. An official reply is still awaited; now well into the twenty-first century.

The SHU exists today, though now only in one location. The Quebec Region of Correctional Service Canada has the dubious distinction of housing the "dangerous" inmates from the federal penitentiaries across Canada. I would be amiss not to mention that one among these inmates is a man who has now passed his seventy-fifth birthday. One is aghast to discover that an organization that proudly defines itself as an international leader in the correctional field has yet to discover an alternate method to cope with such a threat.

*   *   *

When I came to John Howard late in 1980, I knew nothing of its history here in Quebec. I was invited to a meeting of the Advisory Board early on and eventually had an overview of the evolution of the organization. I realized how different it was from other John Howard Societies across Canada.

During the years 1973-74, provincial legislation had been introduced that altered the status of private organizations that provided adult social aid services. Bill 48 brought the John Howard Society of Quebec into the provincial social service network. On the one hand, salaries would not only be guaranteed but also increased to the level of provincial civil servants. Furthermore, unionization would make certain that the appropriate employment levels would be respected, thus assuring pay equity. On the other hand, the JHSQ, one of the oldest John Howard Societies in Canada, would lose its status as a private, non-profit corporation. Its anchor in the community, represented by the volunteer Board of Directors, would virtually disappear; it would now be an Advisory Board.

As a Service Unit within the para-public parent organization, the Ville Marie Social Service Centre (VMSSC), JHSQ was permitted to keep its name but its foundation in the community had been undermined and its autonomy usurped. The new Board of Advisors was just that; they could advise but had no power to decide. Needless to say, interest waned considerably. The meeting that I had attended in the autumn of 1980 resembled the nostalgic assembly of an old boys' club rather than a high-powered meeting of decision-makers, representing the community-at-large.

By the year 1976, a separate non-profit corporation had been established, The John Howard House Inc.(JHH Inc.) had been set up for the express purpose of opening a halfway house for released offenders. This was to be an autonomous facility, independent of the VMSSC. A grant from the McConnell Foundation was to be available upon locating a suitable site. The first required step, however, was to obtain a municipal permit, a condition that proved to be impossible to accomplish over the following two years. Thus, the non-profit corporation remained extant, but on paper only.

In 1985, the newly elected Progressive Conservative government in Ottawa adopted a policy of increased privatization. Indications were that federal corrections were preparing to expand resources in the community through increased contractual arrangements. I thought it would be wise to be pro-active and had the letters patent of the JHH Inc. expanded so as to include all activities pertinent to a viable, community-based service organization. The move paid off. The following year I was invited to a luncheon meeting with Jean-Claude Perron, Regional Director of CSC at the time. His District Director of Parole accompanied him. Our parole contract at this point was limited to a monthly average of fifty supervision cases. Payment for the work went directly into the coffers of VMSSC who handled the total budget and covered our salary, travel and rental costs. The encounter was a godsend; the end result would open the way to a renewed, albeit partial, autonomy and afford the opportunity for an amplification of services.

I was elated at Perron's proposition. He asked if JHSQ was willing and able increase its supervision service to a maximum of two hundred cases. My head was spinning with the realization that with such numbers the private corporation could be activated. The one stipulation, on my part, was that there had to be two contracts: one with VMSSC for fifty cases to be supervised by the current staff and a separate contract with JHH Inc., which would hire new personnel to supervise the balance. Agreement was reached and, on April 1st 1987, the JHH Inc. opened an office in downtown Montreal. As director of both offices, a five-minute walk apart, it was easy to coordinate the activities of the two. Five experienced professionals from the field were engaged to carry out the supervision while the daily tasks at the new office were efficiently handled by a secretary/receptionist. Although the

JHSQ and the JHH Inc. were separate legal entities, their activities overlapped. Joint case conferences facilitated an even flow from the clinical intervention of institutional work to coordinated supervision in the community. The interaction between the two afforded a more complete continuum of services.

In summary, the spring of 1987 augured well for the future development of a well-funded, comprehensive service for adult offenders and their families. The combined staff complement eventually surpassed twenty. Apart from supervision work and the evaluation of community resources, both directly related to the continuing institutional work, a specific family program for wives and children was in place. Public Education frequently took the form of information sessions in schools and various social and business gatherings. The criminal justice system, at both the provincial and federal level, was well served by this total, community-based operation. The combined efforts of the two offices were well represented in the field, principally through participation with colleagues in *l'Association des services de réhabilitation sociale du québec* and *la Société de criminologie du québec*. These interchanges kept us abreast of both the clinical work and the research carried out by other practitioners in the field.

In 1988 we participated in the bi-annual congress of *la Société de criminologie du québec*, held in Quebec City. Aside from taking an active part in the various workshops and training sessions, we thought it useful to highlight our presence through a social activity. We organized a hospitality suite at the host hotel, providing an "open house" at the end of each of the two days of structured conferences. It proved to be a popular respite from the arduous discussions of the day. In a casual setting, uplifted by hors d'oeuvres and a libation of choice, the attendees gathered over a three hour period to make new and renew old acquaintances in the field. Exchanges ranged from the rib-tickling antics of would-be comedians, through the vocal strains of frustrated *chansonniers*, to the more serious banter of convinced theorists. Bureaucrat and practitioner, private sector or government representative attended; all seemed to have a good time. It was not until some weeks later that the murmurs of some petty, jealous rivals filtered through, ". . . look how they spend the money we give them." I disregarded such small-mindedness at the time; in fact though, I was failing to recognize the tip of the iceberg of envy and control.

The three-year span from 1987 through 1989 was a peak period of the JHSQ. The increased parole supervision caseload afforded us the opportunity to provide a service, based on a longitudinal approach, to a greater number of offenders. Prior to this, many of the men we had followed throughout their sentence were simply abandoned by us upon release. We had no say in the matter; our contract was limited to a monthly average of fifty cases. No new case would be added until one had been completed in some manner or another. CSC controlled the numbers.

Now with the expanded caseload and services provided by the two offices, we were able to monitor more offenders over a protracted period. We had a worker placed in the Parthenais Detention Centre one day a week. The accused were held there prior to and during their trial. This is a particularly trying time due to the trauma of arrest and the uncertainly of the outcome. The task for our worker was to adopt a supportive role in which an attempt was made to assure that appropriate legal assistance was available, that contact with the family was maintained and, finally, that we were prepared to provide a continuing presence throughout the ordeal, including the sentence. Our worker would establish contact with former clients and introduce our services to the recently accused, previously unknown to us. A monthly list was compiled that specified where each individual was to be sent after sentencing. Those sentenced to less than two years remained in the provincial system and could be contacted by our representative worker in either Bordeaux Jail or Waterloo Prison; those sentenced to two years or more were sent to the federal system where we had representatives present in the various penitentiaries. Thus, the institutional service was well coordinated and, for many offenders, segued into the after-case service of parole supervision. Unfortunately, we were not permitted to exercise provincial parole supervision, an undertaking carried out solely by the government agency, the Quebec Probation Service. Nevertheless, we offered voluntary post-release counselling to those released from provincial prisons.

This three-year interval was also an enigmatic time for our agency. The launching of the JHH Inc. office permitted us to revert, at least partially, to the relative independence of private status. At the same time, however, there was an insidious encroachment upon our autonomy lingering furtively in the background. It assumed the guise of standardization. The pretence was the setting of specific normative benchmarks so as to ensure a basic quality of service. The reality, however, simply guaranteed mediocrity under bureaucratic control.

Parole supervision is fundamentally a clinical technique based on an interpersonal relationship between supervisor and parolee. It is an intervention designed to help the individual reintegrate into the community in a socially acceptable manner. This is a learning process beginning with a growing realization of the need for change and dovetailing into an increasing ability to alter a self-defeating behaviour pattern. Ideally, the supervision should be the second phase of an ongoing process, which had begun during incarceration. The dynamics of the delinquent personality must be recognized and dealt with in a therapeutic manner while the offender is imprisoned. The post-release supervision then becomes a supportive relationship directed towards the reinforcement of newly acquired living skills, now to be applied in the reality of living in freedom. This ideal, however, does not exist. Prisons and penitentiaries are not venues in which personality dynamics are recognized and dealt with appropriately; they are simply bastions of suppression and coercive measures. Despite the myriad programs that have sprung up over the past several years, the incarceration process inhibits the development of personal responsibility and effectively precludes a smooth adjustment to the demands and restrictions of society. Thus, post-release supervision takes on a different meaning. At best, it is an attempt to undo the harm brought about by the deprivation of liberty and, at worst, it becomes a surveillance technique designed to look for fault, ultimately feeding the vicious circle of re-incarceration.

At John Howard we were trying to make the best of a difficult challenge. We attempted to follow the individual offender as intensely as possible. Where circumstances allowed, we made contact during pre-trial detention, maintained it throughout incarceration and carried it into post-release supervision. Although the intervention was continuous, it was not maintained by any one person; it was carried out by a closely-knit team of professionals, linked by a common purpose and strengthened through regular clinical case conferences. The case conferences also served to enhance learning and improve technique.

We recognized that positive contact at any stage of the process was contingent upon a strong personal relationship. During incarceration, in an environment of imposed structure and demands, offenders perceived the voluntary nature of our encounters as a welcome change. More importantly, it provided the worker with an opportunity to create a proximate ambiance, best described as confrontational within a supportive setting. Confrontation lay in compelling the individual to face the reality of previous self-defeating behaviour patterns that led to incarceration; the supportive setting was the worker as a concerned source of understanding and reassurance. The offender was not obliged to see us; he came because he decided to do so. He was not expected to behave in any pre-ordained way; free expression of feelings was encouraged and subsequently explored. The ultimate aim of the sessions was directed towards increased awareness of personal responsibility for one's actions. Because we were apart from the decision-making system, and perceived as such, there was less chance of eliciting rehearsed responses; as representatives of a community-based organization, the focus of our intervention remained constantly on the future demands of living in freedom, rather than the immediate exigencies of institutional living. Thus, the counselling provided by us during the offender's incarceration was a preparation for post-release adjustment.

Working with offenders is never an easy task. They may be affable and verbally compliant but, fundamentally, they are "unwilling clients." In fact, during incarceration they are a truly captive audience; while under post-release supervision they report because they are obliged to do so, rarely because they feel a need for help. Obviously, the balance between external demands and inner needs varies among individuals but that very balance can be tipped one way or the other, depending upon the quality of the interpersonal relationship. The more recalcitrant offenders are the persistent delinquents. These are individuals who have manifested behavioural difficulties since adolescence, some since the pre-puberty years. Often they have spent more than fifty percent of their adult life incarcerated and the majority have experienced the punitive measures meted out by the juvenile system as well. It is unrealistic to believe that setting a series of restraining conditions guarantees adherence to these demands. The delinquent personality is characterized by a need for immediate gratification, impulsive reactions and reluctance to abide by impositions and restrictions that conflict with the underlying pleasure principle. Some form of clinical intervention is imperative. This is particularly difficult, given the nature of a character disorder, rendered more difficult by years of neglect or, worse yet, through years of reinforcement by the unhealthy process of incarceration. Time, effort and a certain expertise are required to try and effect change; none of these fits a predetermined schedule or answers to bureaucratic measures. Moreover, the inherent danger in a bureaucratic yardstick is its tendency to expand. Standardization, which had begun as a guideline, gradually evolved into a requirement; what had been a quantitative measure, eventually unfolded as an evaluative tool of quality. Bit by bit, the bureaucratic procedure would eclipse in importance, the very task at hand.

*   *   *

As I mentioned previously, delinquency is a phenomenon that does not embody the notion of motivation towards internal change. The source of deprivation and discomfort is projected upon external conditions and, galvanized by a need for immediate gratification, the individual seeks relief through manipulation of the environment. Most mental and emotional maladjustments interfere with daily living, creating a certain inner malaise, which impels the individual to search for equilibrium. Traditional therapeutic techniques assume this underlying premise of incitement to personal change. The character disorder, however, does not incorporate this and an alternate form of intervention is required.

Supervision of persistent delinquents in the community, a form of intervention, is an arduous task for a myriad of reasons, not the least of which is that one is beginning at the tail end of a continuum. Individuals who manifest symptoms of any sort are best treated as early as possible. The social factors that nourish the development of delinquent symptomatology should be recognized and corrected if one is to hope for a healthier society. Similarly, individual traits must be properly diagnosed and treated at the earliest possible stage if there is to be some realistic chance of stemming the evolution of a long-standing, persistent pattern of delinquent behaviour.

Those who have reached a point where incarceration has become necessary are usually those who have manifested serious behavioural problems in the past. Unfortunately, the traditional punitive remedy has proven to be counter-productive in the long term; punishment does not treat the underlying problem but may well reinforce and aggravate the symptoms. Thus, supervision of an offender released to the community after years of incarceration is particularly difficult. The internal determinants of behaviour have never been addressed; moreover, the process to which the offender has been subjected has reinforced these same causal factors.

There are certain expectations inherent in conditional release. The primary one is an anticipated compliance with the demands and restrictions of the provisional release. The assumption is that the released offender has attained a certain degree of maturity and autonomy. This requisite capacity for discernment and accountability, however, is an unrealistic expectancy for men who have undergone a lengthy process that has effectively stripped them of personal responsibility. The supervisor must be aware of this debilitating predisposition, tolerant of initial setbacks and prepared to provide the needed support; change cannot simply be imposed from without. Nonetheless, correctional systems are largely based on coercion and imposition. Despite this approach, change is expected and the proponents are surprised, indeed exasperated, when it does not come about. The typical reaction is to up the ante; increase the demands and restrictions. Thus, a vicious circle is created and a revolving door syndrome perpetuated.

It is within this anomalous context that supervisors are required to function, working with offenders released to the community after years of incarceration; individuals set free in a competitive society with skills attuned to the exigencies of controlled, institutional living. Today all those released from federal penitentiaries are placed under supervision. Those paroled by the National Parole Board are subject to a set of mutually accepted conditions; those discharged on Statutory Release have had their conditions imposed unilaterally. Neither group has lived an institutional experience conducive to the assumption of personal responsibility; both groups have indeed been seriously disadvantaged by subjection to a suppressive system that militates against personal growth and autonomy.

The supervisor is faced with this enigmatic situation. The released offender has been conditioned to respond to a regimented life of the penal institution but now expected to contend with the demands of freedom. This leap from an artificial milieu of institutional control into the reality of living in society is practically instantaneous, cushioned only by the professional acumen of a designated supervisor. Despite this quandary, the supervisor must be a catalyst to change and not simply an authoritative figure delegated to impose change from without. This role, performed diligently, is one of delicate balance requiring certain clinical skills.

Pierre Dupuis was a Criminologist with more than fifteen years experience in corrections when he came to work with us at John Howard in 1983. After leaving the university, he began his career as a Parole Officer with the former National Parole Service. He later did institutional work as a Classification Officer in a maximum-security penitentiary, a position that brought him into daily contact with inmates. He eventually served as a part-time member of the Quebec Parole Board. Thus his experience was extensive; he had supervised the released offender, had worked with the incarcerated offender and was later to be in the position of a key decision-maker in determining how certain offenders would complete their sentence. In addition, he was fluently bi-lingual and proved to be an asset in the varied work our agency undertook. His strongest suit, however, was in the supervisory work he carried out with persistent delinquents.

I had first met him when he worked as parole officer for Jean-Guy in the early 'seventies. I had been impressed by his natural talent in maintaining that delicate balance between tolerance and control, so necessary in the clinical supervision of delinquents. Jean-Guy had completed more than thirteen straight years when released on parole. His institutional record was voluminous and highlighted by periodic violence. This background was threatening to those who simply supervised a "case" rather than a person. Pierre recognized Jean-Guy for who he was: an individual who had responded to his immediate environment. On many occasions the response had been a violent one. Pierre was fully cognizant of Jean-Guy's past, both institutional and familial, and used his clinical skills to help a highly institutionalized individual integrate into the relative freedom of society. Success, in difficult situations as this, is best measured by honest effort. Pierre more than passed the test as far as I was concerned.

Over the years at John Howard, Pierre supervised many released offenders. Some were clear-cut successes, others abject failures. The majority fell somewhere in between. People don't change fundamentally; we are who we are. Our basic values, interests and attitudes change little after we reach adulthood. Fortunately, most of us are able to modify our behaviour when we realize that we are sometimes the source of our own problems. The delinquent, however, perceives life situations differently; we endeavoured to help the individual realize that his lifestyle was considerably less than a success and only he could change matters.

Our regular case conferences at JHSQ were more than a clinical discussion of individual cases. The sessions were also a learning process as staff members shared pertinent information with regard to institutional and supervisory experiences. It was evident the most difficult hurdle for any supervisor was the deep-seated mistrust that offenders bear. Persistent offenders, in particular, have not developed basic trust. The successful completion of this developmental stage, a prerequisite to the later emergence of empathy and compassion, is fundamental to the gradual unfolding of interpersonal relationships, relationships that are not exclusively self-serving. Furthermore, the survival mechanisms learned during incarceration reinforce this underlying mistrust of others. We had a twofold advantage in dealing with the issue of trust. In the first place, we were not perceived as part of "the system," a moniker with a negative connotation; secondly, we were recognized as an enduring resource, having established contact with the offender as early as possible in the criminal justice proceedings and maintained that presence over a protracted period.

Case presentations were made on a rotation basis so as to assure follow-up. Evidently, some cases would come up more frequently than others either because of a lengthy supervision or because of the intricacy of the case dynamics. Thus, every caseworker made regular presentations and the ensuing discussions would be of benefit to all. They usually took place on the last day of the workweek, a time that allowed for a profitable change of pace from the customary routine and were an opportunity for the staff to assemble as a team.

Claude served twenty-three consecutive years in the penitentiary. He had begun with a life sentence for a murder committed during an armed robbery. Less than a year into his sentence he murdered a penitentiary inmate and received an additional life sentence. This second murder was particularly problematic, both for Claude and the penitentiary authorities, because institutional violence of any sort carries repercussions that may last for years; stories abound, sides are drawn up and the potential for retributive violence rises. In this case some believed that the murdered inmate, one of Claude's partners in the original hold-up, was about to bring in evidence that he had given information to the police; he adamantly denied this allegation and claimed the opposite to be true. The complete story is lost in the equivocations and outright lies in this milieu of treachery and deceit. Nevertheless, battle lines were drawn based on perception of strength more than certainty. Regardless of the total picture, Claude was special. Most of his incarceration was served in one form of isolation or another. He was placed in Segregation because of the murder and its consequent reverberations in the institutional milieu. Throughout the years he was frequently banished to Dissociation, usually after verbal altercations with guards. He was finally transferred to the Special Correctional Unit, a more permanent form of Segregation. I had followed him through much of his time in Segregation and later included him in the group I worked with in the SCU. He was not adept at group interaction and his participation was limited to outbursts against the system. Any attempt to encourage introspection would have been difficult in the best of circumstances; given the extreme deprivation of the SCU regime, any allusion to personal responsibility would have rung hollow. Thus, the purpose of the intervention was purely cathartic.

Claude had been raised in a highly delinquent area in the east end of Montreal. He was one of eighteen siblings. The sporadic presence of an alcoholic father was due to out-of-town jobs and out-of-home binges. The profits of his work were squandered in heavy drinking and gambling, leaving little for the large family. Disciplinary measures were in the hands of an overly taxed mother, whose inconsistency in this domain was as expected. Claude's behavioural problems surfaced during the early school years. He spent more time with truant friends than in the confines of a classroom. Poor performance was reflected in an inability to complete the fourth grade, despite several attempts. Permanent absence from school followed and functional illiteracy was assured. The newfound freedom, however, allowed him to contribute to the family finances with earnings from a delivery-boy job at a local grocery, an income supplemented by petty thievery from his employer. Early abandonment to the neighbourhood resulted in well-honed street smarts by early adolescence. He lived out his adolescent years uninhibited by conventional fetters, much less with any positive guidance, as he avoided the control of youth protection services.

The basic delinquent lifestyle, assumed as an adaptive mechanism to cope with the immediate environment, climaxed with a penitentiary sentence at twenty years of age. The ensuing experience simply widened his horizons in crime. Upon release he worked as bouncer at several nightclubs along the Main, solidifying and expanding his connections with the criminal milieu. His muscular physique, supported on a six foot two inch frame, served him well. This was the late fifties, a time when disputes were usually settled by physical prowess rather than through immediate recourse to lethal weapons. This work kept him in the centre of criminal activities and finally led to his involvement in the hold-up which resulted in homicide and a consequent life sentence at the age of twenty-six.

During his incarceration, the lengthy years of intense isolation finally took their toll. The build-up of diffuse hostility, a common reaction to the extreme deprivation of liberty, took an unusual turn from aggression directed outwards to psychological withdrawal. While at the SCU, Claude suffered a reactive depression, an acute state requiring hospitalization in the psychiatric department of the Pen. Medication raised the curtain of despondency in due time but the basic character disorder remained untouched. It was during this difficult period that his mother died. She had been seriously ill for several months and her demise was not unexpected. Attempts were made to arrange a visit to the hospital and later to the funeral parlour. Both requests were denied. It is unfortunate an opportunity like this was squandered, mainly because the decision-maker was far removed from the immediacy of the situation. In this instance, the decision was made at the Regional Office. As a result, an occasion to show compassion in a concrete way was denied those working with Claude on a more intimate level. It is often by simple but genuine acts of caring and concern that a defensive carapace is pierced and a spark of trust and confidence is ignited.

Although Claude remained in the psychiatric unit for more than a year, it was more a case of the authorities not knowing what to do with him than a real need for ongoing treatment. The previous concerns as to his incompatibility with the general inmate population had not dissipated and precluded placement there. In any case, he did benefit from the relative freedom of psychiatry, as compared to his previous status at the SCU, and his overall attitude and behaviour gradually improved. Finally, that perennial panacea of displacing the problem was put into effect with a transfer to the Ontario Region. Although able to adjust marginally to this anglophone environment, in the long run it proved too much for this unilingual francophone and he was eventually transferred back to the Quebec Region.

Serendipity may also play a part in the life of a penitentiary inmate. What turned out to be the most significant experience of Claude's numerous years of incarceration was a transfer to *l'Institut Philippe Pinel*. This maximum-security psychiatric hospital is for the evaluation and treatment of mentally ill offenders. However, in the early 'eighties they opened up a unit for offenders who were not mentally ill but who had been incarcerated for lengthy periods. The hypothesis was that they had reached a saturation point and were possibly amenable to a designed psychosocial, treatment modality. The attending clinicians, a multi-disciplinary group, were not naive and expected no miracles. They were facing a formidable challenge in attempting to unravel a lifetime of reinforced, anti-social behaviour. Claude, now forty-eight years of age, was deemed a suitable candidate. His stay on this specialized unit was just over two years. He obviously made some progress, enough to convince the National Parole Board to release him on full parole. During his time at *Pinel* he had met a well meaning, if somewhat naive, volunteer visitor. Jeannine was a member of an organization that provided a visiting service for inmates who had little or no resources of their own. Occasionally a volunteer would fall prey to her own feelings and become bent on transforming an adult deliquent into a model citizen through goodwill. Usually the transformation affected the helping agent more than the intended subject. In this instance, Jeannine and Claude decided that their destiny was to live as a couple and they were married before his release on parole. Unfortunately, the realities of married life in the community proved to be different from the mutual promises and speculations of a couple living in separate worlds. After release, the former marital bliss quickly transformed into marital blitz and the union was eventually dissolved.

The John Howard was not tasked with Claude's supervision when he was first released on parole. A month or two after his release, however, he telephoned me and set up an appointment so as to introduce me to his new bride. It took mere minutes to recognize a severely stressed relationship. You could cut the tension with a knife. Early on in the interview I got up from behind my desk, placed a chair between the antagonists and sat on it. I knew of Claude's singular inability to deal with hostility and aggression in an appropriate manner; it was not a quantum leap from verbal to physical expression. Claude is a big man but I was relying on our long-term relationship. If he were to revert to his usual impulsiveness and make a move on Jeannine, he would have to get by me first. I knew he could while hoping he wouldn't.

We did provide some solace to Claude and Jeannine over the ensuing weeks as they gradually but steadily grew apart. The tact we used was simply to leave the door open to either and both of them. We wanted to create a climate of acceptance and understanding of any reasonable eventuality. As it turned out, the two parties made use of our counselling service, both by telephone and through direct contact in the office and in the community. The final rupture came about with relative ease and Jeannine stayed in touch with us by telephone over a two-year period. Naturally, Claude was more readily in our sights, mainly through his behaviour. His social adjustment deteriorated as he returned to his former haunts. This was a man who had no legitimate work record whatsoever, was functionally illiterate and knew virtually no one outside the criminal milieu. The best intentions were not enough. He gradually drifted toward familiar faces and places, slipping into what he experienced as an atmosphere of ease and concurrence. The end result was a new conviction for armed robbery. This time, however, Claude was on the receiving end of a fusillade with the police. The three bullet wounds hospitalized him for several weeks before his eventual return to the penitentiary.

He was in his late fifties when released once again on parole. This time he was under our supervision and it took the team approach of our office, spearheaded by Pierre Dupuis, to guide him over rocky terrain. It was obvious from the outset that the task would be a challenging one. His most recent years in the penitentiary had not better prepared him to live in the community-at-large but, rather, had reinforced his basic anti-social attitudes and interests. He possessed few tools to compete effectively in society. Pierre used unorthodox methods in dealing with this complex situation. We were aware that Claude tended to resort to alcohol as a means of alleviating stress but with diminished inhibitions he could easily fall into an impulsive and erratic behaviour pattern.

Despite this danger, Pierre argued to allow him to work as a waiter in a tavern. We finally deferred to Pierre's expertise, particularly with the phenomenon of alcoholism among delinquents, and the outcome was a positive one. Claude's drinking habits changed. He never drank while working and it was soon evident that the casual nature of the tavern setting afforded him a much-needed sense of security and acceptance.

Pierre monitored this procedure carefully, appearing randomly at the tavern but always conveying a spirit of caring and concern as opposed to one of strict surveillance. This sensitivity, bolstered by meetings at the office and elsewhere in the community, proved to be the key to maintaining a balance of tolerance and control. This symmetry is a principal feature of clinical supervision, an element which distinguishes it from the purely control approach of the official Intensive Supervision. The former is based on a healthy interpersonal relationship that incorporates mutual trust and acceptance; the latter is a technique founded upon the unilateral imposition of limits with little or no tolerance for error. The road was not always smooth. Claude experienced several minor regressions. I emphasize the word minor since they were of a more personal nature. Supportive, in-depth counselling was used to treat periodic alcoholic binges and occasional emotional outbursts. These were recognized for what they were: expected reactions of someone subjected to a suppressive style of institutional living over an extended period. Incarceration is sometimes necessary but those who enforce it must acknowledge the deleterious consequences of the deprivation of liberty.

As it turned out, Claude remained under our supervision until the termination of our parole contract in 1995. Since that time, however, he has remained in contact through monthly telephone calls to the office. When some major incident is reported in the media, he makes it a point to enunciate his views on criminal justice with the abandon of unrestrained emotion. One might say that he has a biased point of view but, then again, who hasn't? I had the pleasure of sharing a coffee recently with Claude and his current wife. They live in a six room flat in the southeast end of Montreal, the very district where he worked the streets as a youth. I was particularly pleased to learn that he is an active member of Alcoholics Anonymous, attending three meetings a week. He has now been sober for three years. The emotional short wick, however, is still alive and well, as evidenced by his immediate anger response to the sudden clanging of the telephone. Claude felt that our conversation shouldn't be interrupted. It was encouraging to see how his wife, tenderly but assuredly, confronted him on his emotional outburst. It was even more encouraging to witness his response; he listened, apologized and made a calm but clear reference to his past. We had come a long way from the need to place a chair between combatants.

The story of Claude illustrates the fact that even the most persistent of offenders, including those with a history of repeated violence, are recuperable. It would be pretentious to claim to know all the contingencies that led to his eventual adjustment, marginal as it may be. The intricacies of human nature in general and delinquency in particular are decidedly abstruse and preclude any facile interpretation. However, I would like to think that our efforts played some part in the overall scenario.

I do strongly believe, though, that if the myriad convolutions of the delinquent process are to be gradually unravelled, the cornerstone of research and treatment must be individualized. Although it is impractical and unnecessary to think only in terms of individual treatment, it is imperative and certainly feasible to implement a diagnostic and treatment model attuned to the realistic needs of the individual offender. The current trend to categorize offenders, principally based on type of crime or criminal associations, obliterates individuality. This tendency has led to the application of assessment scales based on group norms, frequently with disregard for the essential in-depth evaluation of the specific person in question. As a consequence, a plethora of institutional programs, masking as therapy and treatment, have arisen while the prevailing culture of suppression and antipathy remain. This course feeds the voracious appetite of an ever-increasing bureaucracy and the self-serving aims of political expediency. It does not, however, prepare the offender for release to the community. Equally important, it does not provide an authentic portrait of the offender for the decision-makers at the parole hearing. These people, under the authority of law, are tasked with the important and difficult decision as to whether the candidate is able and willing to complete his sentence in the community. This weighty responsibility requires powers of discernment that must be underwritten by factual information and a competent evaluation of significant change.

Serious flaws in assessment and treatment of offenders within the correctional institution directly affect supervision of the released offender as well. Much of the subsequent supervisory work in the community consists in helping the individual unlearn specific destructive attitudes and behaviours, which have been reinforced throughout incarceration. The slight advantage we had was that we were relatively small and community-based. Treatment of the offender is inherent in our singular allegiance to the organization. Our foremost intent is to contribute to the prevention and control of crime and delinquency; our principal vehicle, treatment of the offender. This issue is not as clear-cut for the government agency workers. Their allegiance is diversified and can change with management, union and offender demands and pressures. On the other hand, the disadvantage we are under is that adherence to our principles and goals is contingent upon our autonomy and this autonomy depends to a great extent upon the good will of the government agency.

Partnership is a term that has been bandied about over the years, supposedly to reflect a more or less equal relationship between the community and government sectors. At the best of times, the government agency has always been the first among equals. The real meaning of partnership is skewed by the simple fact that one side controls the purse strings. Over the past thirty years this one-sided power structure has heightened considerably and its demands for conformity to bureaucratic procedures has encroached upon the fundamental independence necessary for vibrant and innovative community-based participation in the correctional process. As a consequence, correctional work in the community now comes under the official banner of Community Corrections and is completely dominated by the government agency.

It was in the latter half of the 'eighties that these controlling influences became more pronounced. A more centralist position on the part of the CSC authorities in Ottawa, the development of standards and the typical knee-jerk reaction to major incidents, were some of the precipitating factors. At the outset the interference was subtle but gradually expanded. Every community-based organization that contracted with the government agency had a Liaison Officer assigned to them. The role of this person was supposedly to assure that correct procedures were followed, such as frequency of reporting. Quantitative matters in themselves present no problem. It is understandable that the basic modus operandi be standard. Difficulties arise when qualitative issues are questioned and alterations in the handling of a particular case come about as a result of the perusal and interpretation of a case file, usually by someone who does not know the offender in question.

Patrick Altimas was a Criminologist with several years experience in various branches of the correctional field. When he came to work with us our parole contract had just been significantly increased, thus making him one of the originals with the private non-profit corporation, JHH Inc. He had previously worked for the government agency in different capacities. His work as Parole Officer, Director of a Community Correctional Centre and in an administrative position at the Quebec Regional Office afforded him sufficient exposure to the correctional system to be fully cognizant of the pros and cons of the entire process. I believe his real talent and principal interest lay in the hands-on practice of clinical supervision. He had an uncanny ability to sense the more subtle manipulative mechanisms of the better-organized delinquents. Like any competent clinician, Pat would avoid falling into the trap of adopting the adversarial role, even with the most trying clients. Equally important, he could distinguish between manipulation by the offender and manipulation by the system.

One morning Pat appeared at my office door. "Have you a minute Paul?" He went on to explain that Denis, a twenty-six-year-old repeat offender under his supervision, had a special condition on his parole warrant. It required him to see a Psychologist every two weeks. He simply wanted out of it. The Parole Board applied special conditions, over and above the standard ones, at the time of the hearing. They are added on when the Board judges that a further demand would more clearly define the limits and enhance the chances of successful reintegration. It is understood, however, that the realities of living in the community are often best assessed by the supervising agent once regular contact with the released offender has been established. Thus a request to have the special condition removed may be forwarded to the Board, should the one responsible for the supervision consider the change beneficial.

"He think's the psychologist's a little weird," Pat said with an impish grin, knowing my background.

"Nothing new there" I retorted with a straight face, "but what's your reading on him?"

"Frankly, I think I have a pretty good handle on this guy and I don't see the need for anything extra, matter of fact," he continued, "down the line it could even be a hindrance."

I knew where Pat was coming from on that one. There is nothing more counter-productive than two or more working with the same individual, unless the concerned parties are in regular contact and the roles are clearly defined. This is particularly so with delinquents who tend to manipulate one against the other in an attempt to gain control. Our weekly clinical conference contended with this inherent problem.

"If you think it would be better for you to work alone on this one, I'll back you." I had confidence in Pat's judgment.

"Would you like to take a look at him? I mean you're the psychologist, maybe you'll see a need of some sort that I'm missing."

"Good idea. Set up a time and I'll see him."

I didn't believe for a minute that I would uncover something in one interview that Pat would have missed over several. I did think, however, that my opinion, included in a written presentation to the Board, could bolster our position. I spent about fifty minutes with Denis in my office the following week. I certainly was not able to detect any need for a psychological follow-up. As a matter of fact, Denis' file indicated that three different psychologists had evaluated him while incarcerated and their separate reports could have been describing three different people. The common denominator was that Denis was a recidivist and we supervise recidivists. Sometimes we call them persistent offenders but, yes, they're recidivists. Other than that, Denis had as much need for traditional psychological treatment as most persistent offenders: little to none.

Pat wrote the special report, which suggested to the Board to remove the special condition. The procedure was such that our report is forwarded to the local CSC parole supervision office and from there onto the Parole Board. This bureaucratic maze resulted in a three-week delay before it reached the decision-makers. An addendum, written by someone at the government agency, was included with our report and it recommended that the special condition be maintained. The Parole Board followed this latter recommendation but, in their reply to Denis, stated that if he wished to contest their decision he could apply for a hearing. Denis wished; Denis applied. About two days before the scheduled hearing Pat approached me:

> "Would you be able to sub for me at Denis' hearing? I'm already tied up with a parole hearing at Archambault. It's at the same time."

Since I was familiar with the case I readily agreed. At least I had perused Denis' file, had read and countersigned the special report to the Board and, more important, had interviewed Denis. When I arrived at the Parole Board office I spotted him in the waiting room seated next to a young woman. Shaking his hand I asked who the woman was, thinking that perhaps she was a girlfriend.

> "I just met her. She's from the CSC."

I turned to her, held out my hand and introduced myself. She explained that she had been sent to represent the parole supervising office in the absence of the regular Liaison Officer who was on vacation. "I just met Denis now," she stated, "but I have this report written by Louise." Louise was the Liaison Officer who had prepared a report based on information gleaned from the file. I realized that what we had this morning was a pinch-hitter standing in for a designated hitter. Once the hearing began Denis was given the opportunity to present his point of view. He had no problem explaining that he was particularly uncomfortable seeing the Psychologist.

> "He just sits there stares at me; first he asks me why I'm there and when I tell him, 'because they're forcing me to come here', he just sits there an' puts me on the dummy."
>
> "Maybe you should give it more time," one parole member asserted.

"I've been there three times now an' get nothin' out of it. I've no trouble reporting to my parole officer. At least he raps with me."

"But your parole officer wants you to continue with the psychologist," she stated, pointing to the report on her desk. I clued in immediately.

"Excuse me for interrupting but there's a misunderstanding here. The John Howard has the parole supervision and that is not our recommendation. We are suggesting that you lift the special condition. The report you have there was prepared by someone who has never seen this man," I stated forcefully. "The lady here this morning," I continued, pointing to the CSC representative seated on the other side of Denis, "has never set eyes on this man before this morning either."

It was important to dot the i's and cross the t's before the interview got out of hand. The hearing didn't last much longer. I was given the opportunity to cite the reasons for our request. We recessed for about five minutes while the two Parole Board members deliberated. Their decision: withdraw the special condition.

This is simply one example of the encroaching bureaucratic control, which was to increase both in occurrence and in intensity during the ensuing years until it reached the absurd. The position of CSC was that they had direct supervision and, as such, were ultimately responsible for every case; we had indirect supervision that seemed to mean that we did the work and they made the decisions. The quasi-judicial nicety distinguishing direct from indirect supervision was simply a bureaucratic way of exercising control and providing self-protection at the expense of competent, professional work. Although this approach may well suffice in the manipulation of material goods, the handling of the human person demands direct, personalized contact.

Our work at the John Howard offices continued unabated throughout the balance of the decade with a comprehensive approach to the complex problems of the correctional process. Although we harboured a few doubts about the efficacy of institutional programming, we plodded on. We had a worker placed in each of the institutions, two in some of the larger penitentiaries, on a weekly basis. This provided an ongoing contact throughout the incarceration phase and better prepared us for the post-release supervisory work. Our presence in the three provincial prisons, together with our pre-sentence evaluations for the municipal courts in the immediate region, rendered us more inclusive yet. Our family service, which entailed a weekly group session for the spouses of offenders, as well as an individual counselling service, rounded out the clinical picture. Public education on criminal justice issues was carried out upon invitation to schools and various social and business clubs.

In summary, we were running at full tilt. Little did we realize that our Armageddon was just around the corner. We contended with everyday disputes and occasional setbacks fairly easily. It was two major, unrelated blows in the nineties, which decimated our organization and eventually sealed our fate.

THE BUREAUCRATIC EXPLOSION

~ the gathering storm

The 'nineties were to be crucial years in the history of the John Howard Society of Quebec. They would witness its transformation from a representative community-based entity into a diminutive force, casting a mere shadow of dissent. The combined effect of two major happenings, unrelated but equally devastating, would serve as the catalyst to ultimate demise. The final tally for JHSQ, registered only by the mid-nineties, would reveal a truncated organization foundering in a sea of bureaucratic harassment and emerging into a community sector that had been co-opted by immediate enticements of the politico-bureaucratic machine. As for myself, I would eventually return to my roots working face-to-face with incarcerated offenders. The institutional setting would have changed, not necessarily for the better, but the daily work would prove to be personally rewarding.

The year 1989, on the other hand, was an ambiguous one. It began as a harbinger of troubled times, a premonition of gathering storm clouds that would eventually burst in a vortex of insinuation, innuendo and recrimination. Nevertheless, it turned out to be noteworthy for me personally as it was the year I was elected Incoming President of a national organization concerned with criminal justice issues.

Several years before, I had set my sights on age fifty-five as a target date to reach my principal, professional goal: development of a correctional facility that made some sense. An institution designed and staffed to identify, study and work with the intricate problem of delinquent acting-out was both necessary and feasible. The experience of the failed attempt to recreate the Correctional Development Centre in the 'seventies and the unanswered proposal to initiate a Social Development Centre in the 'eighties still rankled. Nevertheless, the dream generated by the experience of the Dannemora project of the 'sixties remained alive. I had become acutely aware that no amount of institutional programming, nor any surfeit of professional expertise, would suffice to furnish tangible correctional results at the individual level. Unless the prevailing culture of "us" against "them" were to be eradicated, the best-intentioned efforts of the most qualified personnel would ultimately go for naught. Treatment-oriented professionals, as well as highly structured therapeutic programs, are of little or no avail so long as the underlying correctional philosophy and consequent practice fail to acknowledge and redress the prevailing dichotomy that precludes meaningful, clinical intervention.

Especially disheartening, however, is that when the topic of institutional sub-culture is brought up it is usually misunderstood. The problem is mistakenly seen as one-dimensional: the inmate alone defines the institutional milieu. In fact, the sub-culture is shaped by various interpersonal relationships, as much by those between staff and inmates as by those among the inmates themselves. Failure to recognize such an integral part of the overall interpersonal dynamic is, in itself, indicative of the unilateral nature of a contrived correctional process and in great part accounts for the evolution of a milieu characterized by suppression and control.

The introduction of women into the traditional custody and discipline role within the institution and the elevated level of schooling among front-line workers have altered the portrait of correctional personnel. The escalating militancy of the union and solidarity within the labour movement in general has affected the decision-making structure and contributed to further role delineation. Ultimately, everyday work performance and expectations have been affected. Nevertheless, staff-related issues such as these are seldom considered in an analysis of the cultural milieu that is an integral constituent of the incarceration process.

Equally important is the composition of the inmate population, an element that has changed dramatically and brought about a shift in the group dynamic as well. The widespread use of drugs and concomitant drug trafficking within the institutional perimeter, have resulted in a significant escalation in the practice of protective custody and brought about the rise of an enigmatic operation, euphemistically labelled "preventive security." The amplification of inmate rights has refashioned staff/inmate exchanges and, along with enhanced physical comforts, has contributed to a fortuitous reshaping of the institutional environment. Interestingly enough, whenever an ultra-conservative wind blows and demands are made for more restrictive measures, the angry insinuation is that the inmates somehow bequeathed these perceived excesses to themselves. In reality, the existing authority has unwittingly allowed the correctional process to evolve in this manner. Lack of foresight and a tendency toward management by crisis, frequently fuelled by political pressure, have succeeded in a helter-skelter growth pattern, rather than a planned development of a comprehensive correctional system drafted to cope with the fundamental issue of crime and delinquency.

Thus, by the end of 1989, I was aware my personal objective would never likely be attained; by the mid-nineties, I knew it as a certainty. The entire correctional field had been submerged under the tight control of the government agency. The stranglehold that Correctional Service Canada exercised was not limited to institutional living. Since the amalgamation of the Canadian Penitentiary Service with the National Parole Service in 1976, the emergent CSC steadily grew into an all-encompassing, costly bureaucratic organization. Its tentacles spread gradually but deliberately into all facets of the post-release phase of the offender's sentence. The input of community-based organizations became less effective due to the imposition of controls that resulted in a cloning of services and techniques. Initiatives from the community quarter were still entertained but those perceived to be outside the myopic view of government bureaucrats, were given short shrift. Anything seen as potentially advantageous to the enhancement of the corporate image would be accepted and later tailored down to a product beneficial to the organizational structure, at the expense of those it had been designed to serve. The muted voice of constructive criticism was gradually silenced through a combination of bureaucratic standards reinforced by remunerated contractual conformity.

*   *   *

One morning in January 1989 I took a call in my office from the District Director of Parole, René Rousseau. He was in charge of all CSC parole supervision in the greater Montreal area. René was an affable man, always trying to please but somewhat nervous, giving the impression of one who wished the daily pressures of work would just disappear. It was no small wonder he was anxious. He had responsibilities imposed upon him by an unforgiving bureaucracy while working in a volatile domain of unpredictable circumstances.

"Paul, the Enquiry Board has scheduled you for three this afternoon," he affirmed without preamble.

"René, I set my own work agenda," I replied tersely.

I immediately regretted my abruptness. I knew it wasn't his fault. He was merely following orders. However there is a tendency to shoot the messenger when he is the only one in one's sights.

"I have a full afternoon but, with a few cancellations, should be able to be there sometime between three-thirty and four," I conceded.

Some two weeks prior to this call, I had gotten wind of an enquiry to be held concerning the operations of a particular halfway house. Phil Young, Senior Member of the National Parole Board (NPB) in the Quebec Region, was both a colleague and a friend. He had mentioned in passing that there was to be a Board of Enquiry, ". . . in a few weeks time. They're looking into the operations of a halfway house that has received some complaints. They may call you to testify." What I didn't know was that an Enquiry Board was not necessarily restricted to a one-item agenda.

Phil was an ex-cop and not easily ruffled. I took his casual manner as simply his usual way of transmitting information. In my naiveté, I assumed that I would be called as one who had worked in the field in various settings, over a long period. Although we at John Howard did not operate a halfway house, I was thoroughly familiar with the concept of a transition facility and had some definite ideas as how it fit into the overall correctional picture. In hindsight, I realize I should have read a hint of caution in Phil's call.

I knew two of the three Board members, personally. Serge Lavallée was a well-informed, long-term bureaucrat at the Montreal office of NPB. At the time, he was Executive Director of the Quebec Region and was later to be appointed Vice-Chair of the Region. Claude Dumaine, a Franco-Manitoban, was Warden of a penitentiary in the Atlantic

Region of CSC. Both of these men knew me on a first-name basis. The third member, a woman out of Headquarters in Ottawa, was unknown to me. This was evidently a National Enquiry.

All in all, the hearing went very well. I was asked many questions, most of them open-ended. Thus I was able to expound on several issues and comment freely on what I saw as problematic in the correctional field; in other words, I was given ample time to put my foot in my mouth. The more specific questions regarding the daily practices of the JHSQ surprised me somewhat because they were common knowledge. I took my leave after some uninterrupted three hours, exiting the room on a friendly note with smiles and hearty handshakes all around. The entire experience as far as I was concerned was a cathartic one, having had the opportunity to ventilate before a competent Board of Enquiry, bent on examining the relevant issues and trying to find solutions that may improve a complex and challenging field; or so I surmised.

Well, I should have been awarded a medal for being pretentious, ingenuous or just plain stupid. When the questions seldom veered from the operations of the John Howard Society of Quebec, my suspicions should have been aroused. There were no allusions to any halfway house. My personal stance with regard to the authority structure in parole supervision and correctional policy in general became the main theme. Although I was beginning to feel closely questioned, I failed to realize I was an actual target of the enquiry.

It was not until some months later that I heard the first echo of my "performance." It was at a cocktail party that an acquaintance sidled up to me,

"I hear you were giving the Minster a hard time," he said with a pasted grin. I thought it was the liquor talking as the comment came out of the blue.

"Put your glass down you fool, you're not making any sense," I retorted lightly.

"I hear you told that enquiry the Minister doesn't know what he's talking about."

At the word "enquiry" I made the connection. The matter hadn't crossed my mind in the intervening months.

"What I said was that we in the field should be informing the Minister and not the other way around."

My clarification carried little import as my informant had already turned around to chat up some female presence. However, this brief piece of gossip was restored to my consciousness the moment I began to read the Report of the enquiry released in the autumn of 1989. It contained a twelve-page section on the John Howard Society of Quebec. It was basically a combination of half-truths, insinuations and inaccurate information. No one topic or allegation was of serious consequence but the summary conclusion was disingenuous and downright malicious. I was hurt, angry, and discouraged. I had been criticized in the past but when I felt it to be unwarranted, was able to consider the source and go on. In this instance, what bothered me most was not the report, in itself. I was able to consider the source. I was familiar with people who sacrifice personal integrity because of an innate lack of fortitude or simply for personal gain. Before the report reached me, however, it had undergone several revisions and had passed through the hands of several people I considered friends or, at least, friendly colleagues. They knew me well enough to recognize the deceitful nature of the allegations. I believe they could have and should have put a stop to it. They didn't. I could name them. I wont. They know who they are.

My initial reaction was to take legal action. I spoke with two lawyers, separately. Both were of the opinion that I possibly had grounds for a libel suit. I didn't pursue it and I'm not certain why. Suffice it to say that the intimation that I was particularly close to the West End Gang is patently false. I was equally close to the French, Italian and Jewish gangs. For that matter, it's what I do, professionally.

The other extremity of this bipolar year was my surprising election as Incoming President of the Canadian Criminal Justice Association. I had been on the Board of Directors since 1984. The Association, conjointly with the host provincial affiliate, organizes a National Congress every two years. A central feature of the Annual General Meeting at congress time is the election of the Executive Committee to work with the incumbent President. The system unfolds in such a manner that an Incoming President serves on the Executive for two years, proceeds to the presidency for the two subsequent years, then completes a final two years on the Executive as Past President. Thus, the person is committed to serve six years in three sequential roles. I was as surprised as those who know me best at my nomination, let alone my election. I have little trouble forming an opinion, letting it be known and insisting on it being adhered to by my subordinates. The position of Executive Director called for this type of management with my staff at John Howard. The leadership role of President of a Board of Directors, however, is entirely different. One brings a certain expertise related to a particular training and experience and thereby has a point of view to put forth. Nonetheless, the role is really akin to that of *primus inter pares* and not that of chief administrator responsible for final decisions. I was used to the latter capacity but this was something new, something with which I was not comfortable. I sensed it at the outset and the future would bear it out.

I would be less than forthright not to admit I was proud to be in this honorific position. Many prestigious personages over the years have held it and to be counted among them is certainly a boost to the ego. In my case, it happened at a delicate interval in my career, some weeks after the release of the Enquiry Report. The election served as a balm to my bruised feelings and helped me regain some self-assurance. Since the report is not published publicly the damage is pretty well limited to within the system. What makes it singularly pernicious, though, is that it rests in the hands of senior decision-makers in the correctional field. Their personal interpretation of the contents is unknown and any specific use of the findings is a mystery as well. Nevertheless, the report remains extant; the respected status of President of a national organization does nothing to alter this reality.

The CCJA, principally through its committees, studies new laws and evaluates modifications to existing laws. As well, it reviews government policies and practices within the criminal justice system and proffers changes where deemed necessary. Policy papers are prepared as a result of intensive study and debate in committee and, after submission to and acceptance by the Board, are presented to the concerned parties. Invited appearances before the appropriate parliamentary committee afford the opportunity for oral presentation and discussion. National issues are thereby dealt with by CCJA, along with the active support of various provincial affiliates. The treatment of matters of concern within specific provincial jurisdiction is normally spearheaded by the local affiliate and usually buttressed by the national body. Prison over-crowding which led to the notorious "double-bunking," Gun Control legislation and the Canadian Corrections and Release Act are examples of points in question that were studied, prepared and forwarded to the pertinent authorities.

The membership of CCJA is composed of people actively interested in criminal justice issues. Some work in the field, others are simply concerned citizens. All represent themselves, not an organization nor a specific interest group. This is especially so on the Board of Directors. In other words, I did not represent the John Howard Society of Quebec; I spoke for myself alone. The experience I gained working with JHSQ is obviously part of my overall package but I was not there to preach on behalf of the Society.

On the whole, my term on the Executive Committee, including the two years as President, was informative and rewarding. It gave me the opportunity to share ideas, opinions and suggestions with others who had interest and expertise in any one or more of the several facets of criminal justice. What had often appeared to me to be a relatively simple problem demanding a clear and concise answer, took on a more subtle hue when seen from the distance of national perspective. This also brought home that regional disparity demands a suppleness, which allows for a degree of autonomy in the development of policy and decision-making. By the same token, this panoramic outlook confirmed that the rationale underlying meaningful policy and consequent decision-making must originate from the field and not the converse. Criminal justice is essentially for those whom it serves and its efficacy is defined by the response to their needs. The inherent danger in any organization, principally one that provides a service to others, is the inadvertent susceptibility to function primarily for the prestige of the system or for the gratification of those who implement it. This systemic flaw has no innate antidote and is neutralized solely by the fortuitous awareness of discriminating members.

As I mentioned before, CCJA membership is made up of persons interested in criminal justice issues who are prepared to take some active role. Since the majority are individuals working in the field in some capacity or other, those elected to the Board of Directors are usually from either the private or the government sector within the domain of criminal justice. However, any member of the organization may attend a Board meeting and participate fully in the discussions with the sole restriction in voting. During my tenure as President, I had the privilege and pleasure of having a special member in attendance on a regular basis.

Gerry Ruygrok was special in many ways. As a private citizen, he did not work within the criminal justice system. He had, nonetheless, come through the system in a most heart-rending manner. He and his family were victims of a failure in the correctional process; his twenty-one-year old daughter had been murdered by a resident of the halfway house in which she was working. The Coroner's Inquest occasioned new and more restrictive measures as to both the selection of offenders for and the operation of halfway houses. These cautionary procedures were designed to help avoid serious errors in the future but provided little solace to the grieving victims. There is no persevering salve for victims of such a tragedy; feelings of loss, anger and frustration persist, as there are no word or actions to alleviate the pain.Some seek comfort by participating more actively in the subsequent judicial proceedings and later correctional process. They thereby hope to attain closure; others simply withdraw to the support of the extended family and circle of friends. Gerry took several concrete steps to activate constructive and realistic changes from the political structure down. His later participation in the CCJA allowed him a double-barrelled approach to this lifetime trauma.

Several people, including those at the CCJA office in Ottawa, had become aware of Gerry Ruygrok's presence. He had been making some headway by unobtrusively, yet resolutely, sensitizing politicians and senior bureaucrats in the government. There was a decided need for more direct input into the criminal justice system on the part of citizens as a whole and victims in particular. During the last several years there had been a ground swell of victim reaction to crime and what was often perceived as inconsequential punitive measures meted out to the perpetrators. Many victims and their advocates believed they were not being heard; that more attention, concern and protection were shown to offenders than to the victims of crime.

Although there was and still is merit to the allegation that not enough is done for victims, the main issue is what best can and should be done. Victims have a much greater say today than previously. However, it is open to question whether their input in any and all phases of the criminal justice system is well founded. It is certainly logical that the victim, as a direct casualty of the culpable behaviour, should have a noteworthy voice during the judicial proceedings. On the other hand, the cogency of a victim's participation in the later decision-making regarding conditional release is disputable.

Gerry Ruygrok's reaction to this traumatic experience was not limited to the normal visceral response to wanton violence. This self-effacing man persevered through endless months, leading into years, mustering all his inner strength to give some meaning to this senseless tragedy. He was encouraged to participate actively on the Policy Review Committee of the CCJA, an undertaking he accepted and worked diligently at for a number of years. In this capacity he was able to contribute directly to the review of current practice and development of new policies, which would ultimately affect the administration of justice in Canada. He was frequently one of the spokespersons for the Committee making presentations before the appropriate parliamentary committees. Apart from the considerable time and effort Gerry devoted to specific issues, his mere physical presence quickened the conscience of those with whom he came into contact. He was a taciturn, living reminder of the true aim and purpose of a criminal justice system; the furtherance of the human person may be attained, not through vindictiveness and the prolongation of violence, but in a spirit of support, comprehension and relevant change. Therefore, it is incumbent upon all to ensure that our lawmakers and administrators of justice discharge their duties with equity and compassion for both offenders and victims. It is only within this climate of reparation that society as a whole may be bettered.

My own participation in the Canadian Criminal Justice Association, which spanned more than twenty years, proved to be a personal growth experience. The one major regret I harbour to this day, nevertheless, is my failure to have striven arduously enough to alter the balance of power between the government quarter and the private sector. Although political incumbents are duly elected and thereby susceptible to eventual ouster, the bureaucratic structure upon which they depend has a life of its own; often the real power lies therein. I believe that voluntary organizations such as CCJA can and should adopt a role of watchdog, not only with respect to government policy but also to the operations of government agencies. Bureaucracies, necessary as they may be, are notoriously self-feeding. This mitotic process, if allowed to run unchecked, makes the structure an entity unto itself. Accountability ultimately becomes a catchword.

A central difficulty for non-governmental organizations (NGO), however, revolves around funding. NGOs that espouse popular issues, matters that touch the heartstrings, are able to raise funds directly from the general public. They may also benefit from government funding since support for subjects that garner public sympathy carry political value as well. Many NGOs, on the other hand, are frequently tied to important but unpopular or misunderstood matters of contention. The results of public fundraising, in this instance, are generally insubstantial. Thus dependence upon the government for financial support, whether straight from a particular ministry or through a government agency, places the supplicant in an awkward position. The weight of the advocacy role is mitigated by the real or imagined need to avoid biting the hand that feeds. This ambiguous posture leaves the door open for appeasement where a firm stand is called for. This is not to imply that a like situation would necessarily be a conscious reaction; nonetheless, the reality of the threat is present.

It is in this area of governmental/non-governmental relations that I bear an acute sense of frustration and failure for my part on the Board of CCJA. I too often sat mute, as the term "partnership" was bandied about as a palliative for the wounded feelings of those who had, once again, participated in a consultative process after the decision had already been reached. Unfortunately I have nothing to offer but acknowledgement of the fact that I had my chance to run with the ball and fumbled.

*   *   *

Despite the turmoil of the year 1989, the new decade was ushered in with relative ease. The John Howard Society of Quebec had been operating two separate but coordinated offices since 1987. The smaller of the two, whose legal name was John Howard House Inc. (JHH Inc), was primarily involved in parole supervision but occasionally completed community assessments for cases they were supervising. The individual supervisors thus had an opportunity to meet family members of their parolees and evaluate employment resources as well. This small group of professional workers also participated in case conferences with the staff of the larger office. In effect, both offices shared the myriad services provided by the organization as a whole.

The larger office, comprised of some fifteen workers, was my permanent station. Unlike JHH Inc., this was not a private corporation but a service unit within a para-public entity, Ville Marie Social Service Centre (VMSSC). The parent organization had its own Board of Directors and was an integral part of the provincial social service network. Our entire funding for this office came from the Ministry of Social Affairs and the budget was managed by VMSSC. It was this larger office that was in peril though no hint of threat was evident at the beginning of the year. The Executive Director of VMSSC, John Walker, was a pleasant, unassuming individual who did not fit the typical bureaucratic mould. He had no pretensions to expertise in criminal justice matters and graciously allowed us a free hand in operating our business. His only insistence was that I attend a monthly meeting, an information session, with a middle management administrator.

Bruce Garside was a lay back type whose main interest was working with people rather than shuffling papers. A social worker by profession, Bruce gave the impression of one who had been parachuted into this administrative position rather than someone who had actively sought after it. Although he maintained a suitable appearance of seriousness about the task at hand, he never convinced me that he considered our joint assignment any more momentous than I did. He accepted my regularly stated reluctance with patient amusement. At one of our meetings in the early spring, he arrived at the office with a peculiar grin on his face. Before a word was spoken he pulled out some forms from his briefcase and his grin immediately widened. The bureaucratic bosses, at the ministry level, had devised a format that was supposed to assess current operations in the various units and lead to "strategic planning". It made me think of the notorious five year plans in the Soviet Union.

"Bruce this in no way applies to the kind of work we do here. Our bloody clients would have to be included in any strategy; now wouldn't that be something!" I said in exasperation. We had now been at it about twenty minutes.

Garside looked up at me from across the desk, "I somehow thought you'd put up some resistance but it comes down from the top. It's got to be done," he stated with feigned authority. He knew the exercise was fruitless but was in no position to admit it.

"You know damn well this will all go by the wayside eventually. As soon as there's another shuffle at the top of the civil service, the new kid on the block will scrap it and come up with his own stroke of genius," I continued.

Although my obstinacy was the result of a natural disdain for anything but the barest bureaucratic procedures, my words did have a certain prophetic quality to them. It was only a matter of weeks after this meeting that the news broke; a major decision had been taken at the ministry. The Social Service Centres were to be gradually dismantled. The first operational units to go would be those that provided services to adults. All our services were directed toward adults: offenders and their families; juvenile delinquency in Quebec was under the aegis of the Department of Youth Protection. In effect, the John Howard office, officially a service unit of VMSSC, was to be closed. In fact some three months later my personnel, as unionized employees, had been directed to various departments within the remaining parent organization. As for myself, a middle manager in bureaucratic jargon, was dispensable; the one proviso, they were obliged to carry my salary for the next two years. So much for the strategic planning.

In point of fact though, I had some planning of my own to do. I failed to see how this move was to save money for the ministry. In the first place, the salaries of all permanent employees were guaranteed, in our case approximately eighty percent of our budget. Furthermore, ours was the only service unit that actually generated funds. The monthly payments from the federal parole contract went directly into the coffers of Ville Marie and consequently to the ministry. The annual amount almost compensated for the balance of the budgetary expenditures to finance JHSQ. Particularly galling, however, was that this move was never mentioned to me or discussed with any member of our Advisory Board. The last remaining hope was to be at the publicly held VMSSC Board meeting. As it turned out, this was an exercise in futility; a public spectacle where a Board of Directors shamefacedly rubber-stamped a questionable political decision.

In summary, the John Howard Society of Quebec, which had been brought into the public domain through political decree in 1973-74, was now being abandoned by a similar unconscionable edict. The community-at-large was deprived of a valid, comprehensive service in the field of criminal justice by a politico-bureaucratic stroke of the pen. The only work that could continue was that contracted with Correctional Service Canada. Parole supervision and community assessments would now be handled entirely by JHH Inc. Services such as pre-sentence evaluations for the Municipal Courts in and around greater Montreal, along with our long-standing family program would cease immediately. Our regular presence in the federal penitentiaries and provincial prisons in Quebec, the linchpin service that underscored our longitudinal approach to the basic problem, would likewise be terminated. In essence, the composite services that fashioned an extensive, all-embracing approach to the complex problem of crime and delinquency were simply to vanish.

Obviously, adjustments had to be made. The number of parolees to be supervised by JHH Inc., along with community assessments, had suddenly increased significantly. More personnel had to be found to carry the workload. Fortunately, experienced people were available since not all our former staff were prepared to work just anywhere in the Ville Marie system. The social workers could adapt fairly easily to a different clientele since their university training had been diversified. This was not the case with those with a background in criminology. Thus, through mutual assistance, we were able to fill the gap and complete the contractual work.

The John Howard Society of Quebec was once again a private corporation. Our Board of Directors was necessarily revived as they would now have power to make decisions, as opposed to the former Advisory Board which had no real say whatsoever This would make our organization similar to the John Howard Societies across Canada. The one significant difference would be in the sensitive area of funding. The other Societies had a solid base in their own communities. We, on the other hand, had been virtually excised from community support by the law change in 1973-74. Furthermore, we did not have access to the federal grant, administered by John Howard of Canada, during our years in the para-public system. It was not in 1990 that we could expect the other Societies to divvy up the grant in a new manner and diminish their own income so as to finance us.

At that instant, however, funding was not the central issue. We were able to complete the lease within the year and then move to smaller, less costly premises. The contractual work we had with CSC was sufficient to meet our needs, especially since my own salary would be covered for the next two years. What did trouble me, though, was our complete dependence upon CSC. In fact, they were our sole source of revenue. This was a matter of concern at every Board meeting. As there was no easy solution, we tried to tread softly; evidently, not softly enough. The second devastating happening was a short four years down the road.

I was well aware at the outset of the new arrangement that our organization was now a mere shadow of what it had been. What had distinguished our work from that of most community-based organizations involved in the correctional field had been our comprehensive approach based on clinical intervention. The various services were interdependent. The relatively small size of our operation allowed for a more personal and integrated access to the problematic situation; we knew our clients and their families and they knew us. This was no longer to be. Despite individual efforts to maintain a clinical approach, the total operation had been reduced to a mechanical exercise similar to the approach we censured so vehemently. This had to be a temporary circumstance. In good conscience we could not continue in this manner indefinitely. In fact it was to change; it was to worsen.

It was only a matter of time when I realized things had changed for me personally. My official position remained Executive Director, now a somewhat presumptuous title since I had much less responsibility than before. The staff now totalled six to handle parole supervision and a pool of three to help out with excess community assessments. Except for our secretary, all personnel were under contract rather than engaged as employees. Parole supervision, as well as the completion of community assessments, is frequently carried out at times other than during the normal nine to five workday and often outside the office. The most convenient modus operandi, both for myself as employer and for the workers, was to hire them under contract and remunerate them on a case-to-case basis. Apart from interviews held within the confines of the office, the premises were for secretarial duties and case conferences.

My own involvement, after selecting the personnel, was primarily to assign the cases to the appropriate people and coordinate case conferences. Parole supervision, like any clinical work, is contingent upon a workable relationship between supervisor and client; personalities should be compatible and the experiential background of the individual worker relevant to the case dynamic. Thus, knowing one's staff is of prime importance. As well, the case conference allows for an ongoing assessment of the clinical relationship and an occasion for appropriate adjustments where necessary. Nevertheless, my overall commitment was less intense than before. There was no opportunity to organize and synthesize matters into a cohesive clinical whole, given that there no longer was a diversity of programs. A certain amorphous lethargy was gradually seeping into my daily undertakings. The work was becoming increasingly impersonal and automatic. If it weren't for serendipity at various times over the years, I don't know where my career would have veered at certain junctures. This, as it happened, was one of those moments.

I was doing some routine work at the office one day in the early spring of 1993. The telephone rang. It was George, the old-school bank robber from my Leclerc days in the 'seventies. I knew he had been released from a penitentiary in Ontario some months back and was presently in a halfway house in St-Jerome.

"How are ya' doin' Paul? We're almost back on the street full time now," he used for openers. That imperial we brought back some fond memories. Things had been far from perfect in those days but somehow there seemed to be more optimism and hope then.

"Pretty good George, how about yourself?"

"Well, just about finished with the halfway gig, should be home in three weeks."

George bantered on for a few minutes, always pleasant and polite, then got to the real reason for his call, "There was a guy I met in Joyceville, says he knows you, René, don't know if you remember him?"

"Le jeune," how could one forget? He got this name when he entered Bordeaux at the age of seventeen, in the early fifties. The moniker was not given because of his age; seventeen was not young for Bordeaux in that era. René must have really looked like a kid; when I first met him in 1962 he was three years older than I but had the facial appearance of an adolescent. He was on his third penitentiary sentence then.

"Sure I remember him. I haven't seen him since the early seventies though, how is he anyway?"

"Well he's got six in on a twenty-five year bit but he's in medium so he's okay."

The important thing is to be doing good time; obviously everything's relative.

"What the hell's he doin' in Kingston?" It was not unusual for a Montreal guy to be in the Ontario Region but I knew that René had had some serious trouble there some years back.

"The score went down in TO, so he ended up there. But that's the point, he wants to transfer here and wonders if you can help!"

As it turned out I was able to give a hand, however negligible. I contacted the Warden at Leclerc who not only knew René, but also had spoken to him on a recent visit to Joyceville penitentiary, and had told him that he would accept him anytime. I then contacted his Classification Officer in Joyceville, only to find out the transfer was already in the works. The phone calls may have accelerated matters. In any case, René arrived at Leclerc in August 1993.

It was then I decided to remedy my ennui. I spoke with Warden Pierre Viau about setting up a group for long-term offenders. He had no objection, not only because there was no cost for the institution to bear, but also because Pierre came up through the ranks and knew the value of personal contact with the inmate population. He had begun his career in the now defunct St. Vincent de Paul penitentiary and knew me from there. I believe he appreciated my offer.

I set out on my own in September 1993. My plan was to work a half-day per week with a group in Leclerc. I not only could afford the time but really believed that working directly with the men would give me the boost I needed and, at the same time, give the John Howard some presence in the penitentiary. I set the groundwork by meeting first with René and broached the subject with him.

"I think a group's a good idea," he replied to my query but quickly added, "You know, Paul, there's not much contact with anyone in here."

I didn't realize how acute the problem was. Furthermore, it was only sometime later I became aware that the institutional personnel saw no problem whatsoever. Computers ruled the day. So long as reports were compiled and deadlines met, there was no problem. Who wrote the reports and the authenticity and relevance of their content seemed to have little import in the equation. Thirteen years had elapsed since I had worked within the perimeter of Leclerc and much had changed. Internal and external security controls had been built up considerably. Few temporary absences were now granted and there had been a significant decrease in the number of inmates released on parole. Leclerc seemed to be a real parking lot. The most noteworthy change, however, was in relations between inmates and staff.

Correctional institutions have a built-in dichotomy between the involuntary population and those officially in control. Traditionally, this has been between guards and inmates, the watchers and the watched. As the role of correctional officer expanded and his duties demanded a more proximate working with the inmate, the gulf between the two was bridged physically but with no regard for the emotional and attitudinal contrariety. A comprehensive learning process, encompassing both sides, would be a prerequisite to any success at linking these antagonistic groups. Such an endeavour would presuppose recognition of a problem and acknowledgement that, in a learning process, both sides have something to contribute and to learn. There has never been evidence that CSC, at any level, is aware of the basic problem.

I did not immediately grasp the extent to which this gap between inmate and staff had evolved. I began to ask questions when I heard terms such as criminogenic factors, risk assessments and correctional plans being bandied about without ever being able to put a face on those employing the terminology. I started to uncover case managers who did just that, managed cases. It seemed to be a rarity when they actually spoke to the people whose lives supposedly furnished the information to fill those cases. Psychological evaluations and follow-ups were running rampant but I was never able to unearth a simple, but definite, "there is no need." Then again, it was apparent that anyone could and would request an evaluation or follow-up. Obviously, there was a need; the question was, whose need?

I certainly had fallen into a new world. This was not the Leclerc of the 'seventies. All would agree to that; not all would agree which direction the change had taken. As to staff/inmate relations, what I further observed was that the antipathy was palpable on both sides and, more disturbing yet, had generalized to the institutional personnel as a whole. Customary hostility in the past ran between guard and inmate and, under more specific conditions, it targeted the major decision-makers. However, there had always been a resource person available to act as a buffer between the opposing parties, usually in the person of the Classification Officer.

This was no longer so. The Case Management Officer (CMO) with duties that unwittingly encouraged an impersonal approach to the work, had replaced the Classification Officer. Compilation of information and completion of written reports was a full time job; subsequent entries into the unforgiving embrace of cybernetics completed the major task. Unfortunately, this also provided a haven for those who preferred the solace of a closed office, to the sometimes brusque and demanding atmosphere of a confrontational setting. As a result, frustrations within the inmate population built up, creating pervasive, free-floating animosity, which encompassed all personnel.

Thus, I felt I was stepping into a cauldron simmering in deceit and mistrust. This was not the 'sixties, however. The potential for violence now seemed to remain a potential; there was a facade of calm and well being to the casual observer and those who wished it to be so. This deceptive veneer was disrupted only occasionally by individual acts of aggression. The days of group rebellion seemed to be relics of the past. Some sort of mutual accord on the part of the real powers within the institution had evidently been struck, although it was difficult to ascertain what this *entente cordiale* consisted of in reality. Even though the security perimeter inside the penitentiary had been tightened considerably, there appeared to be almost complete licence within the restricted area. In general, for those interested in simply doing time it was the place to be; for those who hoped to prepare for release, however, the experience was quite to the contrary. This overall state of affairs led to the most absurd situations, which would test the credence of the most gullible.

Even though I sensed a vital change in the institutional life, the full impact did not hit me immediately. I was only in the penitentiary a half-day per week and this time was taken up entirely with the group. It was not until some two years later when my work inside would increase significantly. Although this later, more complete implication was self-satisfying in itself, it was not the result of personal choice. It was, rather, the consequence of a critical happening, which ultimately guaranteed the demise of the John Howard Society of Quebec as a meaningful community-based organization in criminal justice. It also signalled the dénouement of my professional career.

*   *   *

It was early December 1994 when I received a letter from Correctional Service Canada. The appendage Personal and Confidential, clearly underlined on the envelope, caught my attention and immediately raised my anxiety level. I was not used to receiving congratulatory missives from CSC. Although I was not aware of any recent increase in the tension level between our office and the government agency, I opened the envelope with a mixture of interest and apprehension. The communication came from Gilles Thibault, Director of Parole for the greater Montreal area. The message, couched in polite verbiage, was clear: our parole contract would not be renewed for the 1995-96 year. At that instant I disregarded the stated reasons; the bottom line was evident. The very existence of the John Howard Society of Quebec was threatened. The only other source of revenue we had, the contract for community assessments, did not provide enough funding to maintain an office, even one reduced to skeletal staffing.

Patrick Wickham, President of our Board, was the man to contact. Wickham was a notary by profession, trained in law. Now retired, he had completed a successful career in his chosen field and was well recognized as a competent professional. It was through his voluntary work, however, that he made a significant contribution to society as a whole. He spent a lifetime giving of himself to the betterment of the disadvantaged by taking an active part in fundraising, mustering political forces and sensitizing the more favoured to the needs of the deprived. He had been on the John Howard Board for more than twenty years, including the lean years of the Advisory Board, and served as President since 1988.

> "Pat, we have a serious problem. The CSC is terminating our parole contract as of this coming April. I received a notice from mid-management but this has to be coming from higher up," I recounted to him over the 'phone that same day.

I had not mentioned a word to my staff as yet. It was the Christmas season. As a matter of fact our annual Christmas supper at *Ristorante Boca Doro* was two days away. An excess of pasta, veal and wine was in the planning, a welcome respite from the daily work routine. The long-suffering Dante, owner and *maitre* d' of the restaurant, anticipated our appearance with guarded amusement. He would, as always, graciously tolerate our shenanigans, which included boisterous singing and dancing around the tables. This purgative experience helped us to bond and I felt strongly that the festivities should not be marred by the distressing news.

Pat Wickham was quick to recognize the gravity of our situation and reacted immediately, "I'll get in touch with Warren Allmand. He'll go to bat for us!"

The Hon. Warren Allmand had been the Member of Parliament for Notre Dame de Grace for some thirty years. He had served as Solicitor General and assumed a leading role in doing away with the death penalty. At this particular time, he was Chair, Standing Committee on Justice and Legal Affairs. Pat knew him personally and was able to set up a meeting. The three of us met in Allmand's office in NDG before the Christmas break.

I had never met Allmand prior to this. I was certainly aware of his reputation as a fighter, a man of principle. Within a matter of minutes his keen intelligence shone through; he asked few questions but the few were incisive. His strength in this instance lay in his ability to create an atmosphere of warmth and acceptance, an ambience conducive to candid dialogue. He also knew how to listen. This was an insightful man who grasped the total picture quickly.

"I'll bring the matter to the proper authorities. I'm sure you realize nothing can be done before the New Year. Parliament is in recess. Ottawa's a ghost town right now." It was the twentieth of December.

We left the meeting satisfied. I had had the opportunity to express how I saw the problems between CSC and JHSQ. It was a meeting that should have taken place with the correctional authorities themselves; perhaps the current crisis could have been avoided. However, this is not how government bureaucracies work. The top echelon usually delegates downwards, the assumption being that the underlings are necessarily on the same page as those above. Thus open discussion to resolve differences, if they take place at all, occur with individuals who frequently carry mixed messages, have a skewed vision of the total picture and seldom have any real power to make decisions. The end result is that problems are allowed to fester until such time that surgery is seemingly the only option.

The ensuing sixteen months proved to be the most harrowing time of my career. I had worked with offenders of all types, in the community and in various kinds of penal institutions; threatening situations were not foreign to me. However, nothing prepared me for this. The insinuations, prevarications and outright misinformation, whether given maliciously or as a result of ignorance, were overwhelming. Once the battle lines were drawn a protracted conflict ensued and enveloped senior correctional officials, three stand-up politicians and the heads of both a national and a province-wide association. It finally reached the office of the Solicitor General and from that point a solution was to be determined. The final result was that a contract for institutional work rather than parole supervision in the community, was agreed upon and subsequently signed. At first blush, it seemed that fairness had won out. It was only a short time later it became evident where the real power lay and that assurances could be ethereal and proffered only to assuage feelings in the immediate.

When I finally got around to re-reading the original letter from CSC I became aware of the stated reasons not to renew the parole contract. The grounds were threefold: there had been a significant decrease in the number of men released under supervision within the greater Montreal area; as a result of several quality control reports; and, due to the findings of an enquiry board into a specific case. The letter went on to acknowledge my personal implication in the supervisory process and that this direct involvement was not in question. Finally, M.Thibault states his intention to share with me the specific recommendations of the enquiry board.

I spoke with him on the 'phone, Jan.5, 1995 after having carefully read his dispatch of the previous month. I expressed firm disagreement with his decision to terminate the contract and vehemently protested the causes cited for the action. This was the first verbal communication with anyone from CSC since reception of the notice in December. I stated my objections to the three given reasons, in chronological order.

In the first place, any reduction in the number of offenders released on parole was the sole responsibility of CSC in preparing the cases on time and the National Parole Board in scheduling a hearing and arriving at a decision. No community-based organization had any input into this process and should not be penalized because of tardy or questionable procedures. In any case, there was no shortage of candidates for possible release. The overcrowding in penitentiaries at the time had led to the notorious "double-bunking" and was a related problem, best addressed by open and frank discussions that must include community-based partners.

Secondly, the allusion to quality control reports was misleading. JHSQ had contracted for parole supervision for well over twenty years and, during this time, has never altered its basic approach: working with the offender as an individual. What had changed over the years was the CSC approach. It had become an increasingly impersonal, bureaucratic system; an indiscriminate method of offender categories and group evaluative scales based, almost exclusively, on the particular crime. The end result was a management of offender files rather than the clinical supervision of a distinctive person. Repeated efforts had been made by CSC to clone JHSQ to this practice so as to quench the bureaucratic thirst for conformity, masking as quality.

The third point was accentuated when M. Thibault had said he was acting upon recommendations in the enquiry report. I retorted that I had not seen the report, only to be informed cursorily that the recommendations would be forthcoming shortly.

"Gilles, what about the bloody report?" My blood was beginning to boil.

"I've been told you'll have to go through 'Access to Information' to get the full report," he replied sheepishly. Gilles was not a bad guy he was only following orders. Sound familiar?

Well, here we were. Threatened with extinction. CSC had acted as judge, jury, and executioner. A seriously crippling blow had been struck yet we the victims were denied ready access to a supposed catalyst. I kept our Board apprised of the circumstances in a written brief submitted to our President. It was in this missive I elaborated certain points so as to make sure all parties concerned would have a true perspective on the entire matter. Behind the assertion that an important reduction in the number of men released on parole, was the inference that the decision was in part a cost cutting measure; there own employees, whose caseloads had evidently been reduced, could assume the case supervision. In actual fact, however, it is cost-efficient to contract out for parole supervision services. The CSC themselves admit that it costs approximately thirty-five percent more to have the supervision carried out by their own personnel.

By the time I completed this summary of facts, I had received and perused the one page document containing the recommendations of the enquiry board. There were three recommendations, two of which were germane to the John Howard. One suggested that the District Director of Parole and the Executive Director of John Howard establish, jointly, an internal mechanism of quality control to assure compliance with respect to policies, procedures and standards of supervision. The other suggested that, as a minimum requirement, there be a formal case conference including both the liaison officer from CSC and the supervisors of the John Howard for every case supervised by our office. There was not even a hint, in the recommendations of the enquiry board, that the parole contract not be renewed.

On the other hand, what did come through clearly was ignorance of both an oral and a written tradition of supervision by community-based organizations. All parties had always officially recognized responsibility for the clinical supervision of the individual case to rest with the private-sector organization. No self-respecting professional entity would accept otherwise. In point of fact, a joint committee of senior officials of the CSC regional office, together with representatives from community-based organizations involved in parole supervision, had produced a document defining the role of the liaison officer. The "*sous-comité de définition de tâches de l'agent de liaison*" was established principally to assure the autonomy of private agencies with respect to parole supervision. This joint committee dated back to 1989-90. Obviously the enquiry board, despite the fact that it was composed almost entirely of government personnel, was unaware of this agreement or simply chose to ignore it. Their recommendation regarding a case conference between the CSC liaison officer and the case supervisor of the private agency attests to this.

The entire issue of quality control is related to the enigmatic role of the liaison officer. The term "*agent de liaison*" implies a constant figure who represents a particular viewpoint. In fact, this was never the case. The truth of the matter was that, in the year 1994, there had been five different liaison officers, each of whom had brought their own nuance to the role. This nuance ran the gamut from professional respect for clinical intervention to outright attempt at rigid control. What complicated the matter further was the introduction of the "*responsable clinique*" at the local CSC office. These individuals, four over the previous year, had attempted to exert their measure of control over cases assigned to JHSQ as well. Despite the fact that the autonomy of JHSQ supervision in clinical matters was given official sanction, some "*responsable clinique*" had no ethical qualms about altering recommendations made by our office to the paroling authorities; adding comments to reports on offenders they had never encountered was common practice.

The last comment in my brief to our Board was a reference to the closing paragraph of the one-page copy of recommendations I had received from M. Thibault. After enunciating the recommendations, this final paragraph requests that, should the Regional Deputy-Commissioner or the Director of Parole for greater Montreal have any questions as to the exactitude of the facts of the enquiry report, they should be addressed before the 12th of December. Obviously they had no questions since their definitive letter to us was dated Dec. 2nd. I further noted that no comments, questions or corrections had been asked of the target of the enquiry, the JHSQ. Then again, we had not even been invited to read the enquiry report as yet.

This information package was forwarded to Pat Wickham, Jan.16, 1995. Interestingly enough, I received a phone call from Jim MacLatchie, Executive Director of John Howard of Canada (JHSC) that same day.

> "Paul, I heard from Edwards (Commissioner of Corrections) recently that there was a possibility you're parole contract would not be renewed," he said in a questioning tone.

I had not informed Jim of our problem as yet. It must be understood that there is no line of authority between JHSC and any provincial society. JHSC is really an association of the various John Howard Socities throughout Canada, all of who are autonomous. Evidently I recognized Jim as a friendly partner but had not wanted to burden him with our situation right away. It was equally evident that our dispute with the Quebec Regional Office had reached National Headquarters of CSC. This was not all bad; sometimes it takes a few waves to force a large bureaucracy to respond.

MacLatchie related that he had told the Commissioner he would contact me, get more information and see if some plausible solution could be reached. During our conversation he asked me to consider the intervention of a third party.

> "You know, I'm not exactly a disinterested party, so I would not suggest myself but would you consider someone like Jim Phelps?"

MacLatchie was a gracious and self-effacing man. He would not suggest himself because he knew he would not be perceived as an objective source. In fact though, the man he was proposing was a senior CSC official, Senior Deputy Commissioner at the time; at first glance, not exactly "a disinterested party" either.

Jim Phelps was a psychologist by training but had spent most of his career in administrative positions. He was an intelligent man with a vast experience in the correctional field, having come up through the ranks in parole, institutional work and both regional and national office administration. He was known as a strict boss who tolerated neither fools nor shirkers. I knew him as a straight shooter who would not support an organization simply because he was an employee. I readily accepted MacLatchie's idea.

It was about a week later I learned that both Commissioner Edwards and his deputy Jim Phelps were open to the proposal that Phelps act as mediator. In a subsequent telephone conversation he made it clear to me how he saw his role in the matter,

> ". . . I'm not about to tell the Quebec Region what to do but I'll try to open up lines of communication." This alone was a great relief to me, as I firmly believed our point of view had not been heard. The date was January 31st, about 9:30 am. He said he would be in my office Friday, February 3rd. His last words, however, were less encouraging: "I will be seeing Jean-Claude today (Jean-Claude Perron, Regional Deputy Commissioner). If everything is OK with him I'll see you Friday morning. If everything's not OK, I'll get back to you by 'phone."

I received the call at 12:30 that same day. In summary, Perron ". . . was adamant, would not budge. When I said to him *'si la porte est complètement fermée*, Jean-Claude, *il* n'y a *rien* a *discuter,'* he hedged a little." The final compromise, according to Phelps, was that Perron grudgingly said that I could set up a meeting with Gilles Thibault but that if anything could be worked out "they would need written guarantees . . ."

This latest turn of events was less than encouraging. I felt we were back to square one. There still seemed to be a conscious attempt to delay our access to the enquiry report. Also, the recommendations of this report, which were alleged to be part of the reason not to renew the contract, did not seem pertinent to this drastic decision. I found out, shortly thereafter, the meeting in Ottawa on Jan. 31st had not been limited to Perron and Phelps but also included Commissioner Edwards and Perron's principal assistant, Guy Villeneuve. The agreement, among these four officials of CSC, was that I could initiate contact with M. Thibault so as to open up communications. It was further agreed that Phelps was to advise me and Perron was to advise Thibault.

I was literally stunned to discover at a luncheon meeting with Thibault on February 13th that he was unaware of any possibility of contract renewal. In response to my questions, he insisted that the only word he had from Perron was ". . . someone from Ottawa, perhaps Mr. Edwards, would be calling me." He went on to say, however, that he had heard from no one in Ottawa. I knew the duplicitous dealings of CSC had reached new depths when Thibault expressed surprise at the tact I was taking.

> "You know Paul, Jean-Claude has already stated openly to the Union, the ASRS and the Institutional Directors that the parole contract with John Howard will not be renewed."

I now considered the charade over. I left the meeting and later that day phoned Phelps in Ottawa. I recounted to him what had happened or, more accurately, what had not happened at the encounter with Thibault. Certainly no lines of communication had been opened. Phelps reiterated the terms the four CSC officials had agreed to at their meeting and also who was to advise whom. He seemed genuinely dismayed and not a little embarrassed at the deception.

While this pretence was being acted out over the period Jan.16th to Feb.13th, our Board President had not been sitting idly by. He had forwarded summary information to Warren Allmand and, in the interim, had engaged the interest and involvement of another political acquaintance, Clifford Lincoln, Member of Parliament for Lac St. Louis and staunch supporter of community participation. Both men were made aware of events as they unfolded. Pressure was evidently beginning to build and I was invited to attend a meeting to be held in M.Perron's office on Feb.17th, only four days after my abortive meeting with M.Thibault. Obviously somebody above had said something. I didn't know what to expect but had known Jean-Claude long enough to appreciate that pangs of conscience had not been the triggering mechanism to institute this latest encounter. As expected, I went willingly but warily.

The meeting, which included Perron, Villeneuve, and Thibault, was cordial. After all these men occupied administrative positions but were also professionally trained criminologists. They knew how to interview; they allowed me to put forth my point of view. What they were really doing was encouraging me to ventilate. I explained that the difficulties we had with CSC were not with established standards of supervision but with a rigid interpretation of policies and procedures, which led to a direct interference into the clinical supervision of each case. I gave concrete examples to demonstrate the usurpation of our fundamental responsibility; as well, how this course of action resulted in a duplication of services, which was both costly and administratively cumbersome.

At the end of the meeting, Perron suddenly stated he had decided to bring in a three-man team to look into the matter. This was obviously a pre-meeting decision; Jean-Claude was Regional Deputy-Commissioner for good reasons. He was an intelligent and astute administrator. He was also controlling and highly manipulative, with colleagues and adversaries alike. All of these traits served him well in this high-powered position. It was Perron who had approached me personally in 1986 with the proposition to extend our parole contract; it was the same man who now held both the hammer and the nails that could seal our coffin. I expressed surprise and no little apprehension at this latest measure. It smacked of previous "evaluations."

In fact, I was not far off the mark. The three-man team visited our premises on Feb. 27th. I had decided three of our more experienced supervisors would attend the get-together. I believed this would deflect some of the attention away from me, as the confrontation was becoming increasingly personal. I wanted the visitors to have an opportunity to hear from others. Our approach to supervision perhaps could be best explained from the point of view of the immediate supervisor. As well, day-to-day problematic situations as perceived by the John Howard worker could be enlightening.

This was not to be so. The inquisitorial tone of the meeting was set at the outset. The John Howard had a contract containing specific stipulations that were not adhered to in every instance. Any attempt to suggest differing interpretations of standards or particular contractual demands were merely brushed aside with a reference to the fact that the contract must be followed to the letter. This pervasive patronizing attitude poisoned the setting and effectively curbed any constructive discussion. The fact that our supervisors present were university graduates whose experience in the correctional field ranged from fifteen to twenty-seven years had no bearing whatsoever. The fact that we were a relatively small group, who were able to work in tandem, sharing experiences and expertise on a daily basis, carried no weight. It was clear that the veneer of professional respect and cooperation had worn so thin as to belie any notion of partnership.

If the encounter had any benefit whatsoever, it cemented relationships within the office. Our front-line workers, faced with the ongoing interference of petty bureaucrats, now had encountered the harassment of the major league players. I held a session with my staff after the inquisitors had left. Once the initial reaction of disbelief had dissipated we didn't know whether to laugh or cry. The insult was felt; we had to consider the source. I spent the remainder of the evening preparing up to date notes for our Board. The principal message was that we had been hoodwinked once again by the CSC machine, that hypocritical body which imposes such stringent demands of transparency upon offenders under its suppressive control. Equally important in my communication, however, was the admonition that any literal interpretation of the parole contract reduced parole supervision to a mere clerical task. This was unconscionable and we had to carry on.

Perhaps we at the JHSQ had been working under the illusion that the "spirit" of the contract takes precedence over the "letter." After all, we were working in a people business where certainties are the exception, not the rule. We were trying to assist offenders make a crime-free adjustment to life in the community. Our subjects were men with a history of pronounced difficulty respecting the established rules of society. The added constraints and conditions placed on them upon release were basically artificial, supposedly designed to be an aid to reintegration and not to be imposed as a set of hurdles to make the path more difficult. However, as the public image of the government organization began to rank higher than the task on hand, the goal became ambiguous and the means more important than the end. Thus a "one size fits all" mentality gradually supplanted any emphasis on interpersonal relationships.

It was toward the end of March we were made aware of a reply sent by the Hon. Herb Gray, Solicitor General of Canada, to Warren Allmand in response to a letter the latter had sent some time before. The content was in reference to our situation in Quebec. Normally this would be an excellent omen, the very fact that the matter had reached the top. However, one paragraph was disturbing because it was factually inaccurate. Obviously the Solicitor General, responsible politically for CSC, went to them for information and was given one version of the situation. Several points needed clarification, a result that could be attained only through open, two-way communication. This had never come about as yet and, as it turned out, never would. The paragraph, which was completely erroneous, bears quoting:

> "CSC authorities met on several occasions with Montreal J.H.H.Inc. Executive Director, Mr. Paul Williams, in order to ensure that CSC's expectations were clear. Mr. Williams was aware that if he did not meet CSC's supervision standards and procedures the contract would not be renewed for fiscal year 1995-96."

This statement is patently false. The fact is my last meeting with M.Perron, prior to our being advised that the contract would not be renewed, had been in 1990. Similarly, the last meeting with M.Thibault or with M. Saulnier (Office Manager of the local CSC parole office) had been more than a year before. Moreover, the first mention that the parole contract was in jeopardy was the written notice that it would not be renewed, dated Dec.2, 1994. Naturally, Mr.Gray would not have been made aware of any of this. By the time his request for information had filtered down through the bureaucratic system and back up, it is not surprising that a sanitized version of happenings brought forth a skewed picture. After all, the information ultimately emanated from the same office that not only had been stonewalling us but had also refused a request for a face-to-face sit down with two significant representatives of community services.

Mme Johanne Vallée, *Directrice Generale* of *l'association des services de rehabilitation sociale du québec*, along with Jim MacLatchie, Executive Director of John Howard of Canada, had asked for a meeting with the Regional authorities to discuss the impasse. These two representatives of the community-at-large in criminal justice, one at the provincial level and the other at the national level, thought it an important enough issue to warrant an in-depth encounter. The Regional Office of CSC thought otherwise. None of this was related to the Minister.

About this time, a third ally was solicited in the person of the Hon. Sheila Finestone who happened to be the Member of Parliament for the district in which our office was located. Ms.Finestone had a stellar record in many respects, not the least of which was her active support of community-based activities. She was later appointed to the Senate of Canada, Thus, despite the several pitfalls, we had reason and hope to continue on. We knew we were up against a formidable foe but were also aware of genuine support.

Warren Allmand and Clifford Lincoln had tried to arrange a face-to-face meeting that would involve the two of them, Perron and myself. The best they could come up with was a telephone conference call. Anyone familiar with 'phone conferencing knows its value as an economic way of communicating information on generally agreed-upon subjects. By the same token, it is hardly an efficacious manner of settling disputes. For the moment, it was all we had, so we gratefully accepted. The call took place March 31ˢᵗ.

It took a follow-up letter on my part, however, to clarify one important point. During the call it was alleged that I had previously refused to produce certain required reports, an assertion that I categorically denied. The point continued to bother me after the conference call, as I knew that Perron was not one to simply lie about something. While mulling over the matter, I suddenly remembered having recently refused two requests, which I had considered absurd. I explained it in my letter to Allmand.

A parolee under our supervision had been arrested and subsequently charged by the police. His parole was immediately suspended and he was returned to the penitentiary. Some weeks later the suspension was lifted and the parolee returned to the community under our supervision. (It is important to note that CSC carried out both the suspension and the later annulment of the suspension; John Howard could only make a recommendation). Eleven months later the charges were withdrawn. We forwarded the required Special Report along with the court document stating the charges had been dropped. Since we are not permitted to send reports directly to the parole board but must filter them through CSC, we did so. The "*responsable du secteur interimaire*" of the day chose to return the Special Report to our office claiming it was incomplete. The parolee had been back in the community eleven months and the matter explained in a brief Special Report, accompanied by the official court document. I had refused to provide another report.

In the second instance the parolee had likewise been arrested, suspended and the suspension later annulled. The Special Report was completed and duly sent to the parole board via CSC. In this case the parole board exercised its prerogative to revoke the parole and send the offender back to the penitentiary. Some weeks later the liaison officer was asking for another Special Report. The reason for this latest demand was that another interview with the offender might uncover further information that may allow for a Special Report more in line with the parole board decision. This request had also been refused.

I pointed out in my letter that it was quite possible that Perron had not been aware of all the facts because, knowing him as I did, he himself would never have countenanced such bureaucratic time wasting. I went on to opine, however, that he should have been fully apprised of the facts before making allegations. It was in this same letter that I took the opportunity to inform Allmand of the inaccuracies in the Minister's letter and that Mme Vallée and Mr. MacLatchie's joint request for a meeting with Perron had been denied.

One of the last written communiqués sent to Allmand was in May 1995. It put, in summary form, the highlights of the previous five months along with some editorial comments on the part of our President. In essence it was as follows:

> *"Since reception of the letter from CSC of Dec.2, 1994 advising us that our parole contract would not be renewed, we have attempted to ascertain the reasons for such a drastic decision. To date, after several delaying and obstructive tactics on the part of the Quebec Regional Office, we remain in the position of the accused who has not had his day in court. The CSC, acting as judge, jury and prosecutor, has brought forth little other than innuendo, half-truths and alternating allegations in its feeble attempt to explain a decision that is seriously crippling a valid, long-term player in criminal justice. In fact, it is becoming increasingly evident that certain Quebec Regional officials see little need to justify their decisions to anyone.*
>
> *"The original catalyst, the 'Enquiry Report', which we obtained through access to information procedures four months after the decision not to renew the parole contract, in no way alludes to a cessation of contractual agreements. What it does suggest is remedial measures in the light of an acknowledgment of difficulties of a bilateral nature.*

"I believe a summary of events, since the original decision was communicated, is in order. It should highlight basic attitudes on both sides. An elaboration of these happenings has been forwarded to you in previous correspondence.

Dec.2, 1994: Letter from CSC (M.Thibault) stating that parole contract is not to be renewed. This is the *first* communication, written or verbal, alluding to contractual relations.

Jan.5, 1995: Telephone conversation in which M. Thibault advises Mr.Williams that the 'Enquiry Report' may be obtained only through 'access to information' but agrees to forward by fax the recommendations.

Jan.16, 1995: Telephone call from Mr.MacLatchie (JHSC) to Mr.Williams resulting in agreement that Mr.Phelps be approached as possible mediator. Mr.Edwards had spoken to Mr.MacLatchie previously.

Jan.30, 1995: Mr.Williams advised by Mr.MacLatchie that both Mr.Edwards and Mr.Phelps favour Mr.Phelps' involvement.

Jan.31, 1995: Early morning call from Mr.Phelps to Mr.Williams to establish meeting at JHSQ office on Fri. Feb.3rd. Noon hour call from Mr.Phelps stating that M.Perron objected to this measure but reluctantly agreed that Mr.Williams set up a meeting with M. Thibault to open up communications. M. Perron agrees to advise M. Thibault of the same.

Feb.13, 1995: Meeting with Mr.Williams and M.Thibault at which the latter denies having been advised by M.Perron of purpose of meeting; M.Thibault admits that M Perron has recently advised the Union, the Directors and the ASRS that the parole contract with JHSQ will not be renewed; a telephone call from Mr.Williams to Mr.Phelps relates this latest embarrassment.

Feb.17, 1995: Mr.Williams meets with M.Perron and two of his assistants; M.Perron has decided to send a three-man team 'to look into the matter.'

Feb.27, 1995: Three CSC representatives meet with Mr. Williams and three members of JHSQ; proves to be more of an 'inquisition' than a meeting of partners.

Mar.24, 1995: M.Perron refuses to meet with Mme Vallée and Mr. Mac.Latchie to consider possible resolution of problem; matter referred to M.Thibault.

Mar.27, 1995: M.Thibault advises Mme Vallée by telephone that there will be no change in the original decision.

Mar.31, 1995: Telephone conference call among Mr.Allmand, Mr.Lincoln, M.Perron and Mr.Williams.

Apr.3, 1995: Letter forwarded to Mr. Allmand by Mr. Williams to clarify and or respond to the allegations he heard during his portion of the conference call; as well to correct certain information given to the Solicitor General, as reflected in his letter of Mar.16 to Mr.Allmand.

"As mentioned before, the above is simply a sequence of events, in chronological order, since JHSQ was first made aware that its parole contract for fiscal year 1995-96 was in jeopardy. Our position in this matter is more clearly portrayed in the notes prepared by Mr.Williams and forwarded to you over the past few months.

"I do believe, however, that what does come through is a certain obstinacy and arrogance on the part of certain CSC Quebec Region officials which belie professionalism at any level. Statements such as, 'Thus we are in partnership with others such as the police, the courts, the parole boards and the after-care agencies that also comprise our system of justice' and 'In order to be truly accountable, the Service must be open. This means we are committed to providing information in a timely way . . .' become mere platitudes in the light of the above-mentioned, recent events. These quotations, cited from an official CSC publication, portray a healthy state of affairs in which mature relationships, based on mutual respect, develop. The manner in which the matter of our parole contract has been treated gives a new and unacceptable meaning to the role of public servant."

It was not until some ten months later we learned that a tentative solution was proposed; more accurately, that a compromise had been forced upon the CSC Quebec Regional Office. In March 1996 we were made aware that the Minister had instructed the Commissioner of Corrections that the impasse in Quebec must be resolved. The Commissioner, through the Board of Directors of John Howard of Canada, advised us that the Quebec Regional Office was prepared to sign a Service Contract with JHSQ for institutional services. It was made clear that parole supervision was to remain a thing of the past.

Whatever pressures, dealings and machinations went on over this ten-month period remains a mystery to me. However, of one thing

I am certain. Had it not been for the active support of the political forces spearheaded by Warren Allmand, along with Clifford Lincoln and Sheila Finestone, we would never have made an iota of progress. Forget the platitudinous rhetoric of the government agency preaching partnership, concern for the individual, etc. These are merely words; self-serving verbiage and little more. It boils down to a power game at the highest level. The political party of the day, the entrenched bureaucratic machine and the labour unions vie for power in an ongoing balancing act. Partnerships, resocialization of the offender, even the more sensitive issues such as care for victims and special consideration for minority groups are subordinate to the preservation of power.

It is interesting and informative to note the niceties of the procedure of compromise. In our situation, it was imperative that feelings are assuaged and images protected. The time lapse of sixteen months created the impression there had been no imposition from on high. The fact that the dictum had passed through the hands of the John Howard of Canada Board, a group conspicuous by its silence throughout the crisis, rendered a cushioning effect on the CSC Regional Office by keeping JHSQ in its place. Finally, the government agency had won in maintaining its decision not to renew the parole contract while we at John Howard were victorious in securing a contract that would prolong our life. What was not resolved, and what was in reality a significant loss for all concerned, was the basic issue of the status of non-profit, private corporations involved in criminal justice. In this instance, was the John Howard Society of Quebec, a community-based organization, competent to design and carry out services to offenders and their families? Could it create services parallel to but not in opposition to those afforded by CSC? The ultimate question that remains unanswered is: are private organizations representative of the community-at-large and can they remain autonomous and remain true partners with government in the overall administration of justice?

A meeting was set up in the office of Jean-Claude Perron that included two of his assistants, Denis Cloutier and Laval Marchand. I had been asked previously to present the outline of a proposal of my choice. Since my own preference had always been to work directly with the offender and primarily with the persistent offender, my proposal was in this vein. The target population would be the long-term offender; the venue would be the four major medium security penitentiaries in the region; the time allotment would be two and a half days per week in each institution; and, the service would be in-depth counselling on both an individual and a group basis. The three basic, immutable stipulations were that the service was to be autonomous, voluntary and confidential.

Eyebrows were raised immediately upon mention of the three conditions, but I was ready. I was not about to jump from the pan into the fire. I went on to explain that autonomy was necessary to ensure a service conducted by an independent, community-based entity and not simply another institutional program subject to limits imposed by whoever happened to be responsible for programming in a specific institution at any given time. The voluntary aspect was equally important. The inmates were to participate of their own volition and not only because they had been sent there. Since we would remain apart from the decision-making apparatus of the institution, we could eliminate the effects of secondary gains that resulted from rewarded institutional compliance. Thus we could anticipate a more genuine response on the part of the participants. The goal of the counselling was neither to enhance institutional adjustment nor to facilitate early release but, rather, to focus on personal responsibility with respect to future adjustment in society.

The most sensitive demand was that of confidentiality. Before I had a chance to explain our rationale, one of the assistants queried,

> "How often will you provide reports, weekly, monthly?"
> "No reports, no reporting," I stated definitively.

I knew this would require some explaining. CSC was not accustomed to allow anything to develop outside their control. I was aware of innovative techniques that had been introduced in the past from outside. It had only been a matter of time before they were either watered down or taken over completely by institutional staff. It is not a question of whether the institutional personnel have the competence to carry out the endeavour but, rather, that there is an inherent value in an exercise that emanates from outside the institutional system and remains so. It is perceived differently and since we are talking here of interpersonal relationships this is of prime importance. Our position begins with the basic premise that we are to provide a service to inmates, not to the institution. Our technique is fundamentally a confrontational one. It is imperative that a climate of trust is developed. It is not a mere truism to state that trust can only evolve in an ambiance of confidentiality, a reality that cannot be overstated, particularly within the customary penitentiary milieu.

I believed then, and still do today, that Perron could see the reasoning behind my insistence. He was well aware that my demands, while exceptional in that the larger organization normally did not willingly allow such latitude, were logical if one is to attempt to carry out an approach that is more than a carbon copy of what is currently in place. Furthermore, both of us were equally aware that an agreement had to be reached.

Nevertheless, they had to show some resistance and they did. The first hitch came when Perron promptly cut the project in half. It could be carried out in two penitentiaries rather than four. Then Marchand added that his budget did not allow for the proposed costs:

"I have nothing more than fifty thousand dollars left for the coming year," he declared petulantly.

I started to get out of my chair.

"There's obviously nothing to discuss here," I replied with undisguised annoyance. I knew very well they were trying to save face by offering as little as possible. Our former parole contract was in the range of 350,000 dollars and my proposal came in at less than $240,000. Perron reacted in an instant.

"Sit down. I'm sure we can come to some agreement." "You know very well, Jean-Claude, we can do nothing with $50,000."

He was aware as I that the primary reason our political pressure had any effect was because it would have been politically embarrassing to allow the John Howard Society to shut down in Quebec. It would have amounted to the federal government having to explain why the John Howard existed in every other province in Canada; that the JHSQ had provided services for more than a hundred years; and that, though traditionally perceived as an anglophone structure, it was the only community-based organization in criminal justice that provided services in the two official languages of Canada, within the officially unilingual province of Quebec; a political minefield.

Thus, for all the wrong reasons, we struck an agreement. The service would be provided an average of two and a half days per week in the Leclerc and Archambault penitentiaries. It would be a service of in-depth counselling with long-term offenders. It would be directed toward awakening in the offender a sense of personal responsibility for his life situation. We would remain autonomous, completely independent of the contrived correctional plan imposed on each inmate. In the spirit of cooperation, however, I suggested we hold case conferences with the case management team of each man we followed. There could be possible benefits on both sides. The proviso was that the conference would include the participation of the concerned offender.

Thus, the John Howard Society of Quebec started out on a new mission, one of rebuilding. It was not that we were unfamiliar with institutional work but we had neither the means nor the mandate for a logical follow-up. There was much to be done if we were to rebuild and, as we would discover once again, little was within our control.

DENOUEMENT

~ *silence in the community*

I was fifty-eight years of age and in my thirty-fifth year working in criminal justice. Much of my time and effort had been spent in the correctional field. In fact, with the new contract I was now involved in the same undertaking as at the beginning of my career: hands-on work with penitentiary inmates, both individually and in groups. In one sense it seemed I had regressed; a one hundred and eighty degree turnabout that led to the past. On the other hand, I realized this face-to-face work forms the basis of all clinical practice and research. Had it not been for my original experience as a front-line worker in St. Vincent de Paul penitentiary, the Dannemora project of the later 'sixties would not have had the same relevance for me personally. As it turned out, that experiment in milieu therapy proved to be the essential element of complementary training and practice in my professional life.

Prisons and penitentiaries exist because of and for those incarcerated therein. Ironically, the truth of this axiom is obscured by its self-evidence. A corollary of this is that policies, procedures and programs earn their validity to the degree in which they respond to the needs of the target group. Anything short of this creates and perpetuates an entity unto itself whose self-serving demands become insatiable.

Leclerc penitentiary in the 'seventies had been a beehive of activity as it carried out a daily commerce with the world outside. Inmates were frequently released on temporary absence and, if sometimes for frivolous reasons, it nevertheless afforded a break from the monotony and automatism of institutional routine. This brief exposure to the reality of everyday life in the community was often carried out under escort with a staff member, thus opening up an avenue of opportunity to initiate or strengthen a more meaningful link between rival factions.

By comparison, Leclerc of the 'nineties revealed a rather bleak, even morose milieu. Inmates were lethargic in their acceptance of contrived counsel and personnel were passively engaged in a technocratic compilation and questionable interpretation of nebulous data. The dissenting posturing had inflated on both sides widening the void ever more between inmates and personnel. Dynamism had expired, only periodically resurrected by an individual inmate's refusal to comply with a debilitating process of depersonalization and consequent staff reaction. Such defiance was eradicated by immediate displacement. Inmate removed and problem solved; ingrained practices seemingly remain forever.

The beginning of my commitment to a two and a half day week in Leclerc was actually an extension of what I had begun in 1993. Since autumn of that year, I had conducted a group session on a weekly basis. I would now continue with the group and use the inmates therein as my principal source of referral. Inmates, although usually inept at recognizing and accepting deficiencies within themselves, are uncommonly adept at spotting the foibles of others. It is simply a matter of creating a climate of confidence and concern that usually encourages them to signal an individual in need. After all, if Harry was able to surface from the dungeon of Segregation in the Pen of the 'sixties and alert me to a problematic situation, I knew it would be a minor challenge to develop a positive milieu within a group at the medium-security facility of the 'nineties. In fact, such an ambience had evolved by April 1996 and it was easy to fill the required time with serious referrals.

This is something the larger organization fails to recognize. In its myopic view of institutional issues it has all the answers, oftentimes before having heard the questions. The exhaustive list of criminogenic factors gleaned from research with large numbers of offenders can be an excellent indicator of group trends and is invaluable as such. The validity of specific factors, however, dissipates rapidly when group factors are used out of context and wielded gratuitously. Similarly, the widespread application of programs by anyone and everyone has brought about an ersatz setting wherein written description impresses all but the discriminating and discerning eye. Clinical tools are only as good as the competency of those applying them, whether they are used for evaluation or treatment. The impositions of incarceration in the 'nineties produced more subtle effects than those of the 'sixties. Gone were the widespread acting-out of auto-mutilation, predatory sexual behaviour and open revolt; the material gains accrued over the years had gone a long way in suppressing these reactions. Nevertheless, the insidious process of depersonalization prevailed and surreptitiously undermined the possibility of a healthy process of reintegration.

The service to be provided by JHSQ to long-term offenders was one of professional in-depth counselling. Our definition of long-term offender was more inclusive than that of the government agency. They used the one static criterion of length of sentence, ten years or more. We looked at the longitudinal profile of the individual and included those who, regardless of the length of the current sentence, had served several sentences. These offenders had spent relatively little time in the community-at-large to where they would eventually return. The counselling process centred on the effects of the deprivation of liberty, as well as the consequent difficulties in coping with the demands of freedom. The principal characteristics were voluntary participation in a confrontational process that remained strictly confidential. The voluntary nature of the contacts, reinforced by a respectful confidentiality, helps create an ambience of trust and transparency that enables confrontational intervention. The aim is directed toward the offender's recognition and acceptance of personal responsibility for a pattern of anti-social behaviour that has been ultimately self-defeating. This approach is facilitated by the fact that it is provided by a community-based organization that stands apart from the decision-making authorities. The uncontrolled variable of inmate response to institution-generated needs and rewards is rendered negligible.

We never for a moment believed that this project would make a significant dent in the complex armour of delinquency. We were convinced, however, that we could make realistic inroads into the daily life of some individual inmates and, perhaps, even influence some institutional workers. We organized an information session for personnel at both penitentiaries right at the outset, describing our technique, defining our objectives and stating a willingness to participate actively in case conferences that would include the inmate. We had been led to believe, erroneously for the most part, that Case Management Teams met with each inmate on their respective caseloads, on a regular basis.

Nevertheless it was imperative that we enunciate certain premises, if only to clarify our position. Delinquency was defined as a dynamic process that permeates the total personality, rather than a solitary act. The persistent delinquent, those with whom we would be working, represented the basic unwilling client in whom motivation to change is of low intensity at best. Thus it was our belief that mere exposure to a variety of programs, or participation under duress, simply elicits a superficial, temporary response. Any hope for a more substantial modification of attitudes and behaviour would be contingent upon regular and sustained participation in an ongoing process, over a protracted period. Motivation, then, would not be considered a prerequisite but, rather, a goal inherent in the treatment process itself. The difficulty to recognize and accept internal factors as a primary cause of problematic life situations is symptomatic of delinquency. Thus, in-depth counselling continually challenges the tendency to project causal factors solely onto the external environment.

Since we were to conduct our counselling service both individually and in groups, a decision had to be made as to who was best suited for what. Unlike the government agency, we did not impose one form or another. It has always been my style to allow the inmates to choose their own group members. There are many reasons for this, the most important being that if one is to develop a process that will eventually have participants confronting one another, it is wise to begin with individuals who share common interests and attitudes or, at least, are compatible enough to accept a measure of basic criticism. Once the participating inmates have made the initial choice, it becomes my task to develop the interpersonal exchanges by encouraging leadership while discouraging control.

In the closed world of institutional living some subjects are best discussed in the comfort of a one-on-one encounter. This may lead to later involvement at the group level, depending upon the subject matter and the individual concerned. Thus some inmates are seen in both a group and on an individual basis. Obviously the group approach is not for everyone; not every inmate and not every therapist. It takes a particular ease in social interaction, especially in a penitentiary milieu, to be able to give and take in a constructive manner. Personal image, often a brittle shell, must sometimes be carefully peeled away and not brusquely fractured, if an overall sense of trust is to permeate the group setting. Similarly, the attending therapist has to be capable of maintaining a balance between the closeness that fosters confidence and the distance required to uphold an objective stance. Thus, clinicians who are not comfortable in a group setting should have the common sense and professional integrity to resort to alternate techniques. By the same token, offenders who are not at ease with a particular therapeutic method should not be compelled to participate. Obviously, malingering must be identified and dealt with but not simply assumed. The underlying maxim is: if the treatment doesn't work, consider changing the prescription.

Prisons and penitentiaries invariably have an influential group within the inmate population. It is a heterogeneous assembly as to race, ethnicity, language and type of crime; the unifying factor is power and the ability to use it. There has been an evolution in this process over the years. During the 'sixties control was exercised for the most part by the physically endowed, in a direct and brutal manner. The expansion of institutional activities and reduced cell time in the 'seventies and 'eighties gave rise to a more sophisticated form of control. The smarter and better-organized inmates manipulated the muscle of the mesomorphs in order to carry out the lucrative trades that escalated with increased mobility within the perimeter. This power was augmented through greater access to outside resources. The 'nineties witnessed another modification in the unfolding of this process. The emergence of a new power within the institutions was a direct result of a sizeable increase in the arrest and conviction of bikers. The strong allegiances that characterized the various groups, magnified by a biker war on the street, introduced a level of violence to the institutional milieu, unparalleled in previous times. It was not long before the authorities resorted to the short-term solution of physical separation of warring parties, a remedy that was to pose long-term problems. Meanwhile, the biker groups came to realize that if they maintained a superficial calm within the institution where their particular group reigned, they would be in a position to attain tacit acceptance on the part of the everyday institutional regime.

It is naive however to see unofficial power within the correctional institution as one-sided. In fact, along with the bureaucratic expansion in corrections came a gradual shift in the power structure among the personnel. Gone was the autocratic control of a Warden or strong

Deputy Warden. Likewise, the oligarchic direction of senior officers was a thing of the past. It was now the age of delegation of authority. What happens in an emerging bureaucratic structure, however, is an increasing diffusion of power that leads to a situation where it is frequently difficult to pinpoint the real seat of responsibility. Thus what developed over the years, in part as a result of this dereliction of clear-cut authority and responsibility, was the growth of an increasingly powerful union presence. They were to exert an influence that would not limit itself, in time, to the period of contractual negotiations or, in place, to National and Regional levels. This force held considerable, if unofficial, sway over the operational life of the correctional institution itself.

In the early 'sixties Gerry Brennan, then Deputy Warden at the Pen, had taken drastic action against a group of guards for insubordination. Segregation, where the rioters were held, was a hotbed of tension. A hostage taking had occurred in the general population, an incident serious enough to bring the temperature in Segregation to a boiling point. Several guards reacted by refusing to allow the daily walk for inmates in this highly restricted area. At this time it was not a question of inmates' rights but simply a matter of good sense to halt the guards' revolt. Mr. Brennan saw each guard individually. As a long-term resident of the town of St. Vincent de Paul, he knew these men and their families intimately, all of who lived and had been raised in the hamlet.

"You're aware that you're refusing a direct order. I want you to think carefully about this. If you continue the boycott, this would be clear-cut insubordination. You know the penalty. Don't force my hand." Brennan was always polite but direct. Seven men were ultimately fired.

It was now the late 'nineties and I was crossing the interior yard at Leclerc when addressed by an inmate I knew:

"Paul, I've been accepted for the minimum at Ste-Anne. Should be leaving by next week."

"Way to go Luc, good way to end up your bit. Remember this has to be the last one," I replied eagerly.

Luc was a Hells Angel. This was his first sentence but he was, as a full patch, well entrenched in the club. I knew he had only a few months left to serve but I took every opportunity to stress the importance of living in freedom. This concept of freedom had a different meaning for someone like Luc but I considered it important that he become aware that another meaning was extant. Maybe it would be only later on that the reality would set in.

Some two weeks later I was crossing the yard at Ste-Anne des Plaines institution, on my way to my bi-monthly group. Luc was trotting toward me.

"Hey Paul!"

"How's it going?" I said elatedly. It was always good to see some progress, however minute.

"I'm going back to Leclerc before the end of the week."

I was taken aback, momentarily thinking I had misheard. "Give it a chance Luc, you've only been here ten minutes."

"They don't want me here. They won't even give me my personal effects."

I was now really stunned. I knew he was serious. Within a few moments I heard his side of the story. He had been told, immediately upon arrival, that Hells Angels members were not welcome at this institution. Two uniformed personnel had confronted him.

"You're gonna fight it, eh? You should take it right to the top," I insisted.

I knew the CSC officially prides itself in its several levels of decision-making committees, supposedly to safeguard the rights of inmates. I knew equally well that certain issues brought by specific groups could outweigh decision-making at any level.

"I'm going back. If the screws don't want me here, I sure as shit don't want to be near them. I have less than a year to go, you know what they can do with their minimum," he replied with an accompanying gesture that left little room for conjecture.

The following week I waved to Luc as he jogged across the yard to his job in the gym at Leclerc. So much for the process of reintegration; so much for the highly touted system of cascading inmates through the various security levels, enticed by a myriad of programs, enforced by a correctional plan and evaluated by contracted psychologists; so much for a system that should make sense.

The system in the 'sixties was at times closer to dictatorship than democracy. Nevertheless one knew to whom to turn in the hope of redressing a seeming injustice. By the 'nineties however leadership had evaporated. One had the distinct impression that, contrary to official word, anyone could make a decision. The problem was that it was difficult, if not impossible, to identify the decision-maker. These two examples simply reflect systemic uses and abuses of power at the extremes of a continuum. Neither is healthy. It is disheartening to see that over a forty-year expanse of time, however, a more wholesome form of authoritative power had not evolved. Close scrutiny would suggest that when the basic raison d'etre of a correctional system is not clearly defined, faithfully respected and conscientiously adhered to, the results become increasingly chaotic and basic principles become a mere print-out for public consumption.

Thus, we had a good idea of what we were up against, a milieu less than propitious for encouraging and bolstering positive change. We had no illusions about the efficacy of our counselling under such circumstances. Nevertheless our initial aim was to introduce a modicum of humanity into a basically sterile environment. It was evident that right-wing political pressures, reinforced by an occasional spectacular crime in the community, had had their intended effect on the criminal justice system. Legislation had expanded considerably, thereby limiting discretionary power in several areas. Policies and procedures, with respect to both corrections and parole, had become more restrictive and less oriented toward the individual. At the institutional level, under the banner of "protection of the public", an antagonistic posture on the part of that segment of correctional personnel who had previously been the helping hand for offenders had evolved. The Case Management Officer (CMO) had now replaced the former Classification Officer. The classification position had been designed to help the inmate cope with everyday demands of institutional life and prepare for eventual release to the community. The new role differed dramatically from the former one. The CMO, as one member of a Case Management Team, was charged with gathering and collating data from various sources stored in a computer. The information saga began when the offender was housed in the Regional Reception Centre and continued throughout his incarceration in the various security levels of institutional existence.

This managerial approach gave tacit approval to withdrawal from personal interaction. Many CMOs, indeed many Case Management Teams, placed undue emphasis on the use of technological devices that gave way to a commensurate loss of immediate contact with the offender. Perusal of a computer screen had become a comfortable substitute with a legitimized avoidance of contention and dispute. An equally nefarious result appeared in the guise of objectivity. Biased perceptions arose from this static view of an uncontested individual profile emanating from unquestioned sources. The final result: expert manipulation of conjecture, an amalgam of fact and opinion, at the expense of direct communication; a veritable management of case files rather than the more arduous task of personal interaction.

*   *   *

Many men found their way to my office in Leclerc. As with any group of inmates the requests varied from simple curiosity of whether this new presence could be of immediate utilitarian value, to a genuine concern about the futility of one's life. The majority of those who made an appearance at my door, fell somewhere within these two extremes. I never took any demand lightly however, since experience taught me that a show of concern for even the most mundane request could have a long-term effect. Sometimes, a more serious issue would arise down the road and the initial spark of confidence could inspire the individual to seek out counsel rather than act out impulsively. On the other hand, it may be the sign of acceptance that would encourage an individual to refer others in need. In any event, I always maintained an open-door policy because I believed it was the right thing to do. My many years in the institutions made me a known presence to both inmates and personnel. Even those of more recent vintage knew me by sight since, apart from business conducted behind closed doors, I frequently chatted with anyone and everyone in the yard, the gym and the shops. In fact though, it was my group that had run continuously for almost three years that really paved my way in April 1996. It included some high-profile cases and the status of these men in the inmate hierarchy highlighted my role in the awareness of others, on either side of the fence.

René was the doyen of the group, the sole remaining member of the originals from autumn 1993; the others had either completed their sentence or been transferred to lower security. He was senior in other ways as well. At sixty-two years of age he had now served more than forty years behind bars and had spent less than three years on the street since the age of seventeen. Despite this background he was an articulate man, fluent in English and French and had a voracious appetite for reading. He had completed a Bachelor's degree in Social Science while incarcerated and had initiated studies at the Master's level at Laval University in Quebec City during the mid-eighties, his last brief sojourn in society. He was presently in his eleventh consecutive year incarcerated, having been sentenced to an additional twenty-three years for his most recent crime and conviction. He was now serving an aggregate sentence of fifty years.

I had first met him in 1962. I was a greenhorn in the business, working as a Classification Officer at the old Pen. As the resident anglophone on staff I received numerous written requests from English-speaking inmates. The volume of internal mail flattered me, outdoing my colleagues by a considerable margin. It was only later I was made aware by these same colleagues that my popularity was simply because I was the new kid on the block, a position typified by naiveté. This trait did not pass unnoticed by the ever-observant inmates; I was an easy mark for tailor-made cigarettes and an occasional 'phone call; the embellishments of penitentiary living were sparse in the 'sixties. I don't remember much about my initial meetings with him. They must have left a favourable impression, however, because I had turned to him for help in working with a troubled Harry in the mid-sixties. Harry was working in the same shop as René and had recently experienced a psychotic break. They knew each other quite well and I took advantage of their firm relationship to maintain a more constant watch over Harry's fragile condition. I spoke with each one individually and the resultant understanding proved beneficial. I was better able to monitor Harry's adjustment and help him avoid pitfalls that could occasion a relapse in his mental condition. I believe René experienced some gratification from his helping role although this kind of sensitivity was not something he would admit to, not even to himself; after all, an image had to be maintained.

René was the second of eight siblings raised in the northeast end of Montreal. The family lived in poverty since the father's wages as a barber were the sole source of income. Financial resources were particularly meagre because the father, although a steady worker, was also an inveterate gambler who squandered most of his earnings in card playing. The long-suffering mother, a conscientious parent, was overwhelmed by the taxing workload in the home. The earliest consequential happening he could recall occurred during the pre-school years. Due to the family's dire economic situation, it was decided that he would be sent to live with a maternal aunt.

"You know Paul, I realize today they were acting out of necessity but in the mind of a four year old, it doesn't come across that way," he stated matter-of-factly.

"I was away about two days, scared shitless, but I wouldn't cry. I decided to find my way home," he continued with a nervous laugh.

"I didn't know exactly where my home was but I started to walk. I couldn't read yet but thought I recognized the street sign, by the size of the lettering I guess. Anyways, suddenly I look up an', sonnovabitch, there's our house a couppla doors down. My mother's on the steps an' when she sees me she runs up to me, hugs me an' bursts out cryin'. I guess she was glad to see me. I was never sent away again."

I had known him about thirty-five years when he related this episode. He did so only the one time. I've never seen any allusion to it in his vast file. In a real sense this is not surprising. He was always emphatic about assuming complete responsibility, to the exclusion of external factors, for his life situation. Anything short of this was perceived as a weakness. In fact, this inability to strike a balance between personal responsibility and the realistic influences of environmental stimuli exemplified a certain intellectual rigidity and reflected a pronounced stunting in his emotional maturation. In the final analysis, it presented as much of an obstacle to internal change as did the opposite disposition of the typical delinquent. In any case, his personal psychodynamics in this respect were advantageous to the group process. "Le jeune" had little difficulty confronting others when he spotted what he saw as "bullshit!"

Two other elements came into play during his formative years, one experienced as a deceitful ploy to control his future, the other as a missed opportunity for self-improvement. Both occurrences would help define his affective mien and have some bearing on the direction his life would take; one would initiate a blocking of emotional contact with authority figures, the other would incur a growing sense of loss of control over his own destiny.

Primary school presented little challenge for René as he led the class. His academic performance passed unnoticed in the general disarray of the home but was recognized in the extended family. A maternal uncle, a diocesan priest, recognized potential in the youth and gave assurances that he would underwrite any future, collegial studies. This promise opened up new vistas to his inquisitive mind and burgeoning ambition; perhaps there was a way out of the suffocating penury. These newfound hopes were dashed mid-way through secondary school. He was made aware of a condition attached to educational sponsorship; further studies would necessarily be directed toward the priesthood. He was emotionally devastated by this sudden disclosure and interpreted it as a conscious deception on the part of his uncle.

Although he continued to do well academically, his interests outside the school setting accelerated and he became preoccupied with activities of the neighbourhood gang. Small in physical stature, he more than made up for this shortcoming with an acute sense of creativity and daring. He was becoming a leader. It was not long before petty thievery expanded into a better-organized system of crime against persons; mock hold-ups of taxi drivers whetted his appetite for more lucrative gain. Nevertheless, the consequent increase in police surveillance in the neighbourhood resulted in his gradual withdrawal from gang activities and a temporary lessening of overt delinquent behaviour. He finally dropped out of school around sixteen years of age. Within a matter of months, however, a nagging feeling of futility plagued him constantly. Acquaintances had been arrested and placed in juvenile detention and, though he had avoided arrest, a general malaise enveloped him. The discomfort was a catalyst to his applying for entrance into the armed forces. The main attraction was a belief that within a military regime he would have access to subsidized education. Whether this was the conscious plan of an intelligent, delinquent adolescent or the musings of an incarcerated, adult offender remains speculative. In any case, it was never to be. His mother brought a letter of acceptance from the Canadian Army to him two weeks before his eighteenth birthday. He was awaiting trial in Bordeaux Jail on a charge of armed robbery. What should have been encouraging news only served to augment an already depressed emotional state. Although unaware of the full impact of his situation, the immediate milieu was ominous enough to enliven feelings of loneliness and despondency at what might have been. In fact he was about to embark on a long journey during which, ironically, he would fulfill his dream of advanced education. Unfortunately he would also spend the greater part of the next forty-eight years within the confines of a penitentiary.

René remained in the group at Leclerc until his transfer to a minimum security setting in the autumn of 1997. By that time he had completed four years in the counselling process. During that time he had appeared twice before the Parole Board and been refused any type of release. His weighty criminal record had been the decisive factor. Adaptation to penitentiary life had been considered above average; previous post-release adjustment had proven to be something else. Throughout his criminal career the crimes had been basically acquisitive. Various armed robberies usually involved significant amounts of money but his almost instantaneous arrest on each occasion accounted for numerous years incarcerated and only brief periods of time in the community. René, with appropriate self-awareness, described himself to the Parole Board as an habitual prisoner rather than an habitual criminal. The Board was hard pressed not to agree with this distinction and aptly pointed out in their written comments that he was highly institutionalized. What they seemingly failed to realize, however, was that their subsequent decision to continue the incarceration simply reinforced the very dynamic they used as part of the rationale to deny parole.

The primary task of a Parole Board is to assess whether or not the candidate before them is capable of completing the remainder of his sentence in the community under supervision. This weighty judgment has obvious, serious implications. The prediction of human behaviour is dubious at best. The odds favouring an equitable decision are enhanced by the degree to which the decision-makers are competent in three areas: knowledge of the dynamics of delinquency, an understanding of the effects of incarceration and an awareness of the availability of relevant resources in the community. Evidently, individual board members cannot know the parole candidate intimately; nor are they necessarily cognizant of the daily workings of correctional institutions or in a position to evaluate specific community resources. Nevertheless, because of their reliance on others in this respect, they must be sufficiently informed as to pose the appropriate questions to the responsible parties. Furthermore, as a legal entity, the NPB should be able to demand changes essential to the enhancement of their capacity to reach informed and fair decisions.

By the time René had been transferred to the minimum security, Federal Training Centre, a number of the men I had followed in Leclerc had reached there as well. In order to give some continuance to the counselling process, I decided to form a group there. The rationale behind CSC policy of cascading inmates from greater to lesser security during their sentence is reintegration of the offender. The underlying philosophy is that the offender comes from the community and is destined to return there. The expectation, one would assume, is that there is an increasing delegation of personal responsibility as the inmate approaches release. One of the preparatory steps in minimum security entails community service. This "voluntary" work, selected and enforced by CSC personnel, is presumed to be an attempt to sensitize the offender to the needs of society's disadvantaged. Suffice it to say that it is an integral part of the official process of reintegration.

René had been working in his prescribed community service for about a month when he accosted me one evening just before our group session.

"Paul, do you eat lunch in the joint or outside?" he queried. Before I could respond he added, "I buy my lunch at a dépanneur near my work and eat it in the park nearby; it's really great, the river runs by and I can feed the birds," he continued enthusiastically, "Would you like to join me for lunch some noon hour?"

He was now about sixty-three years of age and had spent close to forty-four years in the penitentiary. His eyes sparkled like a kid on

Christmas morning as he described his noontime venture. The ability to choose his lunch, the peaceful repose of the park and the freedom of the birds responding to his offerings; this was obviously an idyllic setting.

"I think it's a great idea. How about if I join you at twelve next Wednesday!" I exclaimed with genuine delight.

He had come from a multi-delinquent family and his associates throughout adult life were criminalized. I was one of the few "legits" he knew, certainly the most constant in his life. The proposal was more than attractive. It would be a learning experience for me and undoubtedly for him as well. It was a worthy suggestion to be honoured by acceptance.

I arrived at the church where he worked assisting the maintenance man, at the appointed time. When parking, I noticed him speaking with a well-dressed man some twenty metres away. When he turned and saw me they both started walking toward me.

"Paul, I want to present you M. Ross, my parole officer . . . this is Mr. Williams, he's Director of John Howard."

I immediately extended the conversation while shaking hands. Not everyone knew of John Howard. "What office are you from?" I enquired, more as a way of reassuring the parole officer I was who I was supposed to be and not someone from the criminal milieu. "The Duvernay Office," he replied. I went on to say that I knew his boss, naming him to further confirm my identity. This suspicious demeanour I adopted is not inborn but rather the result of too many years in the business. The process of incarceration takes its toll on all; the difference is merely one of degree.

The pleasantries completed, I suggested we take my car to the dépanneur as a time-saver. His lunch hour was just that, twelve to one and he was obsessive about punctuality. After all, he was a hold-up man; time was of the essence.

"M.Ross is it alright if I go in the car with . . . ?" The parole officer was waving his agreement as he walked away.

Our luncheon *rendez-vous* was, as expected, a pleasant affair. Even the weather cooperated with sunshine and a late spring breeze. It was the first time over a period of thirty-six years that I was able to relate to René in surroundings unfettered by the necessary but forbidding constraints of a penal institution. We didn't discuss courts, prisons, police or parole boards; nor was this a counselling session, though I believe it may well have been more relevant. We probably spoke leisurely of the immediacy of summer and the foreboding fate of the Expos. We did sample silence, truly a rarity in prison; the twittering of birds and the torpid resonance of the passing river enhanced the moment. The experience was rewarding but all too brief. We were back at the church door at one o'clock after this leisurely encounter with nature.

The following week, immediately before our group session at FTC, he caught my eye while preparing the coffee.

"You won't believe this Paul. My parole officer came back the next day. He said I'm not allowed to socialize with anyone, that these are work placements. I'm permitted to speak only with my boss at work, the maintenance guy." This was blurted out in his typical staccato delivery. René was not given to exaggeration but I was sure I had not heard correctly.

"Run that by me again. What's that about socializing?"

I had not misheard. The parole officer had returned the day after our lunch in the park. Work placements were for work. Socializing was done in the institutional visiting room, with authorized groups on special occasions and on temporary absences for resocialization purposes. God forbid that one should socialize while on a humanitarian temporary absence; there's obviously something for every occasion. This attempt to compartmentalize human behaviour reflects a corporate obsessive-compulsive disorder, the natural outgrowth of a bureaucratic mentality run amok. The self-feeding nature of the bureaucratic process, in its need to control, augments the importance of the means in inverse proportion to the value of the end. The written report becomes more important than the subject of the report; contrived programs assume a heightened relevance that outweighs the significance of those they were designed to serve; finally, the organism becomes an entity unto itself. The tragedy in all this is that we are not speaking of untrained individuals. Parole officers, for the most part, are university-trained today. So are their supervisors. I am uncertain whether this absurd counsel was one person's decision or not. It makes little difference; if others on the corporate team were not aware, they should have been. In any case, this is only one example of many that can be cited to demonstrate a system that frequently defies logic. The real threat is that such thinking is infectious and spreads quickly. In fact, by this time, it had already become entrenched in the correctional mentality. Many had been hurt, the number of injured would increase. The victims of this disordered thinking and practice are not limited to the offender population; it is also unsettling to encounter educated personnel, totally unaware of their own professional decline.

René continued on in his community service at the church. Each morning he left the penitentiary around seven-thirty and went back and forth to his work assignment by public transportation. He was less upset than I at the stupidity of the restriction placed on him; then again he had faced the arrogance of control head-on, over numerous years and was obviously used to it. Here was a man who had spent more than ninety-five percent of his adult life incarcerated. He was now in a minimum-security setting, supposedly being prepared to tackle the demands of freedom through a highly vaunted process of reintegration. Nevertheless, he had offhandedly been told to refrain from social contact with his only non-criminalized acquaintance.

The proverbial straw that broke the camel's back, however, came almost two years later at his parole hearing. He had become increasingly aware that his perception of life had altered dramatically. With the last hold-up, that ultimate goal of the "million dollar score" had been attained. Yet, during the three months prior to arrest, he had been left with a pronounced feeling of emptiness, a resurgent sensation throughout the current incarceration. It was as though the dream of instantaneous wealth had no palliative effect whatsoever. In the past, upping the ante on the next pipe dream would fill the void; it now seemed as though the illusion had reached its end and the gap could never be filled with money. In addition to this, he had recently turned sixty-five and was in his thirteenth year on the current sentence. As with all inmates, especially those who have done a significant amount of time, the fear of dying in prison becomes more acute with age. He was not immune to this but fortunately was able to verbalize it in our individual sessions.

The usual alignment for a parole hearing, at least in the Quebec Region, entails a lawyer as the candidate's official representative. The choice is that of the inmate. This legal representation has been in vogue for the past twenty years or more, a practice abetted by the fact that provincial Legal Aid is available for such hearings. The taxpayer underwrites the cost and the venue provides a much-needed opportunity for practice, given the current surplus in the legal profession. The initial rationale had been that the lawyer was present to safeguard the rights of the offender and assure that established procedures were respected. Any divergence from procedure could serve as the basis for review by the National Parole Board's appeal division. Thus procedural steps gradually took on a new significance, sometimes overshadowing more important matters on hand. The atmosphere within the hearing room was changing as well. The former climate of shared information and opinion that characterized the overall exchange was now supplanted by rigid questioning that took on a confrontational tone.

Presentations at parole hearings today are basically limited to three successive phases. The first is comprised of a summary statement usually by the institutional parole officer, reviewing the inmate's file and proffering a recommendation for or against conditional release. The second phase is the candidate's verbal request, interspersed with responses to direct questioning by the Board members and in the third phase the inmate's representative makes the summary plea. The Board members tolerate little debate or discussion during these distinct phases, except for points of clarification. The entire exercise exudes an aura of formality bordering on sterility. This inquisitorial setting places the candidate in an intimidating position, one hardly conducive to open and forthright response. Grandeur and haughtiness now stand in lieu of a dispassionate seriousness, frequently leading to humourless triviality.

When René appeared before the Board it was the late summer of 1999. He had been scheduled to pass, as the first candidate of the day, at eight-thirty. He and his lawyer representative entered the hearing room, only to discover that the institutional parole officer responsible for his case had not arrived yet. After waiting some five to ten minutes, he whispered to his lawyer,

"You can tell them we're ready to begin, she's not recommending me anyway. In any case, they have her written report." As the lawyer repeated his client's request, the immediate response by one of the Parole Board members was,

"We can start now if you wish but with what we have in front of us here," she said pointing to his immense file, "I don't think you'll be going anywhere today."

And I'm pleased to meet you too! He was stunned by this opening gambit and feverishly muttered to his lawyer to ask for a brief recess. This was granted and they both retreated from the room.

"You'll have to ask for a postponement. Did you hear that witch? I could never talk to her."

He was near panic. They returned to the hearing room, the lawyer gave some concocted but acceptable reason for a postponement and the request was granted.

The interviews I had with him after that experience were completely different from the previous ones. He now seemed to be a beaten man. The spark had been extinguished; "le jeune" seemed to have suddenly aged. Prior to this, he had remained upbeat. Despite an appreciation of the weight of his lengthy criminal record and an acceptance of the fact that his life had been a total disaster, he had always held out hope for change. Age and experience had finally caught up with him. Although he would never betray the basic code of the criminal milieu, he had come to recognize that the fundamental lifestyle was more in the realm of fantasy than reality and, for the most part, ultimately self-defeating. Now, however, it seemed as though the bottom had fallen out; there was no light at the end of the tunnel.

As mentioned previously, the prediction of human behaviour holds no certainty and those who think otherwise are foolhardy. The question of releasing someone from prison conditionally is often a coin toss. There are too many unknowns, too many uncontrolled variables. The decision-makers work with what they have. Much is said, plenty is written but little is certain. My regular contact with René over a six year period, along with a study of his evolution over a much longer span of time, led me to believe that he was better prepared for release at the time of his parole hearing than at any time in the past. It was not the direct result of a program, a psychological follow-up or counselling sessions. Something within him had changed. I believe I witnessed it. I also believe it was enough for him to make it.

In the late autumn of 1999, René left the penitentiary for his community service assignment at the usual hour. He was never seen by the authorities again. It is now several years that he is living outside the penitentiary. His previous longest stay in the community had been less than two years and the total number spent in freedom in the past five decades amounted to less than three years. I believe he has been living crime-free, the only reason he is able to remain outside. He is not under some capricious form of supervision in the community but is evidently doing what he expects of himself.

∗   ∗   ∗

The formal reappearance of the John Howard Society of Quebec within the federal penitentiaries in 1996 had been inauspicious. We were limited to two institutions, Leclerc and Archambault, had no formal introduction to the institutional authorities and were simply expected to fend for ourselves. In the same way that the Service Contract had been a direct result of CSC Headquarters in Ottawa pressuring the Quebec Regional Office to settle the problem with JHSQ, our presence in these two penitentiaries was basically an imposition from above and not an invitation on the part of the institutions. The positive side to this was that it inadvertently played into our demand for autonomy; the downside was that many of the institutional front-line workers saw us as competitors rather than as colleagues. As it turned out, our approach was so fundamentally different from that of the institutional personnel, that any attempt to explain our philosophy and modus operandi had little effect. The invitation we extended to share information and technique on individual cases fell on deaf ears. At no time during that first year of operation did anyone approach us for mutual consultation. In point of fact on one occasion, at the request of an inmate I had been following regularly, I contacted his Case Management Officer and asked for a joint meeting.

"Why do you want to meet with me?" was her immediate response to my phoned request.

"Well, I've been working with Joey for some time now and thought we could exchange some ideas."

"We don't work that way at Leclerc. Send me a written report as the other Instructors do."

"I'm not an Instructor", I replied testily and then decided to end the conversation while it still remained civil.

"Well, have a nice day Madeleine," I uttered with moderated sincerity and gently put down the receiver.

I was later to discover that this was less a hostile response to a perceived interloper than a genuine reaction to an unfamiliar request. Every inmate had a structured Correctional Plan. It was the CMO's responsibility to monitor it on a regular basis and be sure it was followed to the letter. Any deviation, such as a follow-up by some unknown quantity as myself, could perhaps be tolerated but certainly not treated seriously. The fact that I was suggesting a meeting that would include the active participation of the inmate would have been especially threatening. Institutional case discussions in the presence of the inmate were rare and the role of the inmate was expected to be of passive compliance.

Our main problem, however, was never really at the institutional level. We had sufficient experience to know how to cope with the expectations of the personnel. We would stay out of their way, yet try to create a positive climate by working directly with the inmate population. I even thought I detected some envy on the part of certain workers. After all, many of them were university-trained and the more sensitive ones must have occasionally experienced pangs of regret at having accepted the position of a glorified clerk, despite the imposing title and better-than-average salary compensation. The Wardens of the two penitentiaries, Michel Deslauriers at Leclerc and Guy Villeneuve at Archambault, were pleasantly accommodating. They allowed us free rein with the inmate population, provided offices with telephones and never questioned our work. If we had any complaint, it would be that they could have more actively sought out our expertise. We didn't necessarily have the answers but, if only because of our freedom from bureaucratic constraints, perhaps we could have posed some thought-provoking questions.

The actual threat lay at the Regional Office. They were the ones whose hand had been forced. Throughout that first year they were conspicuous by their silence. We had submitted a brief mid-year report comprised of some innocuous quantitative data. It had been received without comment. As the month of March 1997 began, signalling the end of the fiscal year and the end of our Service Contract, I had heard no word as yet. I decided to call; I wouldn't have wanted them to think we would simply go away. Laval Marchand was Jean-Claude Perron's principal assistant at the time.

"Good morning Laval, how are you?" I began on a first-name basis, wanting to break the ice immediately.

Marchand's reply was more formal but certainly cordial. He had never addressed me by my first name, an obvious sign of polite reserve on his part. It was the content that followed the pleasantries that stunned me:

"We have decided to send you people to work in our program for long-term offenders at the Federal Training Centre this year." The statement was made with some finality, as though the result of some lengthy negotiation.

"We don't work that way M.Marchand!" I stated categorically. "For a year now," I went on, "we've been following men on a regular basis. Do you think we're just going to wave to them 'so long, we're going to work somewhere else'? I repeat, that's not our style." I was caught up in the moment, "We plan to continue the work we started". I must say that Marchand listened. He calmly said, at the end of my outburst, "I'll get back to you in a few days".

He did. We signed a Service Contract for 1997-98 with the same conditions as the previous year. I knew that if we stuck to our principles we would win out, at least temporarily. Nevertheless, there remained that uneasy feeling that, though we had won the battle, the war was far from over.

*   *   *

During that first year I had initiated an all-Black counselling group. This was a first for me and actually contradicted certain convictions I had held previously. Although I had always encouraged inmates to select co-members to make up a group, I was adamant about any restrictions along racial or ethnic lines. It is no secret that inmates will not tolerate close association with known informers or sexual offenders. The question of excluding informers is reasonable in that it would be impossible to expect a climate of confidence and trust to develop with such an admixture. Their need to disallow sexual offenders, however, is not as easily explicable though just as rigid. Although I have never imposed a sexual offender upon a counselling group, I have never shied from broaching the subject and confronting the group members. The vehemence with which they react to sexual crimes, whether emotionally or behaviourally, defies reason. Thus, I consider it valid subject matter for mature discussion.

The experience in Dannemora had confirmed our belief that racial and ethnic barriers are basically artificial, the result of ignorance and fear, then magnified through incarceration. Although unofficial segregation was practised in New York prisons at the time, we had made it a point to establish a representative racial balance at the outset in our Centre. This was maintained throughout the duration of the project and included the integration of other ethnic groups as well. This planned course also allowed us to meet, head-on, the defensive use of race and ethnicity as a facile explanation of delinquent behaviour.

Earlier in my career, as the lone anglophone on staff at the Pen, I had worked with the few Black inmates, all of whom were English-speaking. In the mid-seventies their number had doubled and they were still mainly English speaking. By the mid-nineties, however, the Black inmate population at Leclerc was multi-national and now numbered about one hundred. Although the majority were French-speaking, there remained an average of thirty to thirty-five English-speaking Black inmates from various countries. All institutional programs are given in French; many, but not all, are in English. Similarly, all personnel speak French; many, but not all, speak English. I knew from the start it was not an equal playing field for all. This realization, however, was not

256

the main incentive which lured me into an English-speaking, all-Black counselling group.

René had always been the central figure in referring inmates to me. He was completely non-discriminatory. Any sentence, crime or age bracket was fair game. Men identified as Hells Angels, Italian Mafia or any other typical label, were ushered forward. All came but not all returned. Those whose only interest was immediate gratification of institutional-generated needs quickly discovered I was of no consequence. Although those individuals did not necessarily come back, they sometimes referred others. Thus, there was never a shortage of clients.

I looked up from my desk one afternoon and gaped inquisitively at an imposing, six foot plus Black man. He sported dreadlocks that ran shoulder-length. His dark complexion radiated a maroon hue, accentuated by a display of straight white teeth and sparkling eyes. I had made out a pass for him at René's suggestion. I had no idea who he was or what he was about. I was soon to find out.

"'ey mon, 'ow ya doin' . . . I was sent by de ole mon, le jeune dey call 'im he say you okay, yeh!"

This was my introduction to Predator. He was to lead me through the intricacies of institutional living for the Black Man and introduce me to some notions of Rastafarianism and Jamaican life in general. This was all completely new to me. My first task was one of basic comprehension. I found the musical lilt to Jamaican-accented English to be pleasantly mesmerizing but sometimes defied understanding. I explained this to him after having asked him to repeat himself several times.

"Mon, me speak patois, lose you totale!" he exclaimed with a grin from ear to ear.

Thus, for the next four and a half years, Predator and I worked hand in hand. He had the cunning and manipulative quality necessary for survival within the criminal milieu but also possessed an innate sense of justice and fair play. These latter qualities, combined with a natural talent for leadership, placed him in good stead with the Blacks and also earned him the respect of several inmate leaders among the overall inmate population. Unfortunately, it created a certain antipathy among some members of the personnel. Here was an inmate who obviously held considerable sway over the Black group; he must be up to no good; he bears watching.

Although this attitude of suspicion and mistrust is understandable among security staff, given the unhealthy climate of the institutional milieu, its permeation of the entire personnel simply precludes any objective evaluation process. In other words, there is a need for diligent surveillance of attitudes and behaviour but always tempered with a recognition of basic, beneficial qualities. The important point is to acknowledge and channel particular strengths, of whatever origin, in a positive direction. The underlying postulate here however would be a genuine interest in the betterment of the individual inmate and not simply the maintenance of a well-ordered institution. As a matter of fact, I strongly believe that the creation of a healthy environment, based on a knowledge of and concern for each and every offender, would allow for the development of a valid resocialization process, while providing a more secure institution in the long term. The short-sightedness of the current system, founded on suppression and control, negates the evolution of a cogent conditional release system and ultimately undermines the concept of societal protection. It was Predator himself who, after several individual contacts with me, suggested an all-Black group.

"Wach' you doin' wit' dee white boys, me I like 'dat for us too." He went on to explain that although tensions between whites and blacks were usually on a one-to-one basis, an individual conflict could easily generalize as sides would be taken along racial lines.

"Dee way I see dee problem, we 'ave dee say in not'ing 'ere. Dee guys are frustrated totale."

Although I knew all inmates felt this lack of control over their daily life, I was now tuning into the fact that this would be immeasurably more so for a minority group. After all, constraints and demands did not come solely from institutional authorities; internal impositions were also placed upon individuals and groups depending upon where they stood in the inmate hierarchy. It really didn't take much convincing. I thought the idea was a good one. However, I cautioned Predator that no miracles could be worked simply by holding a group meeting every two weeks. He dismissed my concerns with a smile and a grand wave of the hand, "dee boys appreciate wach' you doin'," he exclaimed. I had the distinct feeling this matter had been the subject of discussion elsewhere than in my office; the range, the yard or the school seemed to be likely venues.

I remember feeling somewhat elated on the drive home later that day. The idea of such a group was a good one, if only for selfish reasons. I was under no illusions that I would make a major breakthrough as to the high rate of Black inmates; also, the treatment of fundamental contributing factors to crime and delinquency would be on the periphery, at best. On the other hand, I had considerable experience with inmate groups and always considered them to be a primary source of learning for myself, if not always for all participants. I attributed my current euphoria to the fact that an all-Black group would be a first for me; the racial wrinkle would be a novel experience, something different. The group was scheduled for every second Wednesday afternoon from one-thirty to three-thirty in a room above the socio-cultural locale. I was familiar with the area, as I had been holding my other counselling group there for some time now. It was a secluded spot that gave a sense of privacy and confidentiality, important factor within these barren institutional surroundings.

I remember our first group encounter as though it occurred yesterday. I was used to hearing the muffled voices of the few early arrivals to my regular weekly group; the sound carried to the foot of the stairs leading to this second-story room. This afternoon, however, a raucous din emanated from above and carried into the hallway below. Shouts, interspersed with high-pitched peals of laughter, echoed through the hall and into the interior courtyard some fifteen yards away. What the hell was going on? I mounted the steps at a quick pace and stood open-mouthed at the entrance to the room. Some fifteen to twenty Black men were hollering, laughing and gesticulating wildly. It seemed as though no one was listening because none of the verbiage seemed to be directed toward anyone in particular. I stood there for what seemed to be an eternity, probably less than a minute, before anyone noticed me. I believe it was Predator who came to my rescue, not that he perceived it that way:

> "Great turnout mon, dee guys can't wait to git t'ings goin'," he stated with undisguised pleasure. I remained speechless; no one would have heard me anyway. I did wonder, nevertheless, what he meant by the guys getting things going.

Predator then said something in a resounding voice but indecipherable to my ear. Each man suddenly chose a chair and all sat around the table. The silence was deafening. I took this as my cue to introduce myself to the few I had never met and make some innocuous introductory remarks. The men stared at me wide-eyed, hanging on my every word. I went on to explain that this was not a program nor a course, that it would not enhance their chances for transfer to minimum security or obtain a parole and that, finally but most importantly, anything could be discussed in the group but what was said in the group must remain in the group.

"That's cool man" and similar statements of concurrence rang out from various seats around the table. It was obvious the men understood and appreciated the few conditions of group encounter. I then said that if there were no specific questions, perhaps someone could suggest a topic for discussion. And then bedlam broke loose once again.

Since this was our first meeting I gave free rein. After all this was a new experience for the men as much as for me. Over the next two hours, an average of five conversations were carried on simultaneously for periods of ten to fifteen minutes, at which point places were exchanged creating different seating arrangements and new topics of discussion and debate emerged. The meeting ended abruptly at three-thirty. With a brief word and ritual handshake, each man extended his thanks to me personally before withdrawing to the inner courtyard prior to the late afternoon lock-up and count. I wandered back to my office, my ears ringing. "Well this was the first group," I kept telling myself. Allowances had to be made. My drive home was not the usual wind-down after a full day. I was in a state of mild consternation. On the one hand, I knew the meeting had been completely out of control, certainly out of my control; on the other, the response of the men engendered in me a deep feeling of satisfaction. Something good was happening, but what?

These meetings, euphemistically referred to as in-depth counselling sessions, carried on unabated for the next four and a half years. The only break in the rhythm of the encounters came about during the yuletide season or when I was at some conference out of town. Any disruption in the pattern of a meeting every two weeks, however, was quickly brought to my attention by one or another of the Brothers:

"Wat's happ'nin' man, we meetin' this week?" Interest always remained at a high.

Although this particular group was always decidedly different from any other I had ever participated in, it was not simply a constant clamorous scene. There were regular periods of soul-searching, both at the individual and at the group level. Evidently there were times when the race card was played but I quickly learned that a non-judgmental position on my part gradually resulted in one or more members of the group edging interpretations into a more equitable stance. There was so much to learn in this setting. On the surface, the ebullient nature of the encounters at times seemed to belie the gravity of the situation. After all, this was not a social club; these men were penitentiary inmates, some of them doing serious time. Consequently, I finally fell victim to this simplistic way of thinking. Somewhere within the second year of these regular meetings I decided to have a one-on-one with Predator.

"I'm wondering about the group. I don't think the guys are getting anything out of it. They seem to enjoy it . . . but what the hell . . ." I was struggling for a way to express my frustration.

"No mon, you miss dee point", he was up on his feet, eyes flashing, ". . . wach' you mean mon? . . . everyone resepk' you . . . 'dey come because 'dey wan' to . . . not because 'dey're force'".

He stared at me in what seemed to be exasperation. I was the psychologist; I was the one who was supposed to understand.

"Look mon," he continued ". . . you don't know wach' you do 'ere . . . 'dis is dee onliest place men can say wat dey hav' to . . .

261

you t'ink dey not serious . . . mon we do plenty 'a cryin' . . . but
we do our cryin' alone."

This encounter with Predator in the confines of my office at Leclerc
was one of the most instructive in my career. This Black man from
the countryside of Jamaica, of limited formal education but possessing
wisdom beyond his years and station in life, was inadvertently focusing
on the reality of therapy. A true learning process is not limited to the
time restrictions of a formal session or the enclosure of a specific locale.
Furthermore, verbal and kinetic expression are habituated to race and
culture and should not be to designed, professional expectation. The
group continued on, now presided by a less assuming presence.

Over the years I had been an annual guest lecturer in a course
considering correctional options at the McGill School of Social Work.
At the invitation of a former colleague from the Dannemora years,
Dr.Ingrid Thompson, I had been welcomed to address her class,
usually accompanied by one or more inmates. As a result of one of
these presentations, I was later asked to supervise the fieldwork of one
of the students. Thus, for some eight to ten months of the 2000-2001
school year, Karine Gore was under my clinical supervision. Her
official field placement was with JHSQ; realistically she became my
assistant-in-training at Leclerc penitentiary.

Karine was a bright, young woman who, after having obtained a
Master's Degree in Criminology from a university in Ontario, decided
to enrol at McGill for some exposure to clinical work. Her expressed
opinion was that, despite the degree in Criminology, she had yet to
meet a criminal. I had noticed in the past that this anomaly was not
limited to students but applied to some professors as well. My own
approach as a supervisor was simply to introduce her to a number of
inmates and allow her to learn from first hand experience. After all she
came with good credentials: high academic standing, strong motivation
and an obviously out-going, mature personality. She would conduct
interviews on an individual basis and later we would spend considerable
time discussing both specific and general issues germane to the concept
of treatment of the offender in a conventional correctional institution,
as well as specific elements of the particular case. It would have been
unconscionable to exclude her from the experience of group work within
a penitentiary setting. Thus Karine accompanied me to both groups

during her fieldwork. Inmates are always deferential toward women in a group setting. Individual encounters may vary for obvious reasons, one of the main ones being the manner in which the woman carries herself and the quality of her reaction to what is essentially an all-male environment. In the group situation, however, several other elements come into play not the least of which is competition and rivalry in this deprived and bereft milieu. Thus checks and balances arise instinctively as individuals vie for what they perceive as advantageous. All of this is routine but must eventually be dealt with openly.

Although her initial presence in group, especially in the all-Black group, resulted in a temporary stunting of spontaneity on the part of several of the men, it was not long before the high-spirited ambiance returned in this exceptional adventure. More importantly, it became increasingly evident that the men were now better able to deal with personal and family issues. That element of tenderness, natural to a mature and sensitive woman but difficult to reveal in an unhealthy macho setting, was precipitous to some delicate disclosures of significant interpersonal relationships. At times these regular encounters took on the semblance of the more traditional group psychotherapy, temporary digressions that proved to be of considerable value.

My contact with the Blacks at Leclerc was not limited to the conventionality of group and individual counselling. They had occasional social events that included guests from the community-at-large and to which I was cordially invited. These were festive occasions highlighted by West Indian music and food. It gave me an added opportunity to involve members of my family and thereby enhance their cultural education. As well, Karine Gore was to discover a new meaning to the term "field placement." One of the more interesting sidelights to these social events was my introduction to members of an active group in the community-at-large known as the Black Community Resource Centre. They courteously invited me to a meeting at their headquarters that, as it turned out, was located across the street from my office on Côte des Neiges. One evening I spent a profitable two hours trading experiences of institutional and community work from different but complementary points of view.

What I am recounting here happened in the days before CSC organized everything themselves, mainly through the tenor set by their influential department of Community Engagement in Ottawa.

The natural evolution of such a bureaucratic structure brings about increasing control, leading to a demand for conformity and culminating in a virtual strangulation of individual initiative. The ultimate result is one of self-defeat, whereby the governmental system controls the community participation to the point where it is the system influencing the community rather than the converse. Prior to this surfeit of bureaucratic direction, however, our experience at Leclerc was such that the inmates themselves prepared the food with institutional facilities, thereby experiencing a realistic and responsible participation in the ensuing socio-cultural event. In liaison with the community-based cultural organization, they also assumed an active role in selecting traditional foodstuffs. It would not be long before these wholesome initiatives would be stripped from the inmates and placed in the all-embracing hands of a multi-cultural artifice.

One of the first signs of the bureaucratic mentality wending its way into socio-cultural affairs at the institutional level came to my attention in the summer of 1999. New restrictions as to inmate use of institutional kitchen facilities were being imposed. A few of the men approached me on the matter:

> "Say man, we havin' a hassle communicatin' wit' the chick responsible fo' food man; she 'posed to talk English but we can't unnerstan' nuttin' she sayin'".

I didn't know who they were talking about but I did know it would be difficult for someone whose second language was English to communicate with some of these guys.

> "I don't know who you mean but I'll try to find out"
> "Yo man".

As it turned out the task of contacting West Indian restaurants in the greater Montreal area to order food for the next social event, was assigned to a summer student. I met with Lise who was a well-intentioned young woman, working feverishly to do a good job. There were two major problems: she spoke very little English and as a student from Trois-Rivières knew little of Montreal, let alone the location of West Indian restaurants. This is a typical example of bureaucratic thinking put into action: the task is assigned to a position rather than to a specific person. Apart from the fact that these procedures usurp credible responsibility from the inmates, they also dilute the personal element with respect to the staff. It should not be a job description that defines the level of involvement but rather who is best suited to the particular circumstances. The basic question boils down to: are these socio-cultural events an integral part of an authentic resocialization initiative or merely a palliative at the institutional level and deceitful window-dressing at the national level?

It was also in the summer of 1999 I asked for a brief meeting with Warden Michel Deslauriers. He was a polite, refined man who possessed that personal security which allowed him to listen through a potentially problematic issue without thinking it necessary to have a ready-made answer. He had many years of experience in the correctional field, was respectful to the policies and procedures of the system but intelligent enough to realize there were more unanswered questions than some of the facile solutions would suggest. The Black men had been complaining to me they were never granted temporary absence, were not released on parole and that very few even made it to minimum-security institutions. The clear implication here was that the reason was racial discrimination, period. I knew this was not the case and said so adamantly. The reason I was categorical was to avoid simplistic interpretations that led to projections that would be counter-productive. In point of fact, very few temporary absences were granted from Leclerc to any inmate during these years. Paroles were scarce as well; the Parole Board opted for the safe route by insisting the individual be in minimum-security if ready for parole. Needless to say, this created a catch-22 situation for many inmates, as the institutional personnel would frequently use parole denial as a reason for not recommending transfer to lesser security. Finally, I knew for fact there were many Black men in minimum-security institutions, though most had been transferred from institutions other than Leclerc.

Nevertheless there was a gnawing sensation in the pit of my stomach. There was more than a modicum of truth in what the men were alleging. After all, the system had become an unending paper trail and one could easily get the impression that the weight of a positive decision was commensurate with the quantity rather than quality of written reports. Since the overwhelming majority of report-writers were francophone it would not be surprising that some, perhaps a good many, may shy away from the difficulty of attending to the verbally expressed needs of those whose English is strikingly different from the usual. I can honestly state that I, whose first language is English, had considerable difficulty understanding the accent and verbal expression of many inmates. One may safely assume it is more difficult for someone whose first language is other than English. Apart from this rationale, subjective interpretation of what I had observed over a period of time indicated that the men were basically right: proportionally, fewer Blacks were granted temporary absence or paroled from Leclerc and fewer Blacks were transferred to minimum-security. I believed the matter was serious enough to bring to the Warden's attention. I knew quite well these matters were not solely within his jurisdiction. But, following the dictates of an aphorism I had learned in the Pen early in my career, "don't deal with the monkey if you can get to the organ-grinder," I set out for Warden Deslauriers' office.

Michel, an educator by profession, was also a good listener. He quickly agreed the matter was serious and promised to investigate the actual statistics as a start.

> "I know you're a busy man Michel," I said hesitantly, "but if you could find a few minutes to meet with a small group of the Black guys it would really be helpful. They feel like second-class citizens here and, in fact, it's not a level playing field".

Deslauriers surprised me with his quick response, completely free of the common defensiveness. "I'll meet with all of them together," he said while reaching for his agenda. I hurriedly added, "Well perhaps it would be better if you limited it to a representative sample. You know how the guys can get excited at something new and not be able to express themselves clearly." I was thinking of their everyday means of expression. Deslauriers' English was pretty good but not better than mine. I knew he hadn't the time to go through what I had.

> "Whatever you think is best. I'm free next Tuesday afternoon. Do you think one-thirty would be okay?"
> I was floored. "That would be excellent. I'll make the arrangements".

"I'll have to be out of there by three though. I have a meeting about three-fifteen".

Second knockdown. I had hoped for twenty minutes that could extend to thirty if the discussion were lively enough. This was great and I said so with undisguised enthusiasm. I really was no longer used to hands-on tactics on the part of a Warden. The age of delegation was well into high gear.

In fact, Michel Deslauriers, Warden at Leclerc penitentiary, met with five inmates and myself on three consecutive occasions. He was honest and open in his communication, bringing up issues that were of a sensitive nature; in effect, he readily acknowledged weaknesses and failures in the system that applied to inmates in general and others that had decidedly racial overtones. I would like to thank him, once again, for his forthrightness and reiterate the fact that he did more good in those few meetings for inmate/authority relations than all the pompous official pap written up by professional storytellers from the highest ranks down.

Unfortunately a Warden cannot assume the duties that should be carried out by his underlings, on a full time basis. He must depend on his subordinates, in whose appointment he has little or no say. It was when he later delegated responsibility for the meeting to one of his assistants that the bottom fell out. The person had the appropriate job title and was senior enough to make decisions but in reality was unable to do other than pay lip service to change. The five inmates sensed the spurious nature of subsequent encounters. What could have been a breakthrough in the development of meaningful contact between senior management and representatives of a significant minority group gradually faded away. Once again, an opportunity to bridge the gap between "we" and "they" was squandered.

These few meetings with Warden Deslauriers did not bring forth significant, concrete results. The issues of temporary absence, parole and institutional transfer call for input from different sectors, involving several people at varying levels. Any major alteration in policy and practice would require serious deliberation and accord from top to bottom. No one person alone could bring this to pass. Nevertheless the meetings did have a more subtle effect. It was obvious the men took pride in what had come about and not just those who had participated. All knew it was not commonplace for a Warden to meet with a specific but unofficial group of inmates. The easy excuse to avoid a get-together and possible confrontation would have been to claim that it would be precedent-setting, that it would undermine the authority of other segments of the staff or that it would cause jealousy and friction among other inmate groups. Any or all of these reasons could have been put forth to circumvent the matter. They weren't. Instead, Deslauriers showed leadership and the men appreciated it. He had recognized and admitted to the reality of an unfair situation and had opened up communication himself, only later delegating it to underlings. Unfortunately those who assumed the responsibility were of lesser quality, unable or unwilling to see beyond the immediate.

Our own formal group meetings came to an end in the late autumn of 2001. My time allocations had changed considerably with the transfer to minimum security of inmates I followed. I was now spending more time in these other institutions so as to maintain continuity in the counselling process. Karine Gore had completed her field placement by this time and had gone on to more promising employment opportunities. Finally, Predator, my main man, was deported to his native Jamaica at the completion of his sentence. We keep in touch.

Although the all-Black group was discontinued, contact with individuals carried on. With the cessation of the designed group encounters and the simultaneous cutback in my hours at Leclerc, I resorted to a less structured approach. I started making periodic rounds of the various institutional locales, limiting office interviews to requested individual, private contact. This informal approach, looked askance at by some, was an effective way of keeping my finger on the pulse of the inmate population. Despite my time restrictions I was able to keep in touch with more men and stay abreast of important, personal issues. This casual style was probably the main ingredient that ostracized me from the institutional mainstream and paved the way for my ultimate exclusion from this overly controlled environment.

*　　*　　*

In the meanwhile, changes had occurred at the Quebec Regional Office. Apart from the common, sporadic shuffling of the deck that saw institutional authorities transfer to regional positions and vice versa, a more significant change had come about. With the retirement of Jean-Claude Perron, a new Regional Deputy Commissioner had been appointed in February 1998. This was particularly noteworthy for us at JHSQ since our entire funding was dependent upon contractual agreements with the Regional Office. Their higher authority had imposed the contract for institutional work by the JHSQ on them but we had negotiated the actual terms with senior regional officials in 1996. With this new presence at the highest regional level we didn't know what to expect. We were reasonably sure the contract for '98-'99 would come into effect as the due date was April 1st. However, we had no idea how active a role this new personage would play. Richard Watkins was an unknown quantity to CSC as well as to those of us in the private sector. He reportedly had extensive experience in the federal civil service but no official exposure to corrections.

My initial meeting with him, at his request, came in May or June 1998. The contract, late as usual, was only now about to be signed. We met in his office along with his senior assistant at the time, Laval Marchand. After some twenty minutes of pleasant discussion on correctional matters in general, the subject of our contract came up. I had been explaining the work we were doing in two penitentiaries; that we were a community-based organization providing a service to inmates and not a part of the institutional programming. As such we were autonomous and maintained a policy of strict confidentiality while delivering a counselling service to inmates who participated voluntarily. Thus, there were no reports, written or verbal, submitted to institutional personnel.

M. Watkins may have been a newcomer to the correctional field but he was obviously an experienced and astute administrator. He immediately seized upon the fact that, though the JHSQ was working under a Service Contract, it was not subject to the usual constraints and demands. He recognized the wide margin of uncontrolled manoeuvrability, uncharacteristic of official contractual agreements. At that instant, it became evident to me that he was totally unaware of the circumstances leading up to the original Service Contract of 1996; our demands and stipulations had been spelled out at that time and subsequently agreed to by the regional triumvirate of the day: Perron, Cloutier and Marchand. I related this to Watkins, emphasizing our reasons that fell within the framework of the JHSQ correctional philosophy.

> "I understand your point of view Mr. Williams but I have serious reservations about this sort of latitude," Watkins stated, "your position is clear enough, now I want you to understand mine. If I'm asked," he continued, "as chief administrator of a government Service Contract, 'just what are the John Howard doing?', I can't even give them a list of inmates who have participated." I didn't flinch since he evidently appreciated the problematic situation as one that was more his than mine. He turned to Marchand and pleasantly but pointedly queried:
> "Why was this not handled as a Contribution rather than as a Service Contract?"
> Marchand, clearly uncomfortable, cast a glance over at me, "May I talk freely?"
> "Go ahead, if you don't I will but I think it should come from you".

He went on to relate that, in the spring of 1996 an edict had come down from headquarters. The troublesome state of affairs, a dispute between JHSQ and the regional authorities, had been lingering for some sixteen months and the matter finally had to be resolved. With no further debate a compromise had been reached with the JHSQ acceptance of what had already been decreed: an agreement for institutional work. I now joined the discussion, elaborating on the abrupt cessation of the parole contract, through the ensuing political involvement and into the imposition from higher CSC authorities of a solution to the stalemate. If the picture I painted was not an administrator's nightmare, it was certainly not his dream.

Nevertheless, the Service Contract for '98-'99 was eventually signed as a result of this meeting. For my part, I acceded to the request to find new means of operational openness without compromising our ethical concerns. The key points of autonomy, confidentiality and voluntary participation were to remain intact; more precision with regard to hours of actual work and the number of inmate participants was to be articulated. As for his part, Watkins promised that the regional office would look into the possibility of altering the funding from a service contract to the less constrictive model of Contribution.

It would seem that this proposed initiative would be carried out with relative ease, especially in the sycophantic climate of a bureaucracy with a new and unknown commander-in-chief. In fact though, I had to contact the Regional Office, not having heard anything by the month of October. The required forms were finally forwarded to me, duly completed and returned. The result was that the funding for the year '99-2000 was converted to a Contribution. One would think the problem had been solved: the Quebec Regional Office was now funding JHSQ under the form they themselves had proposed and JHSQ would be able to work without the crippling restraints of a service contract. Not so. The following year, 2000-'01, was to introduce a new set of problems.

At application time, around September 1999, it was intimated that perhaps the full amount of the Contribution for the coming fiscal year would not be forthcoming since CSC was undergoing budgetary restraints. Past experience taught us that, without political help, we were dead ducks. The bureaucratic machine could erode bigger and more powerful entities than JHSQ. In addition, we were of the opinion that financial problems experienced by CSC were the fault and responsibility of CSC and no one else, certainly not the private sector. It seemed that, once again, more time and energy was to be expended fighting bureaucrats than fighting crime. Warren Allmand, our stalwart ally in the past, had retired from active politics. The young, dynamic Marlene Jennings had replaced him in his riding. Marlene was relatively new to politics as an elected Member of Parliament but not new to criminal justice issues nor to the wily ways of bureaucratic mentality. This intelligent and compassionate person rapidly became informed of the JHSQ problems of the past, as well as its current precarious position. She was instrumental in securing the necessary funding for the upcoming 2000-'01 fiscal year. It is necessary to point out, however, that the battle had to be renewed each and every year. Bureaucracies don't wear down; they wear others down. Hopefully though, they may eventually implode.

Nevertheless, despite political support, a serious diminution in the Contribution came about in the ensuing years. The years '01-'02 and

'02-'03 witnessed a sixty percent reduction in our funding through Contribution, crippling the JHSQ to the point where it could sanction only a part-time secretary at nominal monetary compensation and one professional worker with little better than reimbursement for incurred expenses. Previously engaged obligations such as rent and contracted basic office equipment used up most of the available money.

It is impossible to state categorically there had been an intentional, concerted effort to close the John Howard in Quebec. Specific individuals in power are gradually replaced through job transfer and attrition. However the overcast of disingenuous conveyance of information, supported by a labyrinthine decision-making structure, remained a constant, irrespective of whoever was in authority. The final result was the same. The demise of the JHSQ, one of the oldest Canadian, community-based organizations involved in criminal justice, coincided with the cessation of the funding Contribution from CSC for the fiscal year 2003-'04. The closing of the doors went unheard in the midst of a silent, cowed community-based sector.

THE AFTERMATH

~ *prevarication*

As mentioned previously, with the severely reduced funding of JHSQ, its functions dwindled commensurately. Activities in the community were limited to the completion of Community Assessments, work carried out by a handful of contracted, part-time help. I handled the institutional work from the autumn of 2001 on, as monies were no longer available to compensate another professional worker. I could now look forward to my pension funds to kick in, with my sixty-fifth upcoming in the autumn of 2002. In fact these last years were personally less stressful. My presence at the John Howard office was simply to read and sign the completed Community Assessments and make out cheques for rent and contracted work. A half-day per week sufficed. There was no longer any realistic hope for a resurgence of our organization as a viable force within the community-at-large. The damage had been done and I believed it was irreparable. My work with the inmates had changed considerably as well. It was now less structured as I realized there was no hope in running a separate but complementary service within the correctional institution. Sharing professional opinion so as to develop innovative techniques was impossible. We perceived and treated the inmate, not only as the source of his own basic problems but also as the fundamental wellspring of his own ascendancy. The initial step was to establish an unequivocal relationship, one in which we could be seen and accepted as a genuinely interested resource. The aim was to help bring about, within this trusting ambiance, an acknowledgment and acceptance of personal responsibility for one's own life predicament. The ultimate objective was to stimulate through positive confrontation, the development of motivation toward behavioural change. The emphasis was always upon treating the individual as such, whether on a one-to-one basis or within the group context. Change is a process that proceeds from the interior to the exterior; both recognition of the problem and its ultimate solution must come from within. External factors can only be precipitating stimuli and supportive signposts, never mere impositions.

The method employed by the federal correctional system is the converse of this. An overall correctional strategy has been mapped out and the individual inmate is subsequently fitted in. The process begins at the Regional Reception Centre where the offender is admitted. The notorious Correctional Plan is assembled here. This document, purportedly the result of a thorough evaluation, is the product of fortuitous observation, controvertible reports and random encounter. Once deposited within the cybernetic control of the modern system, it is rendered indisputable and follows the inmate throughout his incarceration and while he is under supervision in the community. The periodic additions to this blueprint hardly alter its content, as the appendages are more a repetition or recapitulation of previously produced material than a product of direct assessment.

This rigid, impersonal approach is the very antithesis of sound clinical practice. It assumes an in-depth understanding of individual problems with little or no input from the individual concerned and sets the tone for a detached management of cases as opposed to first-hand contact. The undue emphasis on static factors, mainly type of crime and length of sentence, precludes a truly objective assessment of the person and leads to the imposition of corrective measures as the tool of resocialization. These measures come in the form of a plethora of programs, many of which have a certain inherent value but whose validity is lost when applied through coercion, in an environment that militates against self-awareness and personal initiative. So long as the suppressive nature of the correctional milieu predominates, the basic diagnostic and prognostic criteria will be an appraisal of institutional adjustment. Motivation to change, considered a sine qua non rather than a symptom, thus becomes a facile reward/punishment contrivance, so easily manipulated by superficial compliance to external demands. The end result of this artificial course of thinking and action is the growth of a paternalistic attitude toward the offender. The process itself, evident in today's parole hearings and current practice in conditional release supervision, is one that engenders a fawning acquiescence and effectively undermines the development of autonomy and personal responsibility.

One may question the premise that the penitentiary is or should be a centre in which the individual offender's problems and difficulties are to be addressed. It is certainly the opinion of some that the penitentiary should be what the name implies: a place of penance, a retributive detention where, at best, change may come about simply as a result of punishment. The fact is, however, the official position alleges that the penitentiary is a correctional institution within a correctional system. The assertion here is that behavioural change is anticipated, pursued and, finally, demanded. The defined terminology of correctional plan, needs/risk evaluation, resocialization and conditional release are samples of the authorized cant, designed to reflect a system that encompasses the notion of change and suggests a means of carrying it out. The accompanying price tag, conservatively estimated over the one and a half billion dollar mark per annum while supporting this allegation, brings a more pertinent question to the fore: is society duly compensated for this exorbitant expenditure in both fiscal and human terms?

My career in criminal justice, an interval extending across five decades, afforded an exceptional vantage point to witness the evolution of an all-embracing correctional and conditional release system. In fact, it was the amalgamation of two distinct government agencies that produced this unified process. What had originally been the Canadian Penitentiary Service (CPS), primarily concerned with the housing of convicted criminals, and the National Parole Service, tasked with the supervision of offenders released on parole, were later combined into Correctional Service Canada.

The product, however, was not a composite of equal parts. CPS, the larger of the two organizations, carried the day on influencing the evolving theory and practice of the emerging entity. Although material changes in institutional living would come about, they were often a reaction to contemporary circumstance or ephemeral pressures, rather than a consequence of in-depth study and planning. As a result, the nature of the theory and practice remained one of suppression and control, a mind-set that gradually extended into post-release philosophy and praxis.

The other key player in the process, the National Parole Board, was to undergo a number of changes and adaptations over the years. Administrative reshaping and juridical amendments would affect the basic philosophy of parole, ultimately converting the NPB from a releasing mechanism into one whose prime concern is that of detention. The original consideration of whether an offender was now willing and able to complete the mandated sentence in the relative freedom of supervised living in the community, would now be a determination as to whether the inmate should continue his sentence within the physical confines of the penitentiary.

This basic shift in perception is mainly because the fundamental problem of political influence has never been adequately addressed. This is not to imply that specific parole decisions are swayed by political pressure. The influence is more subtle but perhaps more crucial. It lies in the selection of parole board members. In recent years, a screening of applications forwarded by those responding to a publicly announced competition, followed by an in-depth interview of accepted candidates, lends face validity to the exercise. Nevertheless, the overall procedure remains flawed. In the first place, the selection jury lacks autonomy, comprised primarily of senior parole and correctional administrators whose predilection is usually to preserve the status quo. Secondly, the paramount benchmark for acceptance remains overt political support, without which the application is somewhat insubstantial. Finally, the appointment itself rests in the hands of the current Minister responsible for both the NPB and CSC. This link to partisan politics, however tenuous, is a reality and raises a cloud of doubt as to the objectivity required for professional selection.

An essential layer in the bedrock of a free society is a robust criminal justice system, one to which all have equal access. It may be perceived as a living body subject to the fluctuations in public concern, political interests and media scrutiny. Canada has a right to be proud of its system, particularly when seen in contrast to criminal justice practised elsewhere. It must not rest on its laurels, however. As with any organism, its health is contingent upon constant monitoring. One of the most insidious hazards is the surreptitious stripping to the basic essential of a legal quid pro quo; a rendering, no more no less, of what is due. The fundamental components of caring, compassion and restoration, the ultimate benchmark test of a healthy criminal justice organism, are too easily supplanted by a complacent acceptance of retribution and vindictiveness.

A spirit of vengeance can easily be rationalized, not only as just desserts for the aggressor but also as a means of assuaging the extreme hurt experienced by victims of violence. In fact, attainment of closure is a personal psychological process that may be realized through sources of compassion and support, never through the destructive nature of mirror image reprisal. The valid and much overdo movement to redress wrongs visited upon victims has been contaminated by a mind-set of retributive justice. The active presence of victims in the judicial proceedings, including sentencing of the offender, must be enhanced in an informative and dignified manner. However, their involvement in the assessment and determination of ultimate release, conditional or otherwise, is questionable. Their access to information regarding offender exposure to and involvement in correctional programming should be that of any citizen in a free society. Across the board participation in the release process, on the other hand, simply impedes an objective evaluation and obstructs resocializaton, that crucial avenue towards crime prevention.

The inclusion of parties not privy to an offender's experience over a lengthy period of incarceration is not limited to victims. Police, judge and prosecutor also share in the breakdown of a personal element in release decision-making. None is in a position to comment on the current state of affairs of a candidate for possible release, yet all are solicited for their current point of view. In fact, their input amounts to a reiteration of past events and judgments already considered during the judicial proceedings that culminated in the sentence. The fundamental notion of assessment of individual change, inherent in conditional release, is eroded. The view to altering the mode of serving a portion of the sentence as a result of positive change is covertly displaced by the impression that the duration of incarceration is the principal issue. The implication is that modification of the manner in which the sentence is served, is tantamount to an abrogation of the sentence itself.

This fuzzy thinking is alarming though not surprising. The paralysing effect of bureaucratic expansion has been buttressed by over-legislation in the past several years. One result has been a gradual withdrawal from hands-on work with offenders in their management, during their evaluation preparatory to conditional release and within the decision-making hearing itself. The entire process is characterized by a general retreat to the comfort of technological manipulation. A direct consequence of this impersonal approach to human problems is the development of an artificial curriculum that fails to make headway towards viable solutions.

It is only by a return to basic principles that a meaningful correctional process can evolve within a comprehensive criminal justice system. Every effort must be made to assure that the debilitating effects of incarceration are recognized and attenuated and that conditional release is based on an assessment of individual response to a realistic institutional experience. Moreover, supervision in the community must be a personalized helping service, geared towards socially acceptable adaptation to the demands of freedom, if an authentic public security is to be anticipated. Anything short of this as a clear and constant objective belies a common-sense attempt at resocialization of the offender. Furthermore, it paves the way for a blatant abuse of power and absurd remedial measures ensconced in a money-wasting practice.

*   *   *

One of the more popular epithets in the nomenclature of criminology today is Organized Crime (OC). It is now used to run the gamut from juvenile street-gangs, through the numerous titled biker clubs and settles comfortably in television and movie-celebrated mafia. The former boundaries of province, state and country have now vaporized and an international phenomenon has emerged, worthy of our global village.

The fact of organized crime, apart from the lucrative gains accrued by the relative few, has spawned vicarious enterprises. It has stimulated the imaginative skills of screen and television producers, fed the literary endeavours of the print media and enhanced the platforms of all political parties. Consequently, it has been instrumental in eliciting a positive response to the demands of police and correctional officials for significant budgetary increases and expanded powers of control. For the most part, this fallout has had certain obvious benefits; the negative effects, however, have not always been of an innocuous nature. Corrections has proven to be a fertile field in which the spectre of organized crime has stirred the imagination and bolstered the finances of the security bloc, sometimes with dubious consequences.

From my point of view, organized crime has rarely shown its face in prisons and penitentiaries and when it has, it has been handled inappropriately. A constant contention is that the inmate population treats certain crime figures with a marked deference. One has only to know the closed world of institutional living to understand this. What is harder to explain is the official creation of classifications such as "notorious cases" involved in "spectacular events," both of which result in special handling with respect to institutional placement, programming, work opportunity and, ultimately, community supervision. It goes without saying that this practice of management by label spills over into the thinking and policy of the paroling authority. Furthermore, the meagre benefit attained by this system of ticketing, is greatly outweighed by an inadvertent reinforcing of a false sense of self-importance of those who have been so labelled. These personal dynamics, rather, should be identified and perhaps become the object of modification. In fact, those who end up in the penitentiary more suitably represent an aspect of disorganized crime. Another fact is that without the compliance of the "legitimate" side of society, organized crime would not be of the size or power it is today. If this latter reflection were added to the equation of crime prevention, society as a whole may well tip the balance in a true fight against crime.

Mario was in his second year on parole. In his late forties, he had been arrested for complicity in a drug transaction. Although unknown to the police, his associates in the caper were well known and considered active members of an Italian crime group. Mario was convicted, sentenced to seven years and, as a first offender with no history of violence, was eligible for release after serving one sixth of his sentence. His previous work record was impressive, having set up a successful terrazzo and marble enterprise, and where he had worked steadily since his early twenties. He had never before come into conflict with the law. His social preference was the nightclub/bar scene that brought him into contact with Italian criminals. Although he enjoyed "hanging out" in the milieu, his claimed peripheral involvement was supported by a conspicuous absence from the police blotter.

Mario was released to a halfway house at the sixth and remained there, as the law prescribes, until the third of the sentence. Compliance with all rules and regulations, along with a positive approach to work, allowed for a comparatively easy passage from incarceration, through semi-liberty, into the relative freedom of full parole. He was back to full-time employment, conscientiously avoiding previous associates and now reporting regularly to a parole officer in the community. It was during this second year under supervision that he encountered his first obstacle. In a routine interview with his parole officer he mentioned the upcoming wedding of his son:

> "Well, I'll need a list of all invited guests to send to the parole board," was the response to this revelation.

A stunned but still compliant parolee responded:

> "Yeh . . . well sure . . . if it's necessary. But it's gonna' be real pain in the ass. There could be a lotta' people to contact."
>
> "You might have to reduce the number . . . they'll probably want to run a check . . ."
>
> "Hey, wait a minute . . . it's not me gettin' married . . . I've been there once, that's enough! But my son's twenty-four, he does the invitin', wit' his wife naturally. What's this about checkin' up? Not everyone knows I been in the can y'know," added an increasingly exasperated parolee.
>
> "Come on now, you know you've got OC on your file. The Board will want to know if anyone's invited who shouldn't be there."

The upshot of this resocialization tactic was that the number of persons invited was reduced to twenty and one of these was subsequently refused because of a police allegation that he had known connections to organized crime. The fact that he had no criminal record and had previously been security cleared by the institutional authorities, as one of Mario's regular visitors, did nothing to alter the Board decision. Incongruities such as this are of no importance to an impersonal bureaucracy bent on "protecting society" through discriminatory labelling.

This is the result of a rubber-stamp mentality, one which responds to a contrived classification regardless of consequences. The real question is, if Mario is that fragile to need an impersonal edict to monitor and control family relationships, why is he on parole? The logic here would seem to point towards a questioning of the relevance of the law of automatic conditional release, as well as the rationale underlying community supervision. When control measures are exercised on any basis other than individual concern and responsibility, the consequences eventually reveal a hidden agenda of self-serving opportunism and abuse of power. A system that allows anyone to create and enforce rules and restrictions reaches a point where the right hand doesn't know what the left hand is doing, a situation impossible to correct since the specific source of control remains in impenetrable shadow.

Aldo had been tried out in the community several times without success. Work programs, community service, halfway house; none had really worked. He was serving a second penitentiary sentence and was in his early 'forties. An institutional history such as this is not uncommon. The penitentiary is peopled with men who have tried and failed, some because they have never really tried and others because they have not found a hint of a solution as yet. Aldo, though, was different. He had a long-term drug-dependency problem. Nevertheless, this is not what made him different; the difference was that the principal decision-makers considered his addiction problem subordinate to the fact that he was the son of a reputed crime family boss. It was not that the drug use was ignored as much as that any difficulty he had was magnified under the light of the OC label.

With a year to go on his sentence, he was once again released to a Community Correctional Centre where he would be required to reside and seek employment. At the time he was undergoing some changes in his personal life, having experienced the loss of two significant family figures in the recent past and having just assumed a new spousal relationship. The declining health and continuing incarceration of his father weighed on him as well. He knew that one serious step would necessarily be that of legitimate employment, an area entirely unknown to him.

Aldo approached a family friend. Luigi was an ex-offender who had been convicted some twenty years ago. He had since become a successful businessman and professional entertainer. So as to avoid any misunderstanding, Aldo reported the encounter to his parole officer in the halfway house. Her immediate response was that any contact with a person with a criminal record was not permitted. The explanation that this had been an employment-seeking interview with a family acquaintance, who had legitimate connections in the community, was summarily waved aside. Rules were rules and OC was OC.

This frivolous allegation followed Aldo throughout his sentence and was alluded to by the Parole Board at a subsequent hearing. The asinine nature of this episode came full circle when I had the opportunity to meet Luigi about a year later. He was the invited Master of Ceremonies at the thirtieth anniversary event that celebrated the long-term service contract that *CEJEP Marie-Victorin* had with Correctional Service Canada. This well-recognized junior college was instrumental in helping many offenders re-enter the community over the years, one of their graduates being the performing MC. Senior officials of CSC from the Regional Deputy Commissioner down attended this major social event. Penitentiary inmates out in the community, former beneficiaries of the educational service, were also present. I don't know of any who were castigated because of Luigi's presence. Perhaps the appearance of senior correctional bureaucrats attenuated the threat of contamination.

It would be misleading to suggest that the vagaries of the federal correctional system were limited to members of perceived organized crime or any other ticketed group. The problem is more generalized than that. The pigeonholing of inmates, whether it be length of sentence, type of crime, ethnicity or any other tag, tends to diminish their individuality and results in an imprecise assessment. It further feeds into a general breakdown of the way of thinking about and dealing with all offenders.

Jeff, a sixty-five year old offender, was a regular of my bi-monthly group at the minimum security, Ste-Anne des Plaines penitentiary. This was his second penitentiary sentence but he evidently had been involved in crime his entire adult life. Although he was originally from Montreal, his only living relatives were a sister and her family in Toronto.

"Well, I'm going to my sister's place next weekend" claimed an elated Jeff. "It's my first TA so they're sending me with a screw . . . but it's better than nothing."

I was not paying attention to this statement, as it was not out of the ordinary for a man from minimum to be sent home on a TA. But suddenly I remembered Jeff's sister was in Toronto and hadn't he mentioned an escort?

"Did you say you're going escorted?"
"Yeh, we're drivin' down and they told me I have to stay in the local lock-up overnight."

This was becoming more confusing by the moment. Jeff was in minimum-security and the temporary absence was to Toronto. I always had a tough time understanding the rationale behind sending someone from a minimum-security setting who required an escort; the question may be as to why he is in minimum-security. The exception to this would be for someone going out for the first time after a prolonged period of incarceration. In that case the person accompanying the inmate should be someone who knows him well and has a positive relationship with him. This was not the case; Jeff was a recidivist. The fact that he was already doing volunteer work in the community evidently had no bearing.

The outcome of this scenario was as follows: Jeff and his escort went to Toronto by car. After some ten hours on the road, he spent four hours with his sister and her family under the watchful eye of the escort. He was then brought to lock-up facilities where he spent the night. The escort left his hotel the following morning to retrieve Jeff and bring him to his sister's home for another four hours. The return trip was affected over the ensuing ten hours.

A summary of this temporary absence for resocialization purposes would read: twenty hours of escorted travel and twelve hours of detention for a total of eight hours of family visit. The escort costs would include hotel and meal expenses, within a period of overtime pay. This procedure was authorized for an inmate who had been "cascaded" down to a minimum-security setting. This costly procedure was carried out during a period when budgetary restraints that would shortly reduce funding to community-based programs were in the planning stage.

Discussions around the anomalies of penitentiary life would often come up in the group. Bitching was constant but not without reason. If there is any system that sets itself up for criticism, the correctional one is a prime candidate. It is not an easy task for a therapist to divert the attention of a group of incarcerated delinquents away from the lure of extraneous factors and redirect it inwards. I have always felt that the best avenue was a path allowing full rein; never try to defend the indefensible nor explain away the insanity. Simply, intervene regularly in like manner:

"But why the hell did you put yourself into this position . . . not once but several times?" along with appropriate finger pointing.

I usually arrived at Ste-Anne des Plaines around five-thirty. It gave me time to relax before group that was from six to eight every second Tuesday evening. This was supper hour and many of the men used the time to call home as well. Frequently an inmate, group member or not, would come by and chat, sometimes on matters of a more confidential nature. This particular evening it was Aldo who appeared early, quite in contrast to his usual late arrival.

"Paul, I've got one for you you're gonna' really like. I know how you light up at the way they do things here."

He went on to tell the story of an inmate who had been sent out on an escorted TA recently. This one made the absurdity of Jeff's experience pale in comparison.

"If you wanna' see the kid I can get him for next time. I don't know where he is tonight and anyways it's seven now."
"Sure Al next time's fine, I would like to speak with him."

Francois was a twenty-two year old serving a three-year sentence. After failure to adjust in a halfway house setting, the authorities later allowed him a program of seventy-two hours per month on temporary absence as a means of progressive release. He was using the time to visit his father in the Lac St-Jean region, several miles out of the Montreal area. The understanding was that his father who had a commercial enterprise in Alma, Que. was prepared to give his errant son a job opportunity upon release. On the third day of his latest TA, Francois was made aware of his mother's sudden death in Vancouver. He telephoned the institution asking permission to go to British Columbia for the obvious reason. The reply was that he was to return to the institution, reportedly for updated papers, and then could proceed to Vancouver. Upon return from Alma the story had now changed. He was informed that he would be sent under escort and required to remain in detention overnight.

> "But my aunt lives in Vancouver; my mother was living with her" blurted out a tearful young man.
> "I'm sorry but you've used up your TAs for the month. You'll have to go with an escort."

Summary: Result of bureaucratic procedures, possible over-legislation, if not sheer stupidity, a young man's final respects to his mother were paid in the company of a security escort, interrupted by overnight detention and to the exclusion of the comfort of grieving relatives. Apart from these human costs, monetary expenditures included air flight and overtime pay, along with food and hotel accommodations for the escorting officer, all to be assumed by the taxpayer. Francois was an inmate of a minimum-security federal penitentiary at the time of this debacle. He reached his final release date some three weeks later. Case closed.

This mentality of control is rationalized under the guise of protection of society. It is obvious to all but the exponents themselves that these measures are reflections of insecurity at both the corporate and personal level. The real menace, however, lies in the fact that this disposition is generated from above. Politicians have resorted to legislation at the expense of informed discernment and the senior bureaucrats have devised labyrinthine patterns of self-protection. Unfortunately the front-line worker becomes enmeshed in a maze of paperwork and works in an ambience of apprehension. The safest recourse is self-preservation, the repose of technocratic manipulation; the accrued results, though, are manifest in bizarre ways.

Charles is an intelligent, bi-lingual offender with a lengthy criminal record. At the age of sixty-eight, he is nearing the completion of a third penitentiary term. Preparation for release includes some temporary absences. After the mandatory escorted TAs, he is finally allowed a three-day excursion into the community. He has given the address of his daughter Agnes as home base. After completion of the requisite Community Assessment, an on-the-spot evaluative visit to the home followed by a lengthy written report, the case is studied, accepted and the seventy-two hour release is accorded. In recent years the CSC adopted the practice of having the temporarily released offender report to a designated parole office. Originally this procedure had been initiated for select, long-term offenders on their first outing. Naturally, with the inevitable widening of the net it now applies to all offenders on every TA. The logistics of this bureaucratic progression sometimes reach nightmarish proportions. Nevertheless, it provides job opportunity.

Charles arrives at the parole office in the company of another daughter who had come in from Toronto. She awaits him in the waiting room when he goes in for his interview.

"Who's that woman you're with?" enquires a keenly observant parole officer.

"She's my daughter from Toronto. She picked me up at the joint and gave me a lift. We're going downtown for Chinese before going to my other daughter's place. Would you like to meet her?" asks Charles rising from his seat.

"That won't be necessary. You've already broken one regulation and are suggesting another."

Charles' mouth drops in surprise. He didn't think he had ever broken a rule without knowing it. His confused look was recognized.

"The Community Assessment was at your daughter Agnes' house. There was no mention of anyone else. You're supposed to spend the temporary absence with her not someone in from Toronto."

"But she visits me in the pen, that's my daughter Louise out there," says a frustrated Charles, pointing towards the door.

The interview came to an end when Charles acknowledged his mistake, promised to go directly to Agnes' home and agreed that he would go nowhere over the next three days unless accompanied by Agnes. The interview was devoid of any acrimony. It was simply intended to assure that the offender followed the prescribed procedures. I don't know what happened over those three days and, frankly, I don't give a damn. I only know that sixty-eight year old Charles is better equipped to deal with that mentality than this sixty-eight year old. It is not to be thought this need to control remains at the lower levels; repercussions are not limited to institutional bungling or counter-productive measures in community supervision. When the policies, procedures and objectives are skewed, the basic infrastructure of criminal justice is threatened.

Giovanni had served twelve years on a life sentence, was rearrested after thirteen productive years in the community and then sentenced to three concurrent terms that totalled twelve years. Since a life sentence is just that, a sentence that continues for the duration of the offender's life, these twelve years were to be calculated within the context of the original life sentence. The Parole Board is never obliged to release an offender serving a life sentence. When a second conviction occurs, obviously while the offender was under parole supervision, the ensuing sentence is considered under its numerical value with all other elements factored in. In Giovanni's case, he would be eligible for another parole after serving a third of the latest imposed sentence, after four of the twelve years. I emphasize the fact that this is an eligibility date only, not a certainty of release. As a matter of fact, the NPB now takes a more stringent position than in the past. It is rare to see an offender, whose life parole has been revoked because of a new offence, released after a third of the new numerical sentence.

Giovanni had always maintained a stellar penitentiary record. He not only was free of offence reports but also was recognized as an active participant in institutional programming and one who exercised a positive influence on others simply by his comportment. His leadership and ingenuity with respect to community participation was likewise acknowledged. Times had now changed, however; the OC label on his file superseded all other considerations. An excellent institutional record, bolstered by a lengthy stay in the community with steady employment, would remain a positive factor; the spectre of OC, nevertheless, would hover over any assessment and decision-making.

He was now in his seventh year incarcerated and the third in a minimum-security penitentiary. He had appeared before the Parole Board on two occasions. They had granted him a temporary absence program of seventy-two hours a month the first time and extended it for another year the following year. As well, he had been assigned to voluntary work in the community, helping the elderly in a specialized institution, five days a week. Upon return from community work one afternoon, two security officers met him at the front door and peremptorily whisked him away to the detention block of neighbouring Archambault penitentiary. It was after he had been locked in a solitary cell that an explanation was given:

> "We have been advised that your sentence has been re-calculated and the amount of time you have left to do requires that your security level be heightened to medium, possibly maximum security. You'll be placed accordingly when the final determination is made," the tone was not intimidating, simply factual.

Nonetheless, Giovanni was well aware this was not the personnel with whom he could discuss his predicament or a suitable place for in-depth dialogue.

It was three days later when cooler heads prevailed that he was returned to minimum security. The initial action had been precipitated by typical bureaucratic reaction, with no consideration for the individual concerned. Giovanni had a record clear of any escape from custody but t was also well known for his total compliance with any and all regulations; well known, that is, to those who knew him. It was finally through the intervention of an official at Archambault who had known him over a number of years that the previous transfer order to higher security was rescinded and he was sent back to the minimum setting.

The problem, however, had just begun. His temporary absence programme and community-aid efforts were immediately suspended. It was only after some six to eight months of lawyers and courts that the Federal Court of Canada struck down the new calculation of his sentence with the words of the presiding judge echoing the "absurdity" of the government agency position. It had been clearly stipulated by the trial judge at the time of sentencing that the sentences for the three convictions were to be served concurrently, not consecutively, thus amounting to twelve years, the extent of the longest term. The sentence calculation department of the government agency was now claiming, some seven years later, that Giovanni must serve a third of each of the three sentences before being eligible for parole. For purposes of clarification, the Federal Court Judge used a hypothetical example to demonstrate that the position was untenable. If the offender had been sentenced to four concurrent sentences of three years, his term would expire after three years. However, if the above rationale were applied, this same offender would be eligible for parole only after four years, one year after the expiration of the applied sentence.

I find it disconcerting to see with what relative ease the normal flow of an adjudicated sentence can be disrupted and one can only wonder from where the pressure comes. It may be argued that justice won out in this instance but the goal of the exercise remains nebulous. It must be kept in mind that not all incarcerated offenders have the means, the understanding nor the fortitude to challenge complex issues. I believe it is incumbent upon a healthy justice system to monitor, honestly and persistently, all facets of its operations and assure that justice be applied equally to all. Although there rarely is concrete evidence of a direct link between offender labelling and specific decision-making, questions, suggestions and insinuations give rise to doubts. At his last parole hearing, Giovanni was confronted directly by one of the attending board members:

"I have serious doubts that you ever have shown any remorse for the crime you committed in the first place. It was of a serious nature."

Remorse, a psychological reaction to specific behaviour, I believe is best dealt with in a therapeutic setting rather than at an administrative hearing. In any case, the crime alluded to by the parole board member had occurred some thirty-five years before. In the interim, Giovanni had been interviewed and decided upon by this same Parole Board on numerous occasions. There are many parole board members but only one federal paroling authority, the NPB. In the past, the NPB had released Giovanni to a community correctional centre, then into a freer halfway house setting, to be followed by full parole. Some years later, his status had been modified to "reduced parole" by the same authority, a practice used sparingly and only on parolees who were making significant progress. All these decisions were taken while he was serving the original sentence for the crime of a "serious nature." One would assume that the Board members who had made these decisions in the past were fully aware of the seriousness of the original crime. The origin of the allegation now being made and the motivation behind it, at least leaves the door open to conjecture.

The entire management of this case, since the revocation of the original parole, leads to some fundamental questions. The handling reflects a recipe approach to a contrived category rather than the individualized treatment of a specific person. If the NPB believed that Giovanni is a member of a group of organized criminals, why was there decision to release him on a programme of temporary absence for seventy-two hours per month, over a twelve-month period? A man certainly cannot seek employment during these short spurts of liberty. Is this supposed to be a test? The underlying rationale to this type of TA is to reintroduce the offender progressively into the community, normally one who has been away for a lengthy period of time and whose social skills may need honing on a gradual basis. The allegation made against organized crime figures is that they are too organized; that they too easily manipulate the environment with no sense of responsibility as to the effect on others. What better way to carry on in this manner than while released to the community for brief periods of time with little or nothing constructive to do. Would it not be more sensible to skip the TA phase and go straight to release with proper supervision, one supportive of a responsible use of time? The short answer is yes and Parole Board members might act accordingly if they were to treat the individual offender as such and put aside the manufactured formulas designed for artificial groupings.

Had Giovanni been treated as the intelligent and personally organized individual he is, his specific skills within the context of his evolving personal life would have been recognized and become an integral part of a realistic evaluation. The subsequent integration plan would have reflected the genuine needs, talents and deficiencies of a person rather than the largely fictive characterization that emerges from devised clusters.

In the mid-eighties three men were convicted of first-degree murder and sentenced to life imprisonment without possibility of parole for twenty-five years. The law, however, allows for application for a judicial review at the completion of fifteen years. The judicial review is held before judge and jury and the result ranges from, maintaining the eligibility date at twenty-five years, to anywhere along the descending number of years to the current fifteen-year mark. The usual procedure prior to this is that the offender is cascaded down through the institutional system to a minimum-security setting. This procedure, naturally, is contingent upon good institutional behaviour reflected in few, if any, offence reports, positive attitude towards and acceptance of assigned institutional programming and a positive response to work or educational demands. Many of these offenders arrive in minimum security after their ninth or tenth year. If they are planning to apply for judicial review and their overall adjustment has been positive, their case management team, spearheaded by the case management officer, works on a plan of increasing, supervised release as an aid in preparing the application. The usual format is comprised of a series of escorted group outings, escorted individual outings, controlled community-aid work or a combination of the above. The prospective request for and possible acceptance of a judicial review will be enhanced by successful completion of a thorough preparatory phase.

The three men referred to above, however, were treated differently. They had institutional records free of offence reports, had actively participated in assigned institutional programming in accordance with their correctional plan and each had shown a distinct initiative towards educational betterment. Despite this, all three were still wallowing in a medium security setting after having completed fourteen years. The disparate handling of these cases was obviously not because of their institutional performance. In fact, the hindering effect was coming from without the correctional system. Certainly, reports from outside the system itself are acceptable; what is not acceptable is a specific measure being dictated by an outside source. The first clear indications of this became apparent during the twelfth year of incarceration; by the fourteenth year, one of the men sought legal assistance and the end result was a positive reply from the courts. The court applicant was transferred to minimum security within three months; the other two co-defendants in the original trial and conviction were not transferred, however, until some three years later and then only after a final threat to resort to judicial proceedings. The CSC had studiously avoided the high ground and chosen to maintain its adamant and haughty stand despite a clear judicial position.

Although two of the three offenders are Canadian citizens, all three were born outside of the country. Their crime took place in Canada and they were tried, convicted and sentenced under Canadian law. Nevertheless, management of their sentence was directly influenced by international political considerations, hardly an element within the purview of a Canadian correctional and conditional release system. Then again, this is the same system that has all but abandoned any genuine concept of individual assessment and treatment when faced with the allure of categorized labelling. What makes the picture bleak is that this overwhelming bureaucracy has metastasized over the years and corroded the vigour of constructive criticism and informed dissent from without its closed ranks.

*   *   *

Despite the official closing of the John Howard office in January 2004, I continued my institutional work as a volunteer for JHSQ The physical plant was closed but the legal entity remained. I kept in regular contact with board president Pat Wickham who continued on as a member of the Board of Directors of John Howard of Canada, as its Quebec representative. Even though my status was that of volunteer I had the same access to the penitentiaries as before. I had an office in Leclerc penitentiary and easy entry into the minimum-security institutions, Ste-Anne des Plaines and Federal Training Centre. By now, however, I had abandoned Archambault and Montée St-Francois institutions simply out of lack of time.

Although my personal technique was the same with all offenders, my work differed in each institution. At Ste-Anne I did only group work, a collection of some six to eight inmates I had known over the years. Although the individuals changed during the six years I conducted the counselling sessions, there was continuity as new members were usually added before the actual release of others. These bi-monthly meetings targeted difficulties coping with freedom since all members were scheduled for release in the near future.

My work at Federal Training Centre was conducted on an individual basis. Although I had formed a group the first year, the rigidity of this institution's procedures made the logistics burdensome. I reverted to individual counselling on the basis of one day a week, seeing the same men until their ultimate release. Once again, the basic approach was one of positive confrontation within a supportive setting with a view to eventual release into the community. This work continued over six years.

Although the medium-security Leclerc had originally been the hub of my activities, beginning with the contract work in 1996 and later spreading out into other institutions where regular participants were being transferred, it was now the place where I felt the least could be done. It had become, even more than before, a place where inmates were simply "doing time," waiting and hoping for transfer elsewhere. Releases were almost entirely at expiration of sentence; parole, day parole and temporary absence were virtually non-existent. Despite the morose atmosphere, I made weekly appearances of a day or two, usually encountering the men in the more casual setting of the prison yard or gym. The obvious lack of formality however did not detract from the seriousness of my task; a reality acknowledged by most of the inmates but few of the staff.

In fact, though few of the personnel recognized the earnestness of my approach, the number included some key people. Denis Cloutier had replaced Michel Deslauriers as Warden at Leclerc around the turn of the century. The two of us went back a long way, having worked together in the 'seventies. Another former colleague, Robert Massie, now a senior Unit Manager, was also a campaigner from that era. Both of these men knew me and acknowledged the fact that I marched to my own beat in dealing with institutional life. It later came to my attention that these two defended me behind my back, in the face of opposition from the more traditionally oriented within the union and the preventive security forces.

I had just returned from vacation in July '04 when I found out that Cloutier had retired about two weeks before. I was surprised at the suddenness of his decision but really thought nothing more of it. He was still a relatively young man for retirement but I knew his retirement package would have been lucrative. It was at this time when a member of my group at Ste-Anne took me aside at the end of an evening session:

> "Paul, I have something to tell you that is a little embarrassing," he said hesitatingly.
>
> "Let go man, how bad could it be?" I had no idea what he could be leading up to. Sometimes, incarcerated men took things out of proportion. I had just returned so I knew I hadn't ruffled any feathers, not lately.
>
> "Well, it's just that Richard, you know the guy from Lifeline, told me that someone on staff at Leclerc was asking him about you."
>
> I looked at him quizzically, "Asked about me? I was there yesterday, why didn't they come to me?"
>
> "That's what I said to Richard."
>
> "In any case, don't worry about it," I said "I'll speak to Richard when I next see him in Leclerc."

A few minutes later I was in my car driving home. I knew something was afoot; the old paranoia, that reliable preservative, was kicking in. I knew Richard Desrosiers. He was solid. He had done a good amount of time for some serious business but had turned his life around a number of years ago. He was now working with a group known as Lifeline. It was primarily made up of ex-offenders who worked as in-reach workers dealing with men serving a life sentence. The movement had started in London, Ont. under the auspices of St. Leonard's Society and directed by the highly skilled Skip Graham. It had now gained national presence and prominence mainly due to the persistent efforts of the talented John Braithwaite.

About a week later I met Richard crossing the yard in Leclerc. He told me what the preventive security officer had asked:

> "What does that John Howard guy do? How come he roams around the institution talking with all the inmates?"

Since Richard had done time, this line of questioning did not surprise him. He also knew the short answer "because that's his work" could be taken as an affront rather than a mere truism. What he did reply was that I was known by most of the inmates and they felt comfortable talking to me. "Why don't you ask him? He's easy to speak to." I let the matter lie and heard nothing for about a week. I was in the school area interviewing a Jamaican who was uptight about a family situation when the PA system announced, "Mr. Williams, wanted immediately in the deputy-warden's office."

When I had completed the interview on the delicate family matter, I told Rusty I would see him in a week or so. It was never to be.

I went up to Yves Lanneville's office. He was the Deputy-Warden who had come in shortly after Cloutier had taken over as Warden. Lanneville and I knew each other but not well. We had never worked together in the past and our contact in Leclerc over the past few years had been limited to casual greetings. Cloutier was now gone but it never crossed my mind that this call was to introduce me to the new Warden. It wasn't.

> "It's good to see you Mr. Williams," started a pleasant but clearly uncomfortable Deputy. "I have to tell you that some changes need to be made now that you're no longer with John Howard."
>
> "I didn't know I was no longer with John Howard" I toyed.
>
> "What I mean is, now that you're retired, you don't represent John Howard any more and I was told that the John Howard doesn't exist any more."
>
> "Who's been telling you that? I was talking to our President just recently; as far as he's concerned the John Howard still exists and I'm their volunteer representative."
>
> Lanneville grew increasingly uncomfortable, "I want you to understand this isn't my decision it comes from Regional. They say that since John Howard no longer has a contract with CSC you don't represent them but if you're a volunteer," He was clearly floundering.
>
> "Listen Yves," I found that first names sometimes lowered the stress level, "in the first place, John Howard has provided institutional services for at least the forty years I've been in the game, without any service contract or monetary remuneration. The Contribution funding which ended last year was for specific

work in designated institutions. Secondly, the John Howard is still a legal entity regardless of what Regional or anyone else says and I'm their representative on a volunteer basis."

He seemed to have found a way out as his demeanour suddenly relaxed, "but as a volunteer you can still see inmates. There are guidelines for volunteers, however. You must be placed on the inmate's visiting list." I must have looked up suddenly because he was quick to add,

"wait a minute now, the regulations are that a volunteer can be on the visiting list of only one inmate at a time but in your case I'll wave that rule; because of your experience, you can be on the list of any number. What do you think of that?" he added expansively.

"Not much" was my blunt reply.

I left Lanneville's office with a promise I would consider his offer. In fact I was eager to leave, tired of the prevaricating; poor Yves, feeling forced to defend the indefensible.

My weekly visits to FTC were usually on a Tuesday or Wednesday. The procedure was I would telephone the day before and give the names of those I would be interviewing to the visiting room officer. This was to assure a private office. I did so in mid-July, the week following my meeting with Lanneville. When I arrived at the front desk the following morning, however, I was told immediately that I was required to meet with the Acting Deputy Warden and "an escort will bring you upstairs." I turned suddenly and my escort was by my side. I almost extended my wrists for the handcuffs.

The interview was held in the deputy's office. I had never met Joan Malone before but had heard her name; she was accompanied by a non-descript M.Cantin. The opening gambit was similar to that of Leclerc but put forth by Malone in the tone of a disgruntled prosecuting attorney. I guess I wasn't in the mood; I quickly corrected their misinformation, countered their allegations and stated directly:

"I know you hold the big end of the stick and can prevent me from coming in here on any one day. If this is to be discussed further, it will be at another level. What I would like to do now is go downstairs and see the men I have scheduled for interview today and tell them I'll not be back until further notice."

"You can't do any more interviewing, including today," said Malone imperiously.

"Interviews over here," I said, rising from my seat and picking up my briefcase. My parting retort, I realize now, was a waste of breath and beyond the comprehension of such ignorance, "your preventing me from seeing the men I've followed for years shows a total lack of professional ethics." They undoubtedly had a good chuckle at that once they had looked up the meaning of ethics.

Once I descended the stairs, my escort trailing hurriedly behind, I stopped at the waiting room where my first interviewee was:

"I won't be seeing you today Reggie. They won't let me in the joint. Advise the guys that I'm on hold until further notice. Ciao!"

I had been following Reggie, considered a high profile case by the labellers, for the past four years. Although of an impoverished educational background, he exercised a strong native intelligence within the structure of a well-organized personality. He was continually at odds with the system and had some pending lawsuits against certain authorities. He was not a popular figure with the powers that be. Our interviews rarely touched on a specific crime though often on criminality and how, despite undisputed financial gain, it usually played havoc with one's personal life. Reggie was a serious man with respect to his family and, I believe, became more sensitive as a result of our encounters. He was the first person to express concern over my situation. It is not forgotten; he's out now; we keep in touch.

I was able to reach Warden Lise Bouthillier by telephone the following day. She acknowledged responsibility for the decision but was unable to enunciate a clear rationale. The reasons fluctuated from my being a private citizen to the fact that John Howard no longer had a contract, and back. She was explicit however with respect to penitentiary regulations stipulating that a volunteer could be placed on the visiting list of only one inmate.

"But Lise, I was told only last week that I could be put on the visiting list of any number of inmates, the fact that I've been working with them so long. Do penitentiary regulations vary with the institution, or with the person speaking, at any given moment?"

A moment of silence was broken with mumblings of "regional" and "discussing with my colleagues." My contact with Lise Bouthillier ceased after a 'phone conversation two days later. She confirmed her decision that, unless the Regional Office allowed otherwise, I could be placed on the visiting list of only one inmate and that my interviews would be in the general visiting room during the specified hours. When I made it clear that this was unacceptable I requested a final, private interview with each of the men I had been following regularly. It was not necessary to explain my reasons for this; it was simply a matter of being both professional and polite. Nevertheless, the request was denied. The conversation concluded as I called into question the professional standards, not only of an Acting Deputy Warden but also of a Warden who was a Criminologist with some thirty years experience in the field.

Since the word "regional" had been invoked on more than one occasion and by more than one person, I took the liberty of calling the new Regional Deputy-Commissioner, Denis Méthé. Denis was a man I had met on several occasions over the years, mainly since his return to the Regional Office from Headquarters in Ottawa. In summary, he denied knowing about the entire issue and was quick to point out that he was on his way to a meeting. I have no reason to doubt the veracity of this last assertion, one of the few verities in this fiasco.

The evening of my last 'phone conversation with Lise Bouthillier, July 20, 2004, I went to Ste-Anne des Plaines for my bi-monthly counselling session with the group. I was somewhat apprehensive driving there, knowing that the word was out I was, at least to some extent, *persona non grata*. On the other hand, I was also aware that CSC was so overly organized that their communications frequently seemed disorganized. In any case, everything went as normal that evening and continued so for the next six months. It was obvious the inmates were aware of my peculiar status, certainly those in the group were, but the tacit agreement was established and spread, to let sleeping dogs lie.

The first sign of trouble on the horizon arose on December 21ˢᵗ. Upon leaving the institution after the group that evening, the officer at the entrance advised me that the Keeper wanted to see me. My antennae were on red alert.

Keeper Michaud was a polite and respectful man. He remembered me from the Leclerc days in the 'seventies where he had been posted at the time. We had also conversed a number of times here in his office when I would bring back an inmate I had accompanied into the community on some institutional project or other.

> "Mr. Williams, who was it gave you permission for this group in the first place?" he enquired haltingly. "Actually, M.Michaud, it goes back some six or seven years now. It was Beaudry himself," I replied. M.Beaudry had been Warden at the time and had known me for some years, dating back to when he was in charge of programming at La Macaza penitentiary. I had known him as one with a positive attitude towards the inmate population and, hence, the reason for approaching him to get permission for the group.
>
> "I knew you had been coming here for some years now," continued Michaud, "it's no problem just that they want to update your coordinates. You know there are different people on the three shifts and they don't all know you as well as I do," he added as though to assure me. "Just call Breton in the Socio and he'll take the information and the necessary steps."

I knew Michaud was not being duplicitous; he was passing on what he had been told. I also knew that I had neither joined the communist party nor been formally initiated into any criminal organization in the last few years, so the "updating of my coordinates" rang hollow. It echoed with the resonance of bureaucratic proclamation; a sound from afar, at least, a distance farther than the institutional Socio department.

It was not until after the Christmas holidays that I was able to reach Gilles Breton, head of the institutional Socio-Cultural department. He asked where my original security clearance had been obtained. I apprised him of the fact that it had been processed through FTC some years before. I learned that an update was necessary and that he would leave the requisite form at the front door where I could pick it up the next evening of my group. It seemed to him this was nothing but typical paperwork; I suspected otherwise. The following day he telephoned me and embarrassingly declared:

> "I sent your file/request up front and the administration has put it on hold.
> "What is that supposed to mean "on hold'; I didn't ask for anything, you people did."
> Breton was clearly uncomfortable, "I'm caught in the middle here. The administration said your file was on hold and that you are refused entry until the matter is cleared up." I felt sorry for Breton. I didn't know him well but the few times I had dealings with him he was always courteous and pleasant. I realized he was simply the messenger.
> "Who is the administration? Can you give me a name?"
> "It's Mme. Savard. She's replacing the Warden this week."

I thanked him and casually said I would get in touch with her. I was more than a little steamed but didn't want Breton to feel any pressure; he was in no way responsible. The next morning I 'phoned the institution bright and early. Mme Savard was not in her office so I simply left my name and number. By the end of the week I had not received my requested return call. I decided to wait for the Warden's return on Monday. It was not that I knew M.Gougeon. An inmate had introduced me to him while we were leaving for the university several months before. Since this was one of their "notorious cases", a Hells Angel, I thought Gougeon might just remember me. He didn't.

The surest way to get through to a Warden, I had discovered, was to call early in the morning, before the secretary has arrived and when the boss is trying to get an early jump on the day before the interminable meetings begin. It worked. I introduced myself immediately but was uncertain he would remember the name. After a moment's hesitation on his part, I added:

> "we were introduced by the Hells Angel I was taking to the university for you . . ." this got his attention. He may not remember me but he sure as hell remembered to whom I was alluding. "I think I remember you now" he said uncertainly but on full alert. I

went on to relate what had transpired while he was away, as well as the fact that I had been running this group for the past six years. He claimed to be totally unaware of the situation, even after I had explained what had happened at the other institutions some months before."

"I will enquire about the matter and get back to you on it this week. I can't say anything about other institutions but I will let you know where you stand with us," he declared distinctly and politely. I had always felt more comfortable with those who had come up through the ranks. They usually empathized with front-line workers and were understanding of the problems they faced; in other words, they were often more pragmatic about everyday difficulties. I was hoping he would see my work as "front-line".

"I thank you very much for your time. I appreciate that you can speak only for your own institution; that's fine it's the group here I'm concerned with." I gave him my 'phone number even though it was in the institutional file. I wanted to cover all bases.

This conversation took place on Monday, January 17th. 2005. I am still awaiting a return call.

EPILOGUE

Catch phrases and buzzwords are not the exclusive property of advertising agencies. Their brevity and poignancy attract immediate attention. As such they are in vogue in the political arena. Their legitimacy lies in the extent to which they reflect reality; their weakness rests in that their meaning is easily warped and can misrepresent an issue or modify a course of action.

The idea of affording protection to the community-at-large has always been a proposition at the basis of criminal justice. The notion of providing a safeguard against anti-social behaviour that contravenes established law is inherent in the various activities of policing, sentencing, incarceration and conditional release. The level at which the initiative toward public protection is promulgated, however, is related to the particular field of activity. It is present but in greater or lesser evidence, depending on related, equally important factors.

The idea of concrete assistance in the rehabilitation of the offender, on the other hand, has not always been an active ingredient of criminal justice. Punishment and retribution were just rewards for criminal behaviour well into the twentieth century. A common presumption was that the effect of punitive measures might deter the individual in the future and thereby bring about some form of rehabilitation.

The introduction of new approaches based on the social sciences picked up impetus in the second half of the century and an official policy of helping the offender redo his ways was instituted. The National Parole Board was inaugurated in 1959, along with the introduction of classification and psychological services within federal correctional institutions. Reduction in the amount of time confined to a cell and a later increase in sports, educational and cultural activities, dramatically altered the daily routine of institutional living. Emphasis was increasingly placed on ushering the inmate toward the community, with an emerging process of gradual release through temporary absences, day parole supported by halfway houses and the eventual increase in the granting of full parole releases.

On the darker side of the ledger, there was a proliferation in institutional violence during this same period. The escalation in acts of aggression was not limited to individual altercations among the inmate population but also encompassed disruptive group behaviour including hostage taking, escape attempts and general rioting. Reactions from various quarters prompted authorities to tighten up the system that resulted in extended suppression and control. Thus the early 'eighties were characterized by efforts to counteract the allegation that prisoners are being coddled.

It was no longer possible simply to revert to an archaic system of physical suppression and deprivation. Strides made in the area of human rights in general precluded a wholesale retreat to former practices, as proposed by a vociferous minority. Application of the strap as a means of punishment for and deterrence from unacceptable institutional behaviour was buried in the past. Limited diets to accompany the extreme deprivation of liberty within dissociation were also to remain a memory. Something had to be found. Control had to be maintained but rights had to be respected; both were the flavour of the day.

What developed in the mid-eighties and continues unabatedly today, was a subtler form of control, bureaucratic control, a more palatable means of restriction but equally debilitating with respect to personal growth and initiative. Bureaucratic control is insidious in nature, impervious to precise identification. The disseminated decree does not necessarily reflect the actual praxis.Regardless, the federal government agency, Correctional Service Canada, went into full gear. A Mission Statement was proclaimed, Corporate Objectives articulated and Core Values enunciated. Expectations on the part of both staff and inmates were defined, all under an umbrella of glowing respect for the person and with uncompromising conformity to the demands of human rights legislation. The battle plan had now been drawn up and widely published; it remained only for the marching orders to be followed.

It is especially difficult, given the breadth and depth of a federal agency like CSC, to actualize such all-encompassing policies and directives. The demand for orthodoxy may well fall on deaf ears, or at least be up to question, when one considers the diversity of opinion, attitude and perspective of such disparate groups as the workers' union and the inmate population. As well, the endeavour is subject to individual and regional interpretation, existing differences in political aims and the vagaries in media coverage and influence across the nation.

Nevertheless, this gospel of corrections encompassed the two-pronged purpose of protecting society while contributing to offender rehabilitation. The implication was clear from the start that the former took precedence over the latter; the worth of rehabilitation subsists in its contribution to the protection of society rather than its intrinsic value. Although this premise is admissible, the dualism leaves the door open to a false assurance of additional societal protection, should one purpose gradually supplant the other. After all, what better way to protect society than by restricting offender mobility? This ersatz security, however, does not pause to gauge the natural consequence of restraint; it simply curtails movement in the immediate and perpetuates the negative effects of prolonged control. In fact, the two purposes are mutually inclusive. A veritable protection of society comprises rehabilitation of the offender; correspondingly, rehabilitation of the offender axiomatically provides protection for society. It is only when the two are disunited, each one distinct from the other, that they assume a ranking order in the mind of the perceiver and then proceed sequentially into policy and practice.

Over the past thirty years or more, the expression "protection of society" has become a catch phrase, bandied about as though we were a society under siege. It serves the right wing political agenda well; playing on the fears of a public whose knowledge of corrections is too often limited to media accounts of a few spectacular failures. The left wing political agenda has reacted with a decided swing toward the centre and right of centre, likewise espousing the slogan of public protection. When employed in this offhand manner, the notion of safeguards for the public becomes increasingly divorced from the concept of rehabilitation. This splitting of the one issue in two fractures a unitary correctional process. The emphasis on public protection, to the diminution or exclusion of offender rehabilitation, places a disproportionate importance on the neutralizing aspect of incarceration, while reducing its value as a preparatory phase for community reintegration. At the same time, the post-release phase of the sentence assumes a distorted stance, portraying itself as the beginning and sole venue for reintegration of the offender into the community. The end result is that the process of incarceration avoids the close scrutiny necessary to assure that the effects of the deprivation of liberty are acknowledged and given due consideration in the controlled evolution of a meaningful correctional system.

*   *   *

I attended a professional conference under the auspices of Solicitor General Canada in March 2003. In attendance were practitioners and bureaucrats from both the private and government sectors. The title of the two-day affair was, "What Works . . . in Conditional Release and Community Reintegration."

A stellar cast of research professionals from various disciplines across the international scene made presentations. France, Britain, Germany, along with a resourceful complement from the United States, shared the stage with home grown luminaries. For the most part, the format consisted of several panels of three, chaired by competent practitioners and theoreticians. The individual presentations were interesting and informative, yet surprisingly lacklustre if judged by the dearth of participation on the part of conference attendees.

The one glaring flaw that struck me was the Conference's failure to acknowledge, let alone emphasize, the interdependence among the three phases of the correctional process: the experience of incarceration, conditional release and community reintegration. Simply to treat the matter of conditional release and community reintegration begs the question: release from where? It is irresponsibly naive to assume that institutional living is a neutral experience. A positive scenario would be one in which the incarceration phase provides the decision-makers with a clear measure of individual change, the intention being to reach an equitable decision with respect to the candidate's preparedness for community reintegration. A negative scenario would be one in which the process of incarceration, characterized by a punitive deprivation of liberty, is seen as fundamentally counter-productive, rendering the individual less equipped than before to deal with the demands of community reintegration. Undoubtedly the reality lies somewhere between these two polarities. Surely the question of what works in conditional release and community reintegration cannot be suitably addressed without some concomitant assessment of an integral portion of the correctional continuum. This failure to acknowledge the effects of the deprivation of liberty is understandable, though not acceptable, on the part of politicians and senior bureaucrats whose immediate needs and concerns may lie elsewhere. Avoidance of the issue within a conference of this calibre, however, is decidedly disquieting.

A comment made by one of the presenters at the closing session, a senior member of the research staff of Correctional Service Canada, unwittingly articulated this blind spot as to the effects of incarceration. He made reference to a conversation he had previously held with a District Parole Supervisor when the latter person stated, "it's too bad you couldn't design a program that could help prevent our offenders from associating with each other after their release." The allusion was obviously to the ill effects of peer group influence and pressure on the individual after his release. However, there was no evidence of any awareness of the importance of that same phenomenon throughout incarceration.

The paradoxical nature of the subject is of paramount importance. Incarceration keeps offenders in close physical, emotional and intellectual proximity over extensive periods, spanning years. As a matter of fact, an elemental part of the prescribed process of reintegration is residency in a halfway house, again with other offenders. Then immediately upon full release to the community most offenders have a condition of "non-association" imposed on them. The theoretical grounds underlying the provision are clinically sound; the mechanical imposition of the condition, however, can lead to interpretations that defy logic and common sense.

Bill was released from a minimum-security penitentiary to a halfway house in St-Jerome. He worked during the day in the community but was required to sleep in the halfway house on weeknights. One evening a fellow resident approached him,

> "Bill ya wanna get a cuppa coffee across the street?"
> "Sure Jack, be right with you, gonna get my coat."

Two nights later Jack caught up with Bill again and suggested a replay. Bill looked somewhat sheepishly at him as he replied, ". . . look I can't go Jack, my worker told me I'm not allowed to associate with you outside!"

This may seem to be an exception to the rule. Although circumstances may vary, the mentality of literal interpretation and application of rules and restrictions has become alarmingly widespread. I believe this impersonal course is the result of over-legislation and the supplanting of hands-on practice with technological devices and bureaucratic procedures. The entire process has been reinforced by the introduction of computers at the front-line level, guarantors of withdrawal from interpersonal relationships that make some demands and require some effort. Instead of personal encounter, information is compiled, assessments are completed and restrictions imposed from the comfortable distance of technological decree. The most incongruous consequence of this impersonal modus operandi occurs within the institutional setting itself, where inmates are frequently admonished about "hanging around with the wrong people."

Nor is this convoluted thinking limited to front-line correctional workers. Although the institutional personnel usually suggest the post-release conditions, their imposition is within the legal purview of the National Parole Board and are applied at the time of the parole hearing. Thus the responsibility for their clarity and pertinence lies with the members of the Board sitting at the particular hearing.

I represented Guy at his parole hearing a few years ago. I had been seeing him on a weekly basis since his return to the penitentiary for breach of condition. He had been living and working in the community, on parole, over a six year period. There had been no new offence but because he was serving a life sentence and the Board was reacting with more caution in recent years, his parole had been revoked. It was now some fourteen months later and, an in-depth evaluation having been completed, his appearance before the Board was due. The institutional representative, the Case Management Officer, was suggesting his release to a halfway house with a special condition of "non-association." I awaited the Board's questioning of this contradictory proposal in vain. Parole Hearings had evolved in such a way that discussion was somewhat restricted; rather than the free-flowing technique of the case conference, one was now limited to speaking at a specified time. Luckily, I was the last to speak. I pointed out the anomalous proposal of the CSC representative and that Guy's wife at home, in contrast to the residents in a halfway house, had no criminal record and would therefore pose no problem for someone with a special condition of "non-association."

Guy was released on full parole to his home.

This type of thinking is not surprising when the personal element is diminished or extracted completely from the process. The procedure takes precedence over the relevance of the decision itself. The written report becomes more important than the one on whom the report is written. The parole hearing transforms into an affirmation of the importance of the Board, its policies and its members, rather than a hearing that is the property of the particular offender. In reality, it is a hearing mandated to assess whether the individual is now prepared to reintegrate into the community-at-large.

Although the Parole Board is an administrative tribunal, one that determines the manner in which a portion of the sentence is to be served, the parole decision itself is a clinical one. This is not to imply that it is best made by a trained clinician but simply that it targets the assessment of behavioural change. The immediate task on hand is an appraisal of some alteration in attitudes, values and ultimately behaviour. The interpretation of such an assessment clearly must rest with persons having sufficient knowledge and understanding of delinquent dynamics, an appreciation of the effects of the deprivation of liberty and an awareness of the pertinent resources within the community.

Unfortunately, there has been a shift in recent years from the concept of an administrative tribunal to that of a quasi-judicial Board resulting in, or as a result of, an increasing influx and influence of the legal profession. Reinforced by periodic changes in the law, the Parole Board has gradually brought additional forms of conditional release into its ken. Statutory Release may now include an added restrictive measure of assigned residency in a Community Correctional Centre. The most significant change in the Board's authority, however, lies in its power to keep an offender incarcerated, past the Statutory Release date, up to the completion of his mandated sentence. When the new provisions were initiated in the mid-nineties, they were designed for those who posed a clear threat to society. The inevitable "widening of the net" began shortly thereafter. At the time of this writing new amendments are in the offing. The proposal is to have all penitentiary inmates screened for possible detention at their Statutory Release Date. The CSC, naturally, will do the screening. Once again, the deleterious effects of the process of incarceration will escape the scrutiny of an objective body. Consequently, these latter amendments alter the basic nature of the NPB from that of a releasing mechanism to that of an instrument of detention. The resultant medley of quasi-legalistic procedures and pseudo-clinical evaluative techniques continues to give rise to arcane practices and questionable judgements.

*   *   *

My career has now spanned five decades, from the early sixties through the initial years of the twenty-first century. Over this time I have met and worked with many highly endowed, well-intentioned people. They have come from various linguistic, cultural and ethnic backgrounds and have applied their talents with considerable expertise in an attempt to better criminal justice in Canada. Individual solicitude, ability and aptitude have been plenteous whether in the public domain or in the community-based area. Unfortunately, in both spheres of operation a central problem frequently arises with that insidious tendency for evolving programs, techniques and organizations to assume an importance that eventually supersedes the intended objective. The result is a standardization of thinking and practice that ultimately curbs personal initiative, the ingredient essential to wholesome development.

In the correctional field, a tremendous bureaucratic expansion within the government agency has created a monolithic structure which, coupled with an escalated use of technocratic devices, has spawned a mind-set that distances the correctional worker from the offender. The private sector, as well, has not been immune to this erosion of basic fundamental relationships. Their heightened dependence upon government funding has resulted in a commensurate loss of autonomy that threatens a complementary service with becoming a contrived cloned assistance. In addition, the very core of the community-based organization as a voluntary entity, its Board of Directors, has fallen prey to this expanded hegemony. In what appears to be an attempt to mimic bureaucratic government officials, undue emphasis on theoretical board governance and fastidious procedural wrangling, tend to usurp valuable time for discussion of basic criminal justice issues. The end result is that the non-governmental sector is customarily failing in its role to provide a distinct, parallel service and to proffer independent, constructive criticism of a system that is ultimately responsible to society as a whole. Although all organizations are susceptible to ethical implosion, the best safeguard is through honest introspection, a spirit of self-criticism engendered by openness to others and a genuine respect for and acceptance of alternate methods of practice.

In the long run success or failure of a correctional and conditional release process, vital components of a criminal justice system, is heavily reliant upon individual concern and performance. The organization, whether public or private, is simply a vehicle to facilitate and coordinate individual endeavour. Should the organization become an entity unto itself, mixed messages emerge, allegiances are divided and objectives are distorted. In fact, organizations work to get it done, to get it over with, to get on to the next; individuals, alone, have the capacity to fathom the intrinsic value of work and transform it into workmanship.

Criminal justice is essentially a people business, one in which everyone shares to a greater or lesser degree. The transparency of the system is quintessential and its being so is best assured through the interest and involvement of a well-informed public. If we as a society are to be more than onlookers responding to media accounts of titillating events, we must insist upon an accurate depiction of the role of the active participants on both sides of the law. The portrayal of true positive resources must be acknowledged and supported, regardless of whence they originate.

*   *   *

The year was 1966 and though I was still working fulltime at the McGill Forensic Clinic I spent at least fifty percent of my time in penitentiaries. The treatment we practised, the evaluations we made and the professional papers we presented were all of a clinical nature. Because of my previous experience in the Pen, Cormier agreed that my continued exposure to the institutional setting could only be beneficial both to myself and to the Clinic.

I had been running a group of younger offenders along with a colleague, Dr. Reginald Washbrook, for almost a year now. It comprised of six inmates between the ages of fifteen and eighteen. The penitentiary was the Federal Training Centre (FTC), an institution for first penitentiary offenders under the age of twenty-five, in that era. In fact it was Dr Washbrook, affectionately known as Jack, who had started the group and invited me to join in the early stages. Jack had had previous experience in Great Britain working with youthful offenders. His exuberance was infectious and the adventure proved to be a learning experience for all.

I soon realized that these teenagers, damaged as they were since they had already reached the penitentiary level, appeared to be more salvageable than their older, more experienced counterparts at the Pen across the road. The programming at FTC centred on trade training. We knew this was not enough. Kids don't end up in the penitentiary because they don't have a trade; by the same token, they are unlikely to succeed upon release simply because they have learned a trade. The obvious is not always so, when policy is dictated from on high by political and bureaucratic decree.

One of the young men in the group, Bob, was somehow above and beyond the norm. He had that typical tragic background common to many offenders but especially flagrant with youthful ones. He was the issue of a multi-problem family ridden with alcoholism, sexual abuse and mental instability. The miracle was that, if one looked beyond the superficial, Bob appeared to be an intelligent, relatively well-balanced individual. The problem was, and still is, that correctional institutions do not look below the surface. In a setting where behavioural conformity is the expectation, youthful energy and exuberance is interpreted as disruptive hyperactivity, something to be controlled and suppressed. In the case of Bob, the institutional response was to segregate him from his peers. We had to make out a special pass to get him to our weekly meetings. Within the group, once we helped him channel his liveliness, he became a true leader. The positive influence he exerted on others was not through preaching but rather by example; they were able to see someone who had been overly controlled by the institutional regime adopt a more mature role within a different setting.

Despite the progress Bob made in the group, we were aware of an impending problematic situation; his release date was approaching and he really had nowhere to go. He had recently turned seventeen but had no viable resources outside. The family was in tatters and the few healthier members had their hands full fending for themselves. Left on his own to face the temptations and dangers of the streets, Bob exhibited all the earmarks of one destined to a long-term history of persistent delinquency and imprisonment. He was intelligent and had learned well; his abandonment to the streets at an early age had resulted in juvenile detention and subsequent penitentiary incarceration. It was not a matter of exposure to a group therapeutic process alone that would tip the balance.

Raymond Boyer, a colleague at the Forensic Clinic, was a scientist by training and profession. His life experience and personal convictions, however, had led him to live through the effects of incarceration. At the Clinic, he was one of the principal research workers and writers. More importantly, he had a genuine concern for those in need. Phlegmatic in conversations on most topics, he reserved his affect for specific areas of personal concern. One centred on those who had been deprived of their liberty, especially the young.

"I have an important matter to discuss with you, if I may," the ever-polite man continued, "Jack mentioned to me last Friday that we may be able to find a home for that young man in your group. I believe his name is Bob."

My ears perked up immediately. "That is important Ray. He's to be released next month and literally has nowhere to go."

"Jack spoke about a Pastor of a church who knows someone. He's a Mennonite. I don't know if the Pastor's the Mennonite or the someone he knows is."

"What's a Mennonite?" I asked, half in jest. I knew they were a religion of some kind but had never met one.

"Well, if you're up to it you're about to find out. We have an appointment with the Pastor next Thursday morning, at least I do. If you want to come along you're more than welcome."

"I sure do. The kid really interests me and if we can come up with something it'll be a real help."

This was the conversation that led me to the Mennonite Community in Montreal, one of the truly consistent and active forces in criminal justice in Quebec and indeed, throughout Canada. They are auspicious through their actions rather than their words, a characterization that can hardly be applied across the board to all religious groups. Tim Martin was the Pastor, a title I never heard him use. If Mennonites are known by their actions rather than by their words, Tim was their true spokesman: a man of few words. I certainly saw him in action though. We worked together at Leclerc in the 'seventies where we shared some group outings with inmates, traded knowledge and attended a ball game or two when the Expos were still a major league consideration.

This particular Thursday morning, however, I had my doubts about this Pastor. My initial impression though turned out to be off the mark, a fact that I realized only some time later. I had mistaken his polite reserve for shyness, a factor that could prevent him from effectively working with delinquents. My prejudices extended to the person he was about to suggest. Well, I was dead wrong on all counts. This self-effacing man had the strength of character and quality of persistence to work with the most difficult offenders under the most trying conditions. He later did so for a number of years. I was privy to his competent work over several of those years.

"I was told you people are working with a young man about to be released from the penitentiary," he calmly stated in opening the conversation. I had the impression he could have been talking about a young parishioner leaving home for the first time.

"That's right, we've been working with him for over a year now and are concerned because he has no residential facility to go to," I said rather formally and somewhat uneasily. I hurried to add, "I should say at the outset he's no choirboy."

The Pastor's rejoinder was embarrassingly to the point. "Yes, I suppose not if he's coming out of the penitentiary," he intoned.

I looked up quickly, expecting to see a self-satisfied smirk or at least a glint of humour in his eye. I saw nothing but innocent, genuine concern. I privately ate a sliver of humble pie. I was to learn over the years there was never anything duplicitous about Tim Martin. In fact, that quality seemed to be a mark of all the Mennonites I was to meet in this business.

The end result of that meeting was that Raymond and I accepted, sight unseen, the assistance of a certain Harold Reesor and his family. They apparently were prepared to take this seventeen year-old penitentiary graduate into their home. The information we had was that the family operated a farm in the Mascouche area some twenty miles northeast of Montreal. We knew that Bob would be thrilled about living on a farm and working with farm animals. Finally, we were assured by this Pastor, that he would make every effort through the Mennonite Community to establish contact between Mr.Reesor and Bob, prior to the latter's release.

On the ride back to the office the silence was deafening. Suddenly Raymond blurted out, "I don't really know what the hell we just agreed to and, furthermore, under whose authority we were acting but I think we did the right thing." After a suitable pause I added cleverly, "Right on!"

We had no legal mandate and who were these people anyway? We were to find out. In the meantime we would play it close to the vest at the Clinic. Washbrook would be aware of everything; Ol' Jack was nothing if he wasn't a chance-taker. Bruno was something else again. He certainly had the courage to speak out and challenge at any and all levels but his boldness was a planned strategy. Bruno never flew by the seat of his pants and would not be pleased that his employees did, not if the Clinic's name could be tarnished. In this caper we abided by the maxim: silence is golden.

The morning Bob was released I drove him to the Reesor farm. This had been agreed upon between Washbrook and myself since I had a car. It was about noon when we finally arrived. I have the fondest memory of sitting at the table and having lunch with this couple and their five young children, the oldest at ten and the youngest an infant cradled in her mother's arms. What a sense of sharing, that oft-used word whose worth is forfeited unless put into practice. I must admit I had some misgivings that day and for a time later. I was fully aware of Bob's past, the family pathology and the buffeting from pillar to post throughout a lost childhood, all of which resulted in juvenile detention and culminated in penitentiary incarceration at sixteen. I was sure the Reesors knew much of it but it didn't seem to enter into the equation of their value system. But, didn't I have a responsibility at least to make them aware of my qualms?

The fact is I said nothing. Another fact is the happening was a success. I had underestimated basic common sense; more importantly, I had cavalierly discounted loving care. I am not suggesting a naive panacea but am adamantly stating that, without the element of genuine care and concern, treatment is nothing more than a reflection of the narcissism of the one administering the prescription. When I left the premises in mid-afternoon, the last sights and sounds were those of the children and the new addition to the family, rollicking around the kitchen in unfettered pleasure. The entire course of action lacked professional rigour but its unconventional nature certainly outshone the barbarity of segregation.

The next significant communication I had with the Reesor family was when Harold Reesor appeared, unannounced, in my office at the Clinic. I approached him with a certain apprehension and I'm sure the concern showed in my face.

"I'm sorry to bother you Mr. Williams but I was in the area and thought I may drop in for a word of advice."

"Is anything wrong?" I asked anxiously. My contact with Bob over the past year had been by telephone but I had never had any inkling of major problems.

"No problems," Reesor said lightly, "Well, we did have a few minor adjustments to make at first, but everything fit well."

I waited. I remembered Reesor, too, was not particularly loquacious.

"You mentioned something about advice . . ."

"Oh yes. Well, it's been a year now and I'd like to have your professional opinion on how I should deal with Bob."

I was momentarily taken aback. He was the one asking the questions but I felt I was the one who needed answers.

"But he's still working, isn't he?"

"Still working," he repeated, "yes, he's a heckuva' worker . . . does all the chores asked of him, and more."

"Then what is the problem?" I repeated hesitantly.

"Oh everything seems to be goin' fine, but I would like your opinion on how to handle him."

The light began to dawn. This uncomplicated man and his family were handling things in the best way they knew possible. They undoubtedly had some reservations, having heard of treatment programs, therapies, etc. and in all probability had been in awe of, even intimidated by, such august terminology. It was obvious he needed support. I believed that a frank statement was the best.

"Harold what you and your family have done over the past year is incredible. It's not as important to analyse the process as to appreciate the results. Bob is doing well, amazingly well considering where he comes from and I don't mean only the penitentiary." He nodded silently in assent. "We should be the people asking you and not the other way around. In a real sense, you are the expert."

I could see a slight quizzical look on his face but sensed that there was relief there as well. He believed things were going well but needed the assurance they were going well enough.

It was some months later that Bob secured a job off the farm. He had taken an electrical trade while in FTC and apparently had a liking and ability for the work. While he continued to live with the Reesors on the farm, he travelled daily to a nearby town to work an apprenticeship in electricity. This also afforded him the opportunity to develop social skills and gain some autonomy while working in the wider community.

In his third year, shortly before his twentieth birthday, Bob decided to try his wings. Against the wishes and best advice of Harold Reesor, who would have preferred the break from the home environment to be more gradual, Bob set out for the big city. Montreal had changed significantly over the years that had passed since he had lived there. Furthermore, he had never experienced any semblance of a regular home life while living in Montreal as a youngster.

Some months later, he met former acquaintances with similar delinquent backgrounds. He ended up in Court in the Eastern

Townships on a charge of Armed Robbery. Through the intercession of the Mennonite Community, legal assistance was procured, solid representation made and the final resolution was a suspended sentence, along with a return to the Reesor homestead, his sole experience with stable family life.

Bob remained with the Reesors physically for a number of years and emotionally for the rest of his life. He lived through the normal highs and lows of everyday life but learned to avail himself of appropriate help when necessary. He maintained occasional contact with me over the years. One touching event I was privy to was when I attended the funeral of Mrs.Reesor. This taciturn, strong and significant figure in Bob's life was lost to the entire family before her fortieth birthday. His sense of loss was profound but he now had the personal resources to participate actively in the obsequies and undergo a normal mourning process.

Bob married Lisa in his late twenties and, although the couple later underwent marital difficulties serious enough to warrant separation, their deep-seated feelings for each other gradually brought them together again. They were in the process of reconciliation when their lives were abruptly erased in a major motor vehicle accident while away on a second honeymoon. The devastating news reached family and friends shortly after.

I was honoured to say a few words at a memorial service organized by that wholesome, caring community. Bob had experienced an injurious early upbringing, the effects of which were reinforced by a basically impersonal correctional system; he had fortuitously been fostered by a concerned and loving family throughout late adolescence and into adulthood. The persistence of this familial attention was instrumental in bringing out his latent strengths that resulted in his adjustment to life in freedom.

* * *

Late in the winter of 1985 I received a 'phone call at the office on Pine Avenue.

"Hi Paul, it's Johnny. How're ya' doing?"

I knew immediately who it was though I hadn't seen him since I had left Leclerc in September 1980. His voice was distinctive, basically a monotone, always friendly and polite but never effusive.

I had met Johnny when he transferred from Cowansville to Leclerc in 1978. He was then in his late twenties, serving a first penitentiary sentence for a well-planned jewellery robbery in Vancouver some two years before. The score had gone well, the aftermath less so. Most of the gang of six were apprehended shortly after; the bulk of what had been stolen, however, was never recovered.

Johnny did his time unobtrusively. He spoke with many inmates but associated with few. He was introduced to me by one of his partners, a regular member of my weekly group. Johnny himself, although well known to all members of the group, never attended. He would see me alone in my office, always at my request, never his. An easy talker, anecdotes laced with subtle humour, he revealed little of himself and nothing of anyone else.

"How're you doing Johnny, it's great to hear from you," I replied with undisguised surprise.

"I'm hangin' in there, workin' regular, mostly on the road."

I knew not to push for specifics. He had probably completed his supervision by then and, in any case, had never been supervised by our Agency.

"I thought we could meet for lunch some time, there's a matter I'd like to discuss with you."

"Sure Johnny, any time," I replied, pleased but really intrigued. I couldn't imagine him being more expressive while on the outside than he had been while doing time.

We met the following week and shared an extended luncheon in a pleasant Italian restaurant in the north end of Montreal. I had never been there before but the attentive service led me to believe Johnny was a regular.

"Do you ever get to Tanguay, the women's joint?" he inquired.

"We used to send someone on a weekly basis but that's some years ago. Since Elizabeth Fry, the women's organization, has become active here in Quebec, we've pretty well pulled back."

"Well I'd like you to go personally, if you could, because there's someone special there. She's a real stand-up broad but having some difficulties. They consider her a real ball-breaker."

I sat there open-mouthed. Here was Johnny, a guy who gave up little, if anything, paying accolades to a female offender. Although "stand-up broad" is not a politically correct colloquialism, it is highly deferential in certain circles; this was one of them.

Even though our Agency no longer went to Tanguay Prison, I myself was no stranger to it. My first five-year stint with the Quebec Parole Board, a tour that had terminated the previous year, had brought me there an average of once a month. Thus, I was familiar with the place and knew some of the personnel. Johnny's request looked interesting.

"I say she's had some problems," he continued in his low-key manner, "because there's this thing about her escape."

He looked up at me with a smile and, I guess because of the expression on my face, continued hurriedly, "if I didn't think you could handle it, Paul, I wouldn't ask you. She's really a good broad, just got into a serious jam an', ya' know, didn't always handle things as she should have."

I started to ask about the escape when he interrupted, "excuse me Paul but I want you to know she wants to change. As a matter of fact, she's kinda' desperate. She's had a long run and is really tired. She deserves a break, but you know these joints, they'll only bring up her past. If she don't get the help, you'll lose her."

I noticed the well timed, manipulative segue from, "if she don't" to "you'll lose her." Johnny knew me; he believed I could be of help and obviously could fathom what strings to pull. However I knew Johnny too, at least enough to recognize he was for real. He was aware of somebody who needed help someone who, in his estimation, was deserving of help.

I accepted and the following week contacted Louise Bastien, a skilful caseworker at Tanguay who had presented a number of cases before me at the provincial Parole Board. She had impressed me as a thorough worker, one who knew and understood her cases but more importantly one who presented a person and not simply a file during the hearing. Louise was always respectful toward the inmates, with never a trace of condescension.

"I'll set up the meeting for you Paul," Louise replied to my telephone request, "you're going to have your hands full but I'm glad you're coming to help out.

I was beginning to wonder whether I wasn't in over my head. I had never worked with female offenders, other than as a decision-maker with the Parole Board. In fact, the salient recollection I had was that of the whistles and lewd taunts which buffeted my ears the first time I had walked through the offender-filled cafeteria at Tanguay. My crimson-coloured countenance had made me feel like a walking stoplight. This upcoming venture promised to be a challenge on more levels than one.

Manon was a woman in her early forties who throughout the first interview was particularly deferential toward me. She spoke accented English but, nevertheless, was quite articulate. She quietly spoke of her escape at the beginning of her sentence in 1979 but was quick to add that, after some three years on the run, had decided to turn herself in to the authorities.

That first interview was breezing along, after her initial nervousness subsided. What was bothering me, though, was that I could have been interviewing some school matron rather than the person whom Johnny had described in the restaurant. The fact that someone who was connected referred her and characterized her, as a "stand-up broad", would lead me to believe that person was someone other than Mary Poppins. I decided to take the bull by the horns.

"You know Manon, Johnny asked me to see you and I said I would . . . ." As she opened her mouth to speak, I interrupted, "Hang on a minute, I said I would see you and I'm prepared to see you on a regular basis . . . one condition, no bullshit. I don't have the time to come here and listen to nice stories. If you want to do something with your life maybe I can help. But it's up to you. You're not here because you're an angel, you've got to be up front with me."

It was a shot in the dark. She had not been lying to me, not even sugar-coating the truth. But there seemed to be little affect and I had only Johnny's opinion that she wanted to change her life in some way and not simply get out of prison. The response was immediate; I had evidently struck a meaningful chord.

"I really appreciate you're coming here," she blurted out tearfully. "I'm not used to expressing feelings but I'm trying. Johnny's my last hope, he's the only guy I trust and he told me you could help me."

It was now my turn to be up front. "You know, Manon, there's not much I can do. It's got to come from within you. I can only be supportive and maybe point in the right direction at times."

"That's all I want," she sobbed, "I really hafta' get out of this shit. I can't go on this way no more."

The interview ended with a promise on both sides to try and work together. I made it clear that I would be back in a week or two depending upon my schedule at the office. These were the early years with John Howard and I had a large staff and various programs to oversee at the time. Nevertheless, it was approximately two weeks before I saw her again; she had written two information-packed letters during the interval. There was plenty of material to work with in the upcoming sessions.

As it turned out, I saw her on a regular basis for some months after that. Eventually she had a parole hearing scheduled and asked me to represent her. Although the provincial Parole Board at the time was much less repressive than in later years, representing Manon would be a formidable task. Apart from the escape and subsequent number of years illegally-at-large, there had been a prior escape attempt and at one time she had been suspected of bringing drugs into the institution upon return from a Temporary Absence. The nature of her criminality was polymorphous and of long duration. Despite this, I believed she was at the optimal point for supervised release: genuinely fed up with the life-style, increasingly aware of contributing factors to her own criminality and, finally, cognizant of the need for sustained help. The business at hand would be to convince the Quebec Parole Board.

As I have mentioned previously, one important element that helps a parole board reach an equitable decision is a certain familiarity with viable community resources. As it happened, I was known to the Board members and, as Manon's representative, was offering to provide the necessary follow-up at John Howard, if parole were to be granted. Since solely the Quebec Probation Service carried out provincial parole supervision our Agency would provide a clinical service, ancillary to the official supervision. Despite the weight of the case, the Board felt that the overall support being offered was sufficient to justify release. The decision was to send her to a halfway house for six months on day parole. Upon successful completion of this initial phase, full parole would be granted. She was delighted and the transfer was carried out within a few days of the hearing.

Since living in a halfway house is a condition of day parole, I maintained only telephone contact with Manon. The idea was to allow the workers at the house to use their expertise in bringing about a gradual transition to living in the community-at-large. I would establish regular contact upon full release. This period allowed her to experience increasing freedom and provided a covert evaluation of her willingness for on-going clinical follow-up upon release on full parole. Our observations had taught us that with many offenders the most serious resolutions made during incarceration dissipated upon release. This does not necessarily question the earnestness of the inmate at the time the commitment is made but rather that when circumstances change dramatically, one's perceived needs and problem solving may be considerably altered.

In Manon's case the opposite seemed to have occurred. Upon full release she insisted on weekly encounters and was better able to speak more candidly than while in prison. Her regular sessions at the John Howard office were so frequent that her parole officer, after a few months, dispensed with the need for her to report in person for parole supervision. It had become obvious that she was serious about seeking help and the monitoring could be done by telephone. This kind of common-sense flexibility is rare among civil servants but certainly reinforces authentic motivation.

Manon was the younger of two female siblings. The parents separated before she reached her second birthday. During the formative years the girls were placed apart, one raised by various members of the maternal family, the other by the father's side. Neither youngster was provided with any home stability, both were shuffled from one family member to another. This early abandonment prevented any sense of belonging to develop. In its stead, the seeds of deception and mistrust were implanted and ingrained feelings of insecurity gradually emerged. The primary school years were spent in various convents as neither parent had the financial resources to support education and a home life. Many a weekend was passed in gloomy confinement when no one from the family appeared.

Despite this traumatic beginning, Manon never spoke of her parents with rancour. She had little contact with her father during these years but tried desperately to maintain a relationship with her mother, using every excuse possible to remain at her mother's apartment whenever on weekend leave. Around thirteen years of age she adamantly refused to return to the convent. Her mother grudgingly agreed to try to keep her.

Living conditions, however, proved to be far from ideal for all parties. Her mother shared an apartment with a friend. Both worked as waitresses during the day and frequently spent their evenings in the company of various boyfriends. The sudden presence of a pubescent girl seriously cramped their style. This marginal environment was hardly beneficial to Manon either as it failed to provide the acceptance and guidance, so needed by this increasingly troubled young adolescent. As tensions steadily grew she became more sensitive to her interfering presence, a feeling substantiated by her mother's insistence that she "get out and find a job." It was only a matter of time before she acknowledged the compelling call of the streets and their comforting acceptance. It was here that older boys, wise beyond their age in survival strategy, introduced her to a life of easy access to soothing intoxicants, facile friendships and profitable sex. Within a period of months the authorities, alerted by her mother's call to the police, stepped in and a form of juvenile detention was eventually enforced.

Notre Dame de Laval, designed as a haven for the protection of youth, seemed to her like a prison; a punitive institution imposed as a result of her mother's treachery. The basic feelings of abandonment, engendered during early formative years, were now solidified and would colour her interpersonal relationships throughout adolescence and into adulthood. Despite the efforts of qualified educators, the fundamental repressive milieu of this juvenile institution drove the residents and staff into antagonistic camps: the "we" and "they".Peer group pressure effectively reinforced burgeoning delinquent mechanisms. In Manon's case, the positive effect of formal education was outweighed by the surreptitious education in survival techniques, as a preliminary to adult life on the streets. A third and final absconding from detention occurred just before her eighteenth birthday. She now felt better equipped to compete on the streets and was also aware that, because she was approaching the age of majority, the authorities would no longer pursue her and force her return. She was now free and ready to do business.

The next eight years passed in a blur. Prostitution, waitressing in bars and a number of tenuous liaisons were her way of life. Regular usage of soft drugs, along with a growing dependency on alcohol, were an integral part of the scene and did serve to keep the feelings of depression at bay. It was during this period of her life she gave birth to a son. The consequent role of a single parent, both demanding and stressful, was adequately compensated for by a strong sense of accomplishment and satisfaction. Tommy temporarily became the centre of her universe, a force strong enough to push her to try and take charge of a life quickly spinning out of control. Contact was re-established with her mother, prostitution became a thing of the past and her chosen field of work improved as she moved up to a better class of bars in the west end of Montreal. She was now being noticed and accepted by a more organized criminal element.

It was at the age of twenty-seven when Manon met Paddy, a man who was to be a significant figure in her life over the next twenty years or so. Although he worked with a Toronto crew, Paddy was also a part of a well-organized group out of Montreal. Each member had a specialty; Paddy's talent rested in the field of electronics. He was adept at constructing and, more importantly, de-activating alarm systems. He introduced her to a lifestyle that, at the outset, provided thrills, social contacts and fast money. The first step was to gain respectability.

"You don't work in bars, you socialize in bars!" was Paddy's maxim.

This reasoning appealed to Manon. She enjoyed working in bars but was enthralled to live in them, without working. The elasticity in this kind of reasoning failed to take into account the fragile nature of the addictive personality. Her sense of belonging was to be greatly bolstered by this new status; her dependency on alcohol, however, was to be reinforced as well. Over the ensuing years she became a recognized member of this criminalized group. As a woman in this macho milieu, her role was not identical to that of her male counterparts. However it also differed from that of the usual "silent partner" arrangement adopted among criminals and their mates. She participated actively and reached a gratifying level of acceptance and trust, if not equality. In her eyes though, this kind of acknowledgement that had eluded her in the past more than made up for some theoretical status of gender equality. She was a "stand-up broad," knew it and was proud of it.

Despite the thrills of travel, luxurious living and social acceptance, all was not rosy. Paddy was eventually arrested and served time. She was expected to wait. Wait she did but not by staying at home. She had made acquaintances along the way and had learned more tricks of the trade through these new partners. Her involvement in criminal activities ran the gamut from shoplifting, through burglaries, to armed robbery. Although this behaviour lacked the sophisticated pattern of her former associates, the adventures themselves provided the needed buzz as well as a profitable margin.

When Paddy was finally released from the penitentiary they formed a twosome once again. He was insistent, however, that she abandon her wild and reckless behaviour. Planning and timing were of the essence and the bottom line was simple: a lucrative payday. The thrill was in the amount you scored. The consequent style of living was definitely high-class. A life of travel through Canada and the United States appealed to Manon. Her sense of worth continued on the incline as she socialized with Paddy's many contacts. Life was what it was supposed to be, as she kept up her end in the criminal enterprises.

It was after several months of this nomadic existence that the Vancouver proposal came to light. This was to be an all-Montreal operation, a special attraction for Manon. She had been away from the hometown for some time now and though Vancouver was not home, the participants in the caper were all familiar figures. She was to tend to the house needs for the group throughout the elaborate planning phase and carried the important responsibility of guarding the equipment as well. When the score was about to be moved she came back to Montreal, rented a hotel room and awaited Paddy's return. As the saying goes, ". . . and the rest is history!"

Paddy, as well as most of the crew, was arrested. It would not be for a number of months after he had skipped bail and fled to the U.S. that she would join him. The experience of living with a fugitive, however, with all the paranoid-based precautions, proved too much for this relationship. Quarrels for any and all reasons became a daily occurrence and she decided, heatedly, to retreat to Montreal.

It was not long before she returned to former haunts and resorted to previous behaviour. A series of armed robberies, the most spectacular of which involved the use of a rented helicopter and subsequent escape through the Metro system, resulted in her arrest, conviction and imprisonment in Tanguay. Shortly after an aborted escape attempt, she succeeded on a second try, fled to the U.S. and rejoined Paddy. Upon arrival there, she now had certain demands to make. Forewarned by her previous experience, she was no longer prepared to accept the insecure life of an unprotected fugitive. The fact that they both were now fugitives only complicated matters. Their solution was as simple as it was bizarre; they were married under fake identities. Thus, in the early winter of 1980, Paddy and Manon became husband and wife.

The next two and a half years may best be summed up as a living hell. Although there was much travel and some moneymaking, their existence was artificial. The scenario of no home, fleeting acquaintances and a day-to-day adjustment punctuated by a fear they had been spotted or betrayed, gradually took its toll on Manon. The needed support of friends, laughter and reckless abandon were of another life. Now, the tedious daily scramble for financial gain, even when successful, required a subdued style of living, limited in luxury and in social contacts. Fond reminiscence of former good times deteriorated into sombre rumination, as her basically fragile defence system collapsed. Pressure mounted and she resorted to increased use of alcohol, frequently admixed with drugs and steamrolled toward mental breakdown. The initial psychotic episodes received only sporadic medical attention. The situation worsened, getting well out of the understanding and control of the couple. They tried a temporary solution. Manon was to leave and take care of Paddy's ailing, elderly mother who lived on the Canadian side of the international border. In fact, an increase in the frequency and severity of the psychotic episodes occurred. Olfactory, auditory and visual hallucinations eventually brought about brief hospitalisation, followed by some outpatient treatment in the form of controlled medication. During this tempestuous two and a half year period, she had undergone a constant assault on her frail psyche. During the absence from Montreal several significant family figures had passed on. The emotional scars of early childhood, ever remaining just beneath the surface, were brought to the fore during this trying time. However, it was Paddy's sudden arrest that triggered her return to Montreal and surrender to Tanguay Prison. The ambivalence of being alone, while experiencing a certain ephemeral freedom, was overwhelming. Regular doses of prescribed medication had stabilized her to some extent and release from the turbulent lifestyle of living on the run added to a sense of security. In a surreal world, Manon was somehow home.

It was shortly after this that I had made initial contact with her. Our meeting had perhaps been serendipitous for her; for my part, I believe it was due to my work in the milieu. Johnny called me because he knew me and because he knew someone who really wanted help. The best diagnosticians often come from the least accepted resources, the result of professional arrogance and conceit.

I followed Manon for a period of some two years. Although there were some recurrences of emotional instability at times, the appropriate measures were taken and further deterioration was avoided. Nevertheless, the principal agent of change came from within, as she valiantly fought the demons that had plagued her since infancy. There was no return to criminal activity. Some time after she had completed her parole supervision and had been weaned from her reliance upon the counselling sessions, I received a 'phone call at the office. After the initial pleasantries were done with,

> "Mr. Williams, I'm getting married . . . again . . . and you have to come." I was surprised and mildly concerned but before I could comment, she continued, "But I have to ask you something. Do

you think I'm already married, I never got a divorce from Paddy ya' know?"

Well here we go again, there's no book on this one, ". . . you and Paddy were married under phoney names, Manon, I don't think that one counts," I replied with feigned certainty.

"Anyways, I've already made arrangements with a Reverend who's willing to marry us. I didn't tell her the whole story 'cause I was afraid she wouldn't understand."

"Good work Manon, I'm sure you'll be okay, but who's the guy?"

"He's a complete legit stiff who I've known for a long time, steady worker and he really loves me, well whaddy'a expect?" she chortled.

"I think it's great news and I'll be pleased to come!"

It was some two months later I entered a restaurant in old Montreal to attend the reception after the nuptials. It was a veritable "who's who" of the West End Crew. It was a pleasant evening, sometimes boisterous, but with a good amount of non-verbal respect shown to a "stand-up broad" who had decided to hang them up. Call it rehabilitation, resocialization or whatever; it must come from within and any help must be given and accepted willingly and honestly. Manon has now been with her husband for several years. They live outside of Montreal and consciously avoid former haunts. Congratulations!

SHORT BIO

Paul Williams graduated from Ottawa University with a Master of Arts, Psychology degree. His career in criminal justice spanned five decades from the sixties through the early years of the 21st century. He worked as institutional psychologist, clinical coordinator in a diagnostic and treatment centre and parole board member. His last position was that of Executive Director of a community-based organization. He has served on the Board of Directors of l'Aide juridique de Montréal, the Seventh Step Society of Canada and the Canadian Criminal Justice Association. He was President of the latter from 1991-1993.